# AN AMERICAN DYNASTY

THE STORY OF THE McCORMICKS,
MEDILLS AND PATTERSONS

# An
# American
# Dynasty

by
JOHN TEBBEL

1947
DOUBLEDAY & COMPANY, INC.
GARDEN CITY, NEW YORK

To KAY

# ACKNOWLEDGMENTS

It would be impossible to thank the many people who worked with me on this book, but I want especially to acknowledge my indebtedness to Mrs. Mary Crawford and Lois Felder, for their valuable research; to Evelyn Sager, for her research; to Morris Ernst, for permitting me to examine a portion of his then unpublished manuscript; to Keith Sward, for allowing me to use material from his manuscript on Henry Ford; and to the Chicago Historical Society, for its many courtesies.

# CONTENTS

## Part One
### JOSEPH MEDILL AND THE TRIBUNE

## Part Two
### TRANSITION

## Part Three
### THE WORLD OF McCORMICK

ix

Part Four

## THE WORLD OF THE PATTERSONS

Part Five

## McCORMICK, THE PATTERSONS AND
## FREEDOM OF THE PRESS

# LIST OF ILLUSTRATIONS

# A PARTIAL McCORMICK-MEDILL-PATTERSON GENEALOGY

THE McCORMICK FAMILY

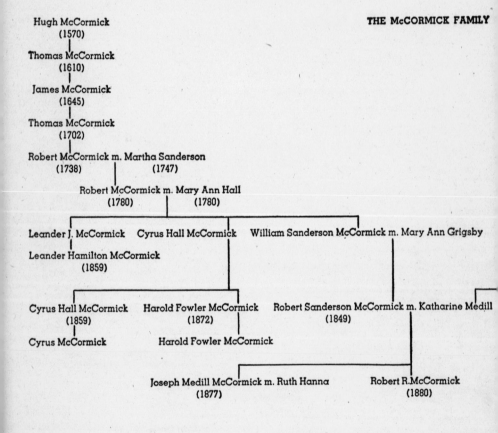

Hugh McCormick
(1570)

Thomas McCormick
(1610)

James McCormick
(1645)

Thomas McCormick
(1702)

Robert McCormick m. Martha Sanderson
(1738)                    (1747)

Robert McCormick m. Mary Ann Hall
(1780)                    (1780)

Leander J. McCormick    Cyrus Hall McCormick    William Sanderson McCormick m. Mary Ann Grigsby

Leander Hamilton McCormick
(1859)

Cyrus Hall McCormick    Harold Fowler McCormick    Robert Sanderson McCormick m. Katharine Medill
(1859)                    (1872)                    (1849)

Cyrus McCormick    Harold Fowler McCormick

Joseph Medill McCormick m. Ruth Hanna    Robert R. McCormick
(1877)                    (1880)

## THE MEDILL AND PATTERSON FAMILIES

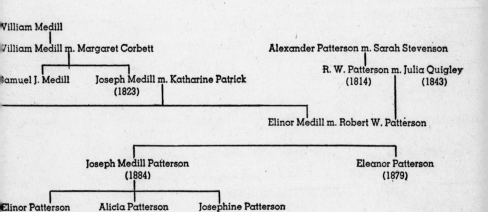

William Medill
|
William Medill m. Margaret Corbett

Alexander Patterson m. Sarah Stevenson

Samuel J. Medill    Joseph Medill m. Katharine Patrick
(1823)

R. W. Patterson m. Julia Quigley
(1814)     (1843)

Elinor Medill m. Robert W. Patterson

Joseph Medill Patterson
(1884)

Eleanor Patterson
(1879)

Elinor Patterson    Alicia Patterson    Josephine Patterson

# Part One

# JOSEPH MEDILL AND THE TRIBUNE

# Chapter 1

## MEDILL, AS EVER WAS

JOSEPH MEDILL walked into the Chicago *Tribune* office for the first time on a spring morning in 1855. He was then a beardless young man of thirty-two with a square Irish face distinguished for its firm, straight mouth and jutting, stubborn chin. His thick dark hair grew low over his ears, with discreetly short sideburns. The black string tie he wore between the wings of his collar, the frock coat and the congress boots, were distinctive parts of his habitual dress.

Medill devoted forty-four years of intense effort to making the *Tribune* a success. For the first eight years he was managing editor, or general manager, as the position was called at the time. He was editor in chief from November 1863 to August 1866, except for brief periods as Washington correspondent. Then he spent a short time in public life, serving first in the Illinois Constitutional Convention of 1869, later on the Civil Service Commission, and as mayor of Chicago. But he devoted himself again to his paper in 1874, when he took complete editorial and financial control and retained both until he died.

The concrete result of his labors was a sound newspaper property. That was the most substantial part of the legacy he left to the family members who came after him. His more intangible assets—the characteristics which enabled him to found the dynasty—he passed on through his two daughters, who married into the Patterson and McCormick families and united the three lines.

Robert Rutherford McCormick and his Patterson cousins, Eleanor and the late Joseph, were the children born to these unions, and it was they who built the empire which is so controversial a part of American life in these times. Their interlocking ownerships of great newspapers—the Chicago *Tribune*, the New York *Daily News* and the Washington *Times-Herald*—and subsidiary interests have established them at a peak of potential power and influence rivaled in our time only by William Randolph Hearst.

It is a position made possible financially by virtue of both inherited wealth and inherited ability. Intellectually it is the contemporary expression of a pattern formed early in the dynasty's history—a pattern shaped by the stubborn, aggressive, eccentric McCormicks; the willful, aristocratic, domineering Medills; and the religiously dogmatic Pattersons.

For the McCormick-Patterson press, and the philosophy it represents, is not simply a political phenomenon of these bitter decades; it is a way of thinking and living which has its roots in the family history of its owners, particularly in the life and work of Joseph Medill, who was the embodiment of the *Tribune* as Colonel McCormick is today. Medill's journalistic philosophy is reflected faithfully in his grandchildren's newspapers, and the powerful financial empire they have built was made possible by the trust he left for them.

Joseph Medill himself was a fighting leader in the era of personal journalism, when that kind of newspapering was consistent with a lusty, growing, brawling America. He was a Midwestern James Gordon Bennett, and his paper was often even more uninhibited. It tried lawsuits in its news columns, used everything short of gutter language in assailing its enemies and stopped at nothing when it advocated a cause.

This description substantially fits the three McCormick-Patterson newspapers of today, modified only by the restraints imposed through the libel laws. These publishers are practicing personal journalism of the Medill variety in a new era when most newspapers are progressing, however haltingly, toward a realizable ideal of objectivity and of full reporting of the news.

Colonel McCormick's approach to the problems of his time is strikingly similar to that of Medill's, and the problems themselves are not essentially dissimilar. Like Medill, McCormick has proclaimed his journalistic ideals in the most high-sounding terms. Medill, on the subject of a newspaper's duty, declared it should be "the organ of no man, however high, no clique or ring, however influential, no faction, however fanatical or demonstrative, and in all things to follow the line of common sense." McCormick's avowed theory, which will be discussed in detail, is fundamentally the same.

Their attitudes toward organized labor are almost exactly alike. Medill denounced the Chicago Socialists as "communistic cranks." Speaking of them, he demonstrated what he meant by "the line of common sense": "As these cranks have now adopted for their watchword increased pay or no work, let us see what that high-sounding phrase really means and what would be the result of such policy. . . . It is a thousand pities there is not some method of incarcerating them in lunatic asylums long enough for their heads to cool sufficiently to enable them to take common-sense views of things."

McCormick could scarcely be more eloquent on the subject of the CIO—or more consistent.

Medill blamed liquor for the workingman's downfall. He called it "the progenitor of all the ills to which the working men of the United States are subjected. No trades unions or other combinations can ever bring relief to them in the absence of temperance and economy. . . ." Further, he believed that reduced working hours would flood the country with a "horde of foreign artisans, and wages would, as a result, fall so low that it would become almost impossible to make a living."

In personality Medill was intensely egoistic and his self-esteem led him into eccentricities as odd as some of those displayed by the present generation of his family. For example, he had a penchant for oddities and curiosities. He was in the habit of clipping miscellaneous items which happened to attract his attention and sending them to the composing room marked "Must, JM."

Just as Colonel McCormick's lack of special training fails to prevent him from assuming an air of authority about everything, Joseph Medill did not let his educational lacks restrain him from taking a bold position on scientific matters. At one time or another he rode a half-dozen scientific or pseudo-scientific hobbies, such as simplified spelling, the sunspot theory and the blue-glass theory. The *Tribune* flew in the face of outraged public opinion for years with such spellings as "infinit," "favorit," "telegrafed" and similar words. Some of these have disappeared, but other phonetic simplifications still appear in the paper today.

Medill loved to converse with real scientists. In several talks with Thomas A. Edison he discussed at length Edison's experiments in saving the energy wasted in burning coal. But he picked the wrong subject when he interested himself in the Keeley cure. Chicago doctors denounced him for advocating a quack remedy and he responded by arranging a special test of the institution and airing the whole matter in the *Tribune*.

Medill attributed all natural phenomena to sunspots until one day he heard of the existence of microbes and immediately adopted this as the new explanation. Soon after, an unfortunate reporter, writing according to *Tribune* policy, asserted that the plague in Egypt was caused by sunspots. Medill went through the copy, crossed out the word "sunspots" wherever it occurred and substituted "microbes."

The man had almost no intimate friends, and he was cordially hated by many people. A friend of Medill's brother Samuel observed charitably that this is true of nearly all editors, and certainly it has been true of many of them, but in the case of Joseph Medill and his publishing descendants it appears to be a family characteristic as well.

The Medills came originally from North Ireland. The name has its roots in England, however, where it was simply Dill. Through his great-grandmother Joseph Medill could trace a relationship directly to Sir Walter Scott. Even more remotely the Medills were probably Huguenots, expelled from France after the revocation of the Edict of Nantes, which eliminated their freedom of worship. In fact Medille is still a French name. A Joseph Medille first demonstrated to the French government that the Mont Cenis tunnel was feasible.

The French Medilles became the English Dills, who migrated northward and became the Scotch McDills, who migrated again and established the Irish clan which spelled its name variously as Madill or Medill. The Irish Medills were Belfast shipbuilders and strict Presbyterians. They passed on both arts from father to son, until trade and religion alike struck a snag in William Medill, an Ulsterite who fell in love with an Episcopalian girl named Margaret Corbett. In the ensuing bitter quarrel with his father William managed to get his way, but it was a hard way. In 1819 he sailed with his bride for America, his only fortune a small patrimony.

William and Margaret settled on a farm near St. John in New Brunswick, Canada. They thought they were settling in America, but this strip of border was in dispute and Canada got it eventually instead of Maine.

Joseph Medill was born on this farm April 6, 1823. Actually he was a British citizen by nativity—a fact which must be a skeleton in Colonel McCormick's mental closet. When Joe was nine years old the Medills migrated to Stark County, Ohio, via the Erie Canal. Joseph lived on his father's Ohio farm for twelve more years, with his two brothers and two sisters. He was graduated in 1843 from nearby Massillon Village Academy, but the family could not afford to send him to college because of heavy losses they had suffered in a fire.

Joseph had to get his education by reading whatever books he could borrow. He read history, especially Gibbon and Hume, and he also devoured travel and biography. Like Lincoln, he would walk miles for a book. On Saturdays he trudged nine miles to Canton for instruction in Latin, logic and natural philosophy from a clergyman. In his spare time he went about his home neighborhood getting subscribers for Horace Greeley's *Weekly New York Tribune*.

At twenty-one Medill began to study law in Canton with Hiram Griswold and Seymour Belden. Admitted to the bar in November 1846, he practiced law for three years in New Philadelphia, Ohio, as the partner of George W. McIlvaine, later chief justice of Ohio. In those days he was surrounded by such men as Salmon P. Chase, later Lincoln's Secretary of the Treasury and Chief Justice of the United States; Edwin M. Stanton, Secretary of War under Lincoln; George E. Pugh; and Henry B. Payne.

But the law went slowly. Medill spent more and more time in the offices of country newspapers, particularly the one in New

Philadelphia. These offices were gathering places in those days for lawyers, teachers and everyone interested in politics; the newspaper was the pulse beat of politics. When he wasn't arguing the questions of the day Joe Medill learned to set type and operate a hand press. He even wrote an editorial now and then.

The newspaper business made him forget the law and everything else. Medill had found his true medium. Looking around, he learned that the Coshocton *Whig* in northwestern Ohio was for sale. He bought it, made himself editor and installed his three younger brothers as assistants. His paper became a powerful antislavery advocate, a strong supporter of the Whig ticket in a Democratic county. Within two years it dominated county politics, but in 1852 Medill backed the wrong horse in the national race by supporting General Scott, whom Franklin Pierce defeated.

In two years Joe Medill ran through country journalism. He moved up to Cleveland and established a Whig morning paper there called the *Daily Forest City*, although by that time he had made up his mind that the Whig party's day was over and its only salvation lay in union with the Free-Soilers. This time he was right. The election of 1854 ended the Whigs and inspired the new Republican party.

Making a practical example of his political ideas, Medill consolidated his paper with a Free-Soil journal edited by a South Carolina abolitionist, John C. Vaughan. They named the new paper the Cleveland *Leader* and dedicated it to the job of uniting all the anti-slavery elements in sight.

Medill campaigned ardently for the formation of the Republican party. Just over thirty, his youthful fire undoubtedly was a real contribution to the party's birth, but whether he was actually its instigator is a matter never proven to the satisfaction of anyone but Chicago *Tribune* biographers.

This is what occurred:

In February 1854 active anti-slavery men held their historic meeting in Ripon, Wisconsin, at which, some historians hold, the Republican party was conceived. In March Medill called a similar meeting in the office of the Cleveland *Leader*. It was secret, and Salmon P. Chase was one of the twenty men who attended.

During the session, it is said, Medill proposed the name "Republican" and the meeting adopted it. In July the party held its first convention at Jackson, Michigan, and Jackson gets credit today as the birthplace of the party.

However, there is some reason for believing that Medill urged "Republican" from the time he bought the Coshocton *Whig*. In April 1853 Medill's *Leader* began a Republican party movement by backing a party of that name in a Cleveland charter election. The Democrats, however, called the new party Fusionist. Republican or Fusionist, the organization gathered up many elements of the German population, combined them with factions hostile to the Democrats, and as Republicans began to carry county elections everywhere in the Western Reserve.

When the Whig convention met at Jackson, it is said, adoption of "Republican" was only recognition of something which already existed in fact. In an interview published posthumously in the *Saturday Evening Post* in 1899, Medill modestly asserted that the honor of naming the party should be divided with Steve Douglas, who he said had hastened the death of the Whig party by "pulling down the bars and letting the South into the free territory. The North united under the name of the National Republican Party to drive them out of it."

Preoccupied though he was with politics, Medill found time to marry one of the girls he had taught during a brief occupancy of the master's chair in a district school, in the late forties. She was Katharine Patrick, a New Philadelphia girl. James Patrick, her father, was Indian agent, land commissioner and county judge, and he was a newspaperman too: he published a Whig paper for more than twenty years.

Joseph and Katharine were married on September 2, 1852. They had three children, all girls. Elinor married Robert W. Patterson, Jr., and Katharine married Robert Sanderson McCormick, thus establishing the present McCormick-Patterson generation. Josephine, the third daughter, did not marry and died in January 1892, two years and a half before her mother's death.

In the fusion of Medill blood with the McCormick and Patterson lines, it is likely that the proud McCormicks felt the other two clans were fortunate. The McCormicks have spent considerable time and money tracing their ancestry, and willing investigators have turned up two lineages, both satisfactory, from which to choose. There is no way of telling which one is accurate, and it makes no difference to anyone except the McCormicks.

One theory says that the line goes back to remote Irish stock, related obscurely to King Cormac, who died in A.D. 260. "Mac Cormac" is genealogical evidence in support of this argument. It is certain there was a Donaugh MacCormac who lived near the beginning of the fifteenth century.

The other theory asserts that the earliest family members migrated from Scotland to Ulster about the time (1607) that James I of England sent out Scottish colonists to establish the so-called "Plantation of Ulster," having first ousted the earls of Tyrone and Tyrconnell from their estates.

Evidence points most strongly to the latter theory, but the story is probably wrong in one detail, because the first accurately recorded McCormick was Hugh, born in 1570, about forty years before the founding of the "Plantation of Ulster." The family must have existed in Ireland, then, some time before 1570. Probably they migrated from unhappy Scotland as did so many of their neighbors, who came to Antrim in the middle of the sixteenth century and established a large Scottish settlement. Hugh McCormick lived there in a place with a Scottish name, Dunmakelter. He belonged to a division of the Clan Maclaine of Scotland, and helped to perpetuate the name "Mac Cormac," an Irish title only recently extinct. The clan bore the McCormick motto, *"Sine timore."*

Hugh's son Thomas was born in 1610. Thomas married and had a son, Captain James McCormick, born in 1645, a sturdy fighter who wrote a bloody name for himself at the siege of Londonderry.

Captain James bequeathed his fighting blood to a son born in 1702, named for his grandfather Thomas. Young Thomas had need of it. Married at an early age to Elizabeth Carruth, he determined to join the flow of immigration to America and arrived here in 1735 with his wife and goods to plunge at once into the

hard frontier life of Cumberland, Pennsylvania. He built a home-
stead and made a good life for himself on the two hundred acres
of limestone soil he took for his own.

The fifth son born to Thomas and Elizabeth, in 1738, was
named Robert. He became the immediate progenitor of those
McCormicks who have made so profound an impression on
American life. Robert lived in Juniata County. From all accounts,
he was a hard-working man who practiced weaving and farming,
meanwhile keeping a weather eye toward improving his fortunes.
He acquired more property and married well. The bride was
Martha Sanderson, the daughter of a Scotch-Irish landowner who
lived near by. But Robert had to leave his acres and his bride six
years later to fight in the Revolution, mostly against Cornwallis in
the advance through the Carolinas which culminated in the great
British defeat at Yorktown.

After the Revolution Robert left his kinsmen in Pennsylvania
and took his family to the Valley of Virginia. There, in 1779, he
bought four hundred and fifty acres and a log house near Midway,
on the boundary line between Rockbridge and Augusta counties.
Family historians, however, record the McCormick home as in
Rockbridge County.

At this point the family history becomes vague enough to accommodate a skeleton. Recorders are careful to point out that
the Robert McCormick who had to defend himself in court against
importunate creditors for the next decade is probably not *the*
Robert. For evidence they point to the growing list of known
properties belonging to the true Robert McCormick, who not
only acquired more horses and cattle but had at least one slave in
1792. Eight years later he owned three slaves and eight horses, an
estate surpassed only by the leader of local society, Colonel James
McDowell, who had thirteen slaves and nineteen horses.

(If Joseph Medill had ever looked closely into the family history of Robert Sanderson McCormick, who married his daughter
Katharine, it might have troubled his conscience to find a slaveholder.)

The first Robert McCormick firmly established the tradition-
alism which his numerous descendants maintained so rigidly in

the Chicago of the eighties and nineties. It appears strongly today in the character of Colonel McCormick, whose devotion to tradition inspires many of his actions.

As his position in the community improved, Robert became a square-hewn Presbyterian elder, an upholder of the true faith. He attended the New Providence Church, where in 1792 his conservative soul was profoundly shocked by the substitution of Dr. Watts's hymns for the Psalms of David. He rallied others to his cause, withdrew from the church and established an Old Providence Meeting House, where he could worship safe from newfangled doctrines.

Five children had already been born to Robert and Martha in Pennsylvania, but on June 8, 1780, they had one more in their new home. He was a boy, named for his father.

Nothing much is known of the second Robert during the first thirty years of his life, but his marriage at twenty-eight was a significant one. It had definite material advantages. His bride, Mary Ann Hall, brought a dowry of horses and cattle worth a thousand dollars. Moreover, she infused the blood of another Scotch-Irish clan into the deepening McCormick stream. The ancestors of Robert and Mary Ann were probably neighbors a century before, back in Hugh McCormick's bailiwick.

The newlyweds lived at first in the log house of Robert's father and began raising a large family. Eight children were born between 1808, the year of their marriage, and 1822. Only two influenced family history. The first-born, Cyrus Hall McCormick, who arrived on February 15, 1809, left an enduring monument to his name in the reaper he invented, and he sired a colorful branch of the line whose members the present Colonel is said to call "the mad McCormicks." The other was William Sanderson McCormick, whose son Robert married into the Medill family; his grandchildren included the Colonel and Medill McCormick, first husband of Ruth Hanna.

All these descendants were influenced by the dominating figure of Mary Ann McCormick, who was called Polly. It was Polly who inspired her children to make a place for themselves in the world; it was she who set the standard of rich living which her grandchildren carried to the height of fin-de-siècle elegance in Chicago.

Polly was a proud woman, and her rich dowry soon made possible the kind of life she required. She liked to see the shimmer of the family silver and admire the peacocks as they strutted across the lawns of the country home which replaced the log house she had come to as a bride. In her handsome carriage she whipped her fine horses at a dashing speed along the rough country roads. She wore lovely dresses and ornamented herself in a way that inspired the gossip of poorer neighbors. Her impulsive tongue sometimes got her into trouble, too, but for all that, she never wanted friends. Her ivy-covered home at Walnut Grove, overlooking the lush Virginia hills, was the scene of a good many gay parties. But Polly was efficient above everything else, and no house was better managed. Most of all, she always found time to listen to her children, and her love for them was something they never forgot.

Overshadowed by his wife, Robert McCormick was nevertheless an admired and respected man in his own quiet way. He was honest and pious, good Scotch-Irish qualities which recommended him to his Valley of Virginia neighbors. Like so many good Calvinists, Robert did not let his religious tenets hamper his business. With one hand he took away his workers' liquor ration and with the other he sold homemade whisky for twenty-five cents a gallon.

His inventive talents, carried to so brilliant a fruition by his son Cyrus, won him a local fame and he had the business ability to double the size of his father's estate. The original McCormick estate flourished under his hand. He bought the 532-acre home farm from his aging father, who lived with him. By 1812 he owned four slaves and seven horses. He built the two-story red brick Walnut Grove house, sixty-five feet across and fifty feet deep, complete with a porch, a service wing and windows with white casements. Polly filled the eight rooms with splendid furniture, from the stores of Richmond and Lynchburg, designed to blend elegantly with the house's high wainscoting, carved wooden mantels and big fireplaces.

Robert was master of this house, and of workshops, barns, slave quarters and mills. His estate was self-sufficient. Its flax, hemp and sheep fed the busy spinning wheels and looms. Brine barrel and smokehouse were filled with meat from the farm's animals, and with such by-products as tallow for candles and oil for soap. Hides from slaughtered animals were tanned near by and made into shoes and harness. The harvested grain was turned into flour at Robert's own gristmill, and into whisky at his distillery. The fruit went into cider. He had a sawmill to cut up his own timber whenever he needed lumber. There was always more than enough stone for building and the limekiln. Robert turned out numerous inventions at the forge and anvil of his smithy, where Cyrus got his apprenticeship in invention. Eventually, in 1830, the Walnut Grove estate contained about twelve hundred acres of land, nine slaves and eighteen horses. It was as complete in itself as the Chicago *Tribune* empire is today with its paper mill, radio station and syndicate service. Robert McCormick's Virginia estate stood in as splendid an isolation as Colonel McCormick later came to believe that Chicago, Illinois and the Middle West would stand forever.

With this kind of aristocratic background, it is perhaps understandable if the McCormicks considered Katharine Medill's marriage into the family as something of a condescension on their part. In the case of Elinor Medill's union with young Robert Patterson's family, however, the ancestral backgrounds were somewhat more similar.

The Patterson family's early history was much like the McCormicks'; later it hewed to a different line. The first Pattersons were hardy Scotch-Presbyterians who endured a century of persecution before they sought religious freedom in America. Alexander Patterson and his wife, Sarah Stevenson, founded the family in this country. They emigrated to South Carolina sometime after the middle of the eighteenth century, but pushed on to Tennessee about 1800, where they settled in Blount County. The Rev. Robert W. Patterson, D.D., most distinguished member of the family, was born there on January 21, 1814. Seven years later Alexander and Sarah became disturbed by the pro-slavery feeling

Joseph Medill, grandfather of Colonel McCormick, Captain Patterson and Eleanor Patterson

Samuel J. Medill, brother of Joseph, and associated with him in the early days of the Chicago Tribune

Robert McCormick, father of Cyrus Hall McCormick

Cyrus Hall McCormick, inventor of the reaper, publisher of the Copperhead Chicago Times, bitter enemy of Joseph Medill

in Tennessee and, casting about for a Free State, decided on Illinois and settled there in Bond County near the close of 1821.

Before he was five Robert had learned to read at home. His mother taught him while his older brothers and sisters were at school. Sarah, like Mary Ann McCormick, was a strong influence on her children, but in a different way. She gave them all religious instruction and undoubtedly directed young Robert's footsteps toward the ministry.

When he was nine Robert went to school, but the death of his father ended his formal schooling before it had lasted six months. Nevertheless, he had learned enough so that he was able to teach school for two or three terms when he was eighteen. He became a member of the Presbyterian Church in 1832 and entered Illinois College the same year, in the preparatory department. He enrolled in the college itself in 1833 and was graduated in 1837. While he was in college Robert fell under the spell of William Lloyd Garrison and plunged into the abolitionist cause. But he convinced himself before long that Garrison was turning away from abolitionist ideals, and his own ardor cooled into a moderate anti-slavery attitude.

Robert's mind was not wholly upon politics. His interest turned more and more toward the ministry, and upon his graduation from Illinois College he went to Lane Theological Seminary, where he studied under such eminent professors as Drs. Lyman Beecher, Calvin E. Stowe, Baxter Dickinson and Thomas J. Biggs.

Even in the seminary, however, he could not escape the sharp divisions of opinion which were the growing pains of an expanding America. There was, first of all, a split in the Presbyterian Church in 1837. Robert followed the lead of his parents and his professors: he sided with the New School. Then the slavery question invaded the seminary. Robert took a middle ground between the abolitionist professors and the secessionist students.

His first pulpit was in the First Presbyterian Church of Chicago, where he substituted for the pastor-elect, the Rev. Flavel Bascom, in the summer of 1840. He went back to the seminary in the fall, spent the next winter there, and after a short interlude in the East in 1841 he accepted a post, on June 1, 1842, at the newly organized Second Presbyterian Church of Chicago.

Like all the Pattersons, McCormicks and Medills, **Dr. Patterson** was a conservative. Yet, like them, when there was a fight, he got into it. In spite of his middle stand on slavery at the seminary, he did not hesitate to preach on the moral aspects of the question when in 1856 the Civil War began to take shape with the question of extending slaveholding. After Lincoln's election Robert came out flatly for the Union, and all through the war he preached and prayed vigorously for that side.

Thus Joseph Medill's two daughters did better than they knew when they married into the McCormick and Patterson families. As for Medill himself, he was well aware that his own marriage was the extra push he needed to enter the journalistic big time. Matrimony and ambition combined to make him seek greater fortune in the West, and at the suggestion of Horace Greeley he went to Chicago in the spring of 1855. One *Tribune* veteran swears that Greeley gave his famous "Go West" advice to Medill. In any event Horace told Medill that it would be a good idea to start a penny paper in Chicago, and he arranged a meeting there with another friend of his, Charles H. Ray, of Galena, Illinois, then the state's metropolis. Dr. Ray had been editor of the Galena *Jeffersonian*.

Medill and Ray arrived in a Chicago of 85,000 population that pulsed with restless, expanding activity. They carried letters to each other from Greeley, and met in the parlor of the Tremont House, where they were introduced by the proprietor, John B. Drake. Their personalities were ideal for a journalistic partnership: Medill was a business and editorial genius; Ray was an ardent reformer. The result of the meeting between Ray and Medill was a historic decision. They decided not to start a new paper but to buy into the up-and-coming Chicago *Tribune*. Medill bought a third interest; Dr. Ray took a fourth.

With that purchase an era in journalistic history began. The *Tribune* was already eight years old, but its real career began when Joseph Medill entered the office. From that moment the Chicago *Tribune* transcended the simple role of newspaper: it became forthwith a state of mind and has remained so to this day.

# Chapter 2

## ELECTING LINCOLN

THE BATTLES over isolationism and the second World War have assured the McCormick-Patterson press a place in history. The struggle over slavery and the Civil War performed the same service for Joseph Medill and his newspaper.

However, there is one important difference. The political influence of the family today is negligible, measured in terms of practical politics, but there is little doubt that Joseph Medill influenced the course of American history in his use of the *Tribune* as a political weapon. By 1859 his paper was surpassed in power nationally only by the New York *Tribune*, and it completely dominated its own part of the country. This power was a prime factor in the election of 1860. The *Tribune* pushed the doubtful Western states into the Lincoln camp, and Medill himself, in collaboration with Dr. Ray and the Illinois politicians, was largely responsible for getting Lincoln nominated in the convention.

The *Tribune* political technique is much the same now as it was in 1855, when it first referred to the Douglas interests as the "anti-American" party. Even at that early date it believed that God was on its side. Medill took over the property just after the *Tribune* had been defeated in a fanatical crusade for prohibition. The anti-prohibitionists paraded by its offices with a band playing the dead march; they carried a black-draped banner lamenting "The Chicago *Tribune*."

Next day the paper asserted: "The Chicago *Tribune* is not dead. If not now, the principles which it supports will by and by be triumphant. We may endure the mortification of a hundred other defeats. The crepe may be borne by our door ninety and nine times, but sooner or later the victory will perch on the banner we carry aloft. The Almighty has ordained it."

Whether Providence can be held responsible or not, victory did begin to come to the *Tribune*, from the summer day in 1855 when Abraham Lincoln walked into the office to take out a subscription. Abe naturally favored the paper because it was on his side, and he told Medill, "I didn't like the paper before you boys took hold of it. It was too much of a Know-Nothing sheet."

As he plunged into national politics Medill displayed his remarkable political foresight by passing over such Republican hopefuls as Senator Trumbull, John C. Frémont and Justice John McLean. He admired them all and would have liked to vote for his friend Salmon P. Chase, but he knew that neither Chase nor any of the others stood a chance to win. "The one committed to the cause and who can concentrate the greatest number of votes is the man," he wrote. The man who could win, he concluded, was Abraham Lincoln.

In taking its stand for the Republicans, the *Tribune* laid the foundation of Midwestern isolationism upon which it has rested ever since. Then, as now, its enemy was the East and Eastern politicians. The *Tribune* declared: "If we are to have the co-operation of the party elsewhere, well; if not, Illinois is sovereign, and her sons can walk alone!" This was taken as a direct threat to Greeley and Seward.

Again, Medill said proudly: "Chicago is the pet Republican city of the Union, the point from which radiate opinions which more or less influence six states." All that a neighboring paper like the Cleveland *Plain Dealer* could do was to reply sharply: "The principal productions of Chicago are corner lots, statistics and wind."

But in spite of its proud declarations the *Tribune* had a narrow escape from financial failure in 1858, when all Chicago business suffered from depression. Medill and his partners pulled through by consolidating with the *Democratic Press*, and the paper was called the Chicago *Press and Tribune* for a time. Given three years by its creditors to pay off debts of sixty-five thousand dollars, the reorganized *Tribune* paid them in twenty-one months, with ten per cent interest, moved into a new building and successfully met current expenses. It was never again in real financial difficulty.

The move also brought new blood into the firm. Medill and Ray were joined by Alderman William Bross, known as the "Deacon," a scientist who was a pioneer in developing the Far West and was lieutenant governor of Illinois from 1865 to 1869. A second addition was John Locke Scripps, of the famous Scripps newspaper family, one of Lincoln's friends and biographers. These were the men who guided the *Tribune* through the critical Civil War period.

Joseph Medill's political character in this period has been described aptly by Professor Tracy Elmer Strevey, of Northwestern University's history department, whose study of Medill is probably the best extant. Strevey writes: "Medill was clearly a devout Republican from the beginning and throughout this entire period never deviated from the platform of his party nor from the principles for which it stood. He was intensely partisan and apt to take extreme views. . . . He looked upon the Republican party as the product, in part, at least, of his own efforts."

His partners were of the same cut. The best evidence is this straight-faced statement from the *History of Chicago* which Bross wrote later in his life. "The course of the *Tribune* during and before the war," he declared, "was the result of the matured opinions of four independent thinkers and hence it was always right. . . ."

By December 1859 the plan to nominate and elect Lincoln had been settled upon in Chicago by Medill, his *Tribune* partners, and the Republican politicians. Medill went to Washington as correspondent, where he planned to write a series of letters which would launch Lincoln as a candidate, and to lobby for him in Congress. Later that month the Republican National Committee, meeting at the Astor House in New York, voted to hold the convention in Chicago on the following June 13. If they had voted to hold it anywhere else, many historians agree, Lincoln might not have been nominated.

On February 16, 1860, the *Tribune* published its famous editorial urging Lincoln's nomination, widely quoted in political histories ever since. It was followed by a Medill letter from Washington designed to clinch the argument. The editorial and letter were enough to alienate Seward. He sought out Medill at a diplomatic reception and denounced him. "I had always counted on you as one of my boys," he remarked bitterly. "I shall never trust you again."

Medill came home from Washington in February and the pre-convention wirepulling began. The date had been moved up to May 16. While the political maneuvering went on Chicago pre-pared for the historic moment by tearing down the old Sauganash Hotel at the corner of Lake and Market streets and putting up a convention building called the Wigwam, with a seating capacity of ten thousand.

The convention itself, in which five hundred delegates and more than forty thousand onlookers participated in one way or another, accomplished the nomination of Lincoln by political buy-ing and selling of the traditional kind. Medill and Ray were leaders in the horse trading. Some of their convention conversation, as reported by Carl Sandburg in his life of Lincoln, is most reveal-ing. Much of it took place in the smoke-filled room of that day, in the plush Tremont House, Lincoln's headquarters, five blocks from the Wigwam.

"We are going to have Indiana for Old Abe, sure," Ray told Medill.

"How did you get it?" Medill asked.

"By the Lord, we promised them everything they asked."

Then they went to work on Pennsylvania. Later that night, about midnight, Medill was sitting in the Tremont House lobby, smoking and waiting for results, when he saw Judge David Davis come downstairs.

"What's Pennsylvania going to do?" he asked.

"Damned if we haven't got them," Davis replied.

"How did you get them?"

"By paying their price."

Ray came along at that point, and Medill asked him for details.

"Why, we promised to put Simon Cameron in the Cabinet," Ray said. "They wanted assurances that we represented Lincoln and he would do what we said."

"What have you agreed to give Cameron?" Medill wanted to know.

"The Treasury Department."

"Good heavens! Give Cameron the Treasury Department? What will be left?"

"Oh, what's the difference?" Ray said. "We're after a bigger thing than that; we want the presidency and the Treasury is not a great stake to pay for it."

When the actual balloting began at the convention these tactics enabled Lincoln to jump from 102 to 231½ of the 465 votes on the third ballot. Medill leaned over to Carter of Ohio.

"If you can throw the Ohio delegation for Lincoln," he whispered, "Chase can have anything he wants."

"How do you know?" Carter asked.

"I know, and you know I wouldn't promise if I didn't know."

No wonder that Honest Abe, who actually intended to live up to all the promises made in his behalf, later asked his friends, "Well, gentlemen, where do I come in? You seem to have given everything away."

That those at the convention were well aware where credit for the nomination was due is shown by the *Tribune's* own account of the victory celebration, which said: "Last night the *Tribune* was illuminated by the glare of a thousand lights. On the east side of the counting room door stood a rail, one of the 3,000 split by Abe on the Sangamon thirty years ago. On the inside two more hung, glistening with lights. On the front of the office and over the main door was suspended an immense transparency with the inscription 'For President—Honest Old Abe—for Vice-President—Hannibal Hamlin.' Crowds shouldering rails marched through the streets to the music of a score of bands. Many other buildings also were illuminated. Everybody was happy. At dark several of the triumphal processions united, parading through Clark Street and stopping before our office."

Medill forthwith began to sell Lincoln to the public before election time. The *Tribune* distributed biographical sketches, pamphlets, speeches, Lincoln's letters, reports on the Lincoln-Douglas debates and similar material over the entire Northwest. All the resources of the paper were enlisted for the campaign.

Meanwhile Medill used plain words to denounce his New York

counterpart, James Gordon Bennett. "Old Man Bennett of the New York *Herald* is again at his stupendous lies, calling Lincoln a ferocious John Brown abolitionist," the *Tribune* reported. Bennett and the other anti-Lincolnites did not prevail against the Republican campaign and the *Tribune* was able to report "The Great Victory" on November 7, 1860. Chicago's Wide Awake Clubs marched sixteen abreast in a torchlight parade and demonstrated military maneuvers in front of the *Tribune's* Clark Street office.

In the interval before Lincoln was inaugurated the *Tribune* took the opportunity to attack President Buchanan for the last time, in terms couched only a little more strongly than those used many years later to attack President Roosevelt. The paper's Washington correspondent reported on January 3, 1861, concerning a Cabinet meeting:

"The row recommenced. The President, like a pusillanimous coward, refused to take sides, and, shaken like an aspen leaf, entreated them not to quarrel, and offered them some old whiskey—his unfailing remedy. The old man has become little better than a sot. He keeps saturated with Monongahela whiskey. He drinks to drown remorse and stupefy his brain as he staggers along with the treasonable gang who have possession of him."

Then as now the *Tribune* did not hesitate to read out of the Republican party anyone who failed to stay in line. In February, Congressman William Kellogg, of Canton, Illinois, who had been close to Lincoln, introduced in the House a bill which would have amended the Constitution to permit taking slaves into any territory south of 36° 30', from any slave state. Next day the *Tribune* dismissed Kellogg, and added a day later: "We are opposed *in toto* to any double-tongued proposition which shall add the crime of swindling to that of compromising with traitors."

On this belligerent note, the *Tribune* entered the war years.

## Chapter 3

## FIGHTING THE WAR

FROM 1861 to 1865, Medill and his *Tribune* preached the Union and emancipation with an increasingly powerful voice. The paper fought against wildcat money. It fought for the development of railroads. And it grew with Chicago.

They were violent years. Medill felt the violence personally in February 1861, as a result of the *Tribune's* attack on Kellogg. The congressman met Medill at the National Hotel in Washington and demanded an explanation, but the editor refused to discuss the matter. Kellogg struck him, knocked him down and began to beat him until bystanders ended the fight. Back in Chicago, the *Tribune* denounced Kellogg all over again, calling him a bully for assaulting an invalid. (Medill suffered from spinal rheumatism.) The paper never forgave Kellogg.

Shortly after the inauguration Medill came home to devote himself to *Tribune* affairs. He had been most unhappy in Washington. It was more to his liking to supervise the installation of a new cylinder press. With the beginning of war this new press was kept busy turning out the *Tribune's* voluminous war coverage, which was so complete that even Medill, Ray and the other editors were frequently at the front as reporters.

In the summer of 1861 Lincoln learned what several others had learned before him—that Joseph Medill and the *Tribune* were ardent supporters of men and causes which were theirs, but God help the man who differed with them. As President, and acting for his own good reasons, Lincoln had countermanded an order of Major General John Frémont setting free certain slaves he had confiscated from the rebels in St. Louis. The *Tribune* not only denounced the President's action editorially, but Medill wrote a letter to his old friend Salmon P. Chase in which, as Sandburg points out, he was apparently so disgusted with Lincoln that he was ready to sound out Chase as a potential Republican party leader.

This was no incident of the moment. The question of loyalty to the President recurred on a much more serious basis in 1864, before he was renominated. There was a strong anti-Lincoln movement opposing his renomination, to which Medill certainly contributed by writing to Congressman Washburne and declaring bluntly that he thought Lincoln should be dropped unless he reorganized his Cabinet along radical lines. He wrote, "Lincoln has some very weak and foolish traits of character. If he had reasonable political sagacity and would cut loose from the semi-copperheads in his Cabinet and about him, if he would put live, bold, vigorous radicals in their places no human power could prevent his renomination."

Much of what Medill was thinking and feeling at this period in his life is revealed in the letters he wrote to his brother, Major William H. Medill, who had come up in the newspaper business with him and left the *Tribune* to join the Union Army. Elected captain of G Troop, 8th Illinois Cavalry, William was killed at Gettysburg, in his twenty-eighth year.

These Medill letters, to William and others, often sound like the utterances of his grandson, Colonel McCormick. It is possible that at least part of the Colonel's anti-British phobia stems from Medill's hatred of the British for daring to help the Confederacy. One letter to William is now in the possession of the Chicago Historical Society.

May 24, 1863

. . . How do you like the glorious news from Vicksburg? . . . I tell you the Kingdom of Jeff Davis totters to its fall. . . . I believe the war is hastening to its close. When we get the devils going downhill the velocity of their fall follows the rule of other falling bodies. . . . There is a great, grand and glorious future to our country when the slave holder's hellish revolt is crushed out. There will never be another rebellion. There never was but one in heaven, and there never will be but one in North

America. The Almighty put the revolted Lucifers into h--l and the loyal people will put the revolted slave holders into as hot a place.

But it is· very possible that we shall have two wars when this one is ended—one to clear the British out of Canada and the other to clear the French out of Mexico. This continent belongs to the Free American race and they are bound to have it—every inch of it, including the West Indian Islands. We have got a taste of blood and learned the art of war and our own tremendous strength and exhaustless resources. Our navy will dominate the seas and our army the continent.

The insults received from England must be wiped out, and the only reparation she can give us is to vacate North America. Peacibly [sic] if she will—forcibly if we must. And as to France, she has taken a mean and cowardly advantage of this nation to crush poor Mexico, which will not be allowed. We shall permit no nation to abuse Mexico but ourselves. We claim the right to turn her up on Uncle Sam's knee and spank her bottom for not behaving herself as in 1846, but will permit no one else to touch her. . . . In future wars black and yellow men will be freely used to fight. We will not be so careful about spilling the blood of niggers. England holds India with Sepoy troops who hate her. How easy for us to hold the South with black troops who love the North and are devotedly loyal. Old Abe says, "Bring on your niggers. I want 200,000 of them to save my white boys as soon as I can get them." Our people are learning sense. The war has pounded new ideas into their heads and old prejudices out. It is a great teacher, and great progress is never made by a people except through war. The tree of Liberty must be watered by the blood of patriots at least once in every three generations.

This last paragraph provides some indication of how much of Joseph Medill's abolitionist crusade was purely political and how much of it was humanitarian.

A letter written to Schuyler Colfax, after the failure of the Peninsular Campaign, shows once more how Medill wanted to run the Cabinet and the war in his own way, and the devil take the President if he didn't stay in line. Medill wrote:

"What a dismal retrospect is the past eighteen months. That

period consists of epaulettes and apathy, imbecility and treachery, idiocy and ignorance, sacrifice on the part of the people, supineness on the part of the Government. McClellan in the field and Seward in the Cabinet have been the evil spirits that have brought our grand cause to the very brink of death. Seward must be got out of the Cabinet. He is Lincoln's evil genius. He has been President *de facto* and has kept a sponge saturated with chloroform to Uncle Abe's nose all the while, except one or two brief spells, during which rational intervals, Lincoln removed Buell, issued the Emancipation Proclamation, and discharged McClellan. Smith is a cipher on the right hand of the Seward integer—but himself nothing but a doughface. Bates is a fossil of the Silurian era—red sandstone at least—and should never have been quarried out of the rock in which he was imbedded. Blair was drawn into a retrograde position by the quarrel of his brother Frank with Fremont. There must be a reorganization of the Cabinet—Seward, Smith and Bates must go out."

Again and again, too, Medill solidified the foundations of Middle Western insularity in his battles with the Eastern papers and their publishers, particularly Bennett's *Herald*. Medill was particularly incensed when the *Herald*, in 1863–64, boomed General Grant as "the People's Candidate" in the coming election.

Editorially he gave the *Herald* some bitter advice: "We claim the right to tell this organ of the Five Points and the Thugs of New York, that it must keep its copperhead slime off our Illinois General. He has no attribute, thought or sympathy in harmony with the *Satanic* [the *Tribune's* nickname for the *Herald*]. General Grant is an old neighbor and friend of President Lincoln. The latter has stood by him with the strength of iron from the first. . . . In return General Grant has been true as steel to his friend and Commander-in-Chief. For the New York *Herald* to bring out General Grant is a gross libel on him and an insult to his friends. Unless it keeps its unclean and treacherous hands off of him, it may expect to get 'tomahawked.' . . . It cannot be allowed to paw and slobber over our Illinois General, and if it has any regard for its 'throat' or its 'fifth rib,' it will take warning and govern itself accordingly." The *Herald*, unable to think of an adequate reply, could only retort that the *Tribune* was "the sewer into which goes everything too dirty for its New York namesake to print."

*Tribune* biographers and uncritical admirers of Joseph Medill like to cite his unabashed criticism of Lincoln and the President's policies as proof of his integrity and of his unswerving devotion to his beliefs. They also call it a splendid example of freedom of the press.

But not unlike the late President Roosevelt, Lincoln let Medill and other editors say what they liked—until they had plainly put themselves in their true perspective, as little dogs snapping at the heels of a big dog. Such an incident occurred in 1865, in one of the war's darkest hours, when the slaughter was at its peak and there was protest over the bloodshed. The protest was in the form of resistance to the draft quotas. Medill headed a committee of three from Chicago, a city which thought its quota was too high, having already sent twenty-two thousand men. Lincoln heard his visitors out quietly, and when he spoke he gave them an unanswerable response. As Medill himself remembered this impromptu speech, Lincoln said:

"Gentlemen, after Boston, Chicago has been the chief instrument in bringing this war on the country. The Northwest has opposed the South as the Northeast has opposed the South. You called for war until we had it. You called for emancipation and I have given it to you. Whatever you have asked for you have had. Now you come here begging to be let off from the call for men which I have made to carry out the war which you have demanded. You ought to be ashamed of yourselves. I have a right to expect better things of you. Go home and raise your six thousand extra men. And you, Medill, are acting like a coward. You and your *Tribune* have had more influence than any paper in the Northwest in making this war. You can influence great masses, and yet you cry to be spared at a moment when your cause is suffering. Go home and send us those men."

For once Medill knew that he had been wrong. Here was something the Almighty had not ordained. He confessed later: "I couldn't say anything. It was the first time I ever was whipped, and I didn't have an answer. We all got up and went out, and when the door closed, one of my colleagues said, 'Well, gentlemen, the old man is right. We ought to be ashamed of ourselves. Let us never say anything about this, but go home and raise the men.' And we did, six thousand men, making twenty-eight thousand in the war from a city of a hundred and fifty-six thousand."

Between 1862 and 1866 Medill was engaged in a subsidiary war. By coincidence, it was a war of the same kind which has occupied so much of Colonel McCormick's time. The conflict arose over the dissemination of news by wire and involved the Associated Press. Some of Medill's pronouncements on the subject must sometimes embarrass the Colonel, if he ever thinks of them.

The basis of the dispute was the formation of a Western Associated Press, in opposition to the New York Associated Press. This, of course, was before the AP as we know it today was born. In 1862 Medill sent out a discreet letter to his fellow Western publishers, hinting that they should meet and organize—but quietly, so as not to make the New Yorkers suspicious.

An initial meeting in Indianapolis in 1862 elected Medill chairman, and the next year another session chose a committee to be sent to New York in an effort to get better news reports. The committee was successful in establishing a news agent in New York, and a year later Medill urged incorporation of the Western Associated Press. It was chartered in Louisville in 1865.

Then the conflict broke out. The issue was whether the Western Associated Press would have an equal voice in newsgathering with the New York outfit or would be independent. Negotiations were fruitless. New York flatly refused equality. The Western group served notice that it would control its own news reports. By 1866 the war for news was at its height.

At this point Medill stepped into the fight (he had resigned as chairman in 1865) and denounced the New York Associated Press as a monopoly—exactly the charge that the government was to bring against the AP in 1944, with Medill's grandson on the opposite side of the fence. Yet Medill spoke in words that would have delighted Colonel McCormick's heart.

"Don't be afraid of independence," he told his fellow editors earnestly. "It is not going to hurt you. It will not be long before these New York birds of paradise will come down from their lofty trees and roost lower."

Eventually the New Yorkers were outmaneuvered, and monopolistic practices of those days were modified to suit the times. But it was a long time before New York relinquished its hold on the news, in spite of the efforts of wiser heads in the Associated Press to reorganize on a sounder basis.

The year 1864 was further enlivened in the *Tribune's* history by its first libel action. The paper fell afoul of one of the commonest causes for such action. It quoted a Chicago alderman's charge of bribery in council affairs, and the quotation included the name of a fellow alderman, J. H. Roberts. The *Tribune* ran its story with the head, COPPERHEAD CORRUPTION, and although the paper made no charges of its own, Roberts sued for twenty thousand dollars.

This action gave the *Tribune* its first opportunity to sound the cry which it has raised ever since, whenever it has been attacked. The libel suit, cried the *Tribune*, was a blow to freedom of the press. Moreover, it said, Roberts had been "egged on" by the *Tribune's* Copperhead enemy, the *Times*. Shortly afterward the *Tribune* attacked Roberts directly, implicating him in a current railroad scandal and calling him a "notorious dandy, windy and ambitious." Roberts thereupon said he would make the charge criminal libel.

Apparently the *Tribune* lost the suit, because the paper's historians do not mention its outcome.

But great events overshadowed this squabble. The war ended, and the *Tribune* announced the news in four columns of page-one bulletins. It called Lee "a public enemy—an average Virginia slaveholder in moral character, nothing more." Discussing Reconstruction, it began an editorial with this characteristic statement: "This has been a rich man's war. We have from the first branded the war as a war of aristocracy against democracy, of slave holders against working men, of oligarchs against the people."

The *Tribune's* war had only begun.

# Chapter 4

## FAMILY QUARREL

THE WAR'S EFFECT on McCormick-Medill-Patterson family history was profound. It elevated Joseph Medill and the *Tribune* to national prominence, and it also established the McCormick family in Chicago. Finally, it involved the McCormicks and Medills in one 'of the most bitter personal conflicts of the times, although little more than a decade later the families were united by marriage.

Within the framework of this larger drama other stories played themselves out. One was the story of Cyrus Hall McCormick, as stubborn a die-hard as Joseph Medill. Another was the tragic life of Cyrus's brother, William Sanderson McCormick, a transplanted Virginian who never wanted anything he achieved. A third involved the schism in the Presbyterian Church, political in origin, which was responsible for the founding of McCormick Theological Seminary and eventually brought the Patterson family into the conflict.

If Cyrus McCormick had remained the quiet inventor he started out to be in Rockbridge County, he might never have precipitated the family into history, but money and fame made it possible for him to back up his political convictions. If he started to fight, he quickly displayed the dominant McCormick family characteristic: an inability to admit that he might be wrong. When his Virginia conservatism came into conflict with expanding, radical Chicago the results were paradoxical; his political defeats were more than balanced by the mark he left upon the city's business and social life. The whole story of Cyrus's amazing life has been told best in William T. Hutchinson's two-volume biography, published in 1930.

Cyrus was only fifteen when he invented a light cradle to help him compete with the grownups in the harvest fields of Walnut Grove Farm; seven years later he was demonstrating his first reaper at the famous public trial on a field near Steele's Tavern, Virginia.

In 1835 his father, Robert McCormick, gave Cyrus a farm on South River, nine miles from Walnut Grove. In the following year the young man built an iron furnace in Augusta County and entered into a partnership with his father, meanwhile improving his reaper. Five years later he sold the furnace, as the result of losses in the panic of 1837. Both he and his father were heavily in debt. By that time, however, his reaper was beginning to sell, mostly because of Cyrus's own salesmanship and demonstrations.

The business began to expand in 1845. He had made connections with Backus Fitch & Co., of Brockport, New York, and with A. C. Brown, of Cincinnati, to sell reapers in upper New York State and Ohio. Within two more years he was able to enter into a partnership with C. M. Gray, of Chicago, for the sale of reapers, and established a factory on the north bank of the Chicago River, near its mouth. The plant was the marvel of its day, shown proudly to visitors by resident Chicagoans. Three stories high, the brick building was a hundred by thirty feet in ground area, and in it a steam engine operated saws, lathes, planing machines and grinding stones. Thirty-three men worked at these machines and the plant's six forges. In eight years the factory grew so rapidly that it had a daily capacity of forty machines; it built four thousand reapers in 1856.

Cyrus had pulled up his roots in 1847 and gone to Chicago to live. Two years later he sent for his brothers, William and Leander. While these men ran the plant and made the family a power in Chicago real estate, Cyrus himself was drawn into the political arena.

He encountered Abraham Lincoln for the first time in 1854 when the Illinois lawyer was among counsel in one of McCormick's suits for infringement of patents. Already Cyrus felt his Virginia gorge rising against the abolition talk he heard everywhere in Chicago. In 1856 he was shocked to learn that the minister in his own church was beginning to argue for abolition.

By this time the inventor was a millionaire, and he further solidified his position in Chicago society through a fashionable marriage in 1858 to Nancy (called Nettie) Fowler. There were only a few guests at the ceremony, but in the evening more than five hundred friends filled the North Side home of Cyrus's brother and sister-in-law, William and Mary Ann Grigsby McCormick, which was already a social center. The reception was impressive proof that the Virginia farm boy had arrived.

The Chicago *Daily Press*, a Republican newspaper which later joined the *Tribune* in attacking McCormick, was almost rhapsodic over his wedding reception. Its reporter wrote: "One of the most pleasant and hospitable residences in the North Division was thrown open last evening, and despite the unfavorable weather the guests gathered and filled the apartments to overflowing. They came and seemed scarcely to add to the number, they went and were little missed, as carriage after carriage deposited its freight of fair women and brave men to take their places. Within, all was gaiety and the sound of music, and the murmur of conversation, and the merry laugh. The party was the largest, and one of the most brilliant of the season, and will be marked and memorable in festive days. . . ."

A year later the *Press* was in a different mood. Cyrus Mc-Cormick had launched three projects, all of them designed to advance the political ideas he shared with Stephen Douglas and the other opponents of Lincoln in the North. He bought the *Times*, dedicated it to Democracy and pitted it savagely against the Republican press. He established the *Presbyterian Expositor*, a religious periodical, as a lever to persuade the Presbyterian Church to adopt Old School views and prevent war. Finally, he endowed four professorships in the Presbyterian Theological Seminary of the Northwest, with the long-range plan of sending into Presbyterian pulpits in Chicago and elsewhere young ministers who would advance the anti-war doctrines of Old School Presbyterianism.

In Cyrus McCormick's mind patriotism, party loyalty and his religion were inextricably tangled. He believed that the Union could not be preserved by force, and in January 1861 he predicted that failure to reach a compromise would mean "all the horrors of a civil war." Still, he shared Douglas's view that coercion was the next best thing if it wasn't possible to avoid the issue.

He presided at a meeting in North Market Hall that January, at which delegates to the Springfield party convention were to be elected. His faction, which the *Tribune* dubbed the "McCormick party," dominated the meeting and succeeded in passing a resolution which declared that "it would be unwise and impolitic to seek by war to compel an unwilling Union."

Until the war began McCormick would not believe that compromise was impossible. He was pleased with the division in the Republican party over the same issue, comforted himself with the thought that the less forthright Seward would guide Lincoln's policies, and believed firmly in the unconstitutionality of secession. The inventor blamed the whole conflict on the politicians of both sides. If the issue could be taken to the people of the North and South through conventions, McCormick argued, the will of the people would be for peace and union. There were others who agreed with him. They were the Peace Democrats of the North, who went through the entire war believing that only a people's convention was necessary to end the conflict and that the common man had been betrayed by his leaders, both North and South. McCormick never wavered in these beliefs for the rest of his life.

But to the Republicans, the position of McCormick and his followers appeared like that of the appeasers in our own time. It was a peace-at-any-price stand. The *Tribune* was furious. It denounced McCormick as a "rebel" and a "slavedriver." These editorial pronouncements, appearing in February 1861, angered Cyrus to the point where he was ready to sue for libel, but the editors of the *Times* pointed out that his paper was almost as violent in its attacks on abolitionists.

On the day the *Tribune's* editorial blast appeared Cyrus happened to be in Washington on patent business, but William and Leander took up his defense in a public letter. They wrote, in part: "A more Demon-like production [meaning the *Tribune's* editorial] could not be hatched this side the infernal regions. . . . Cyrus H. McCormick is interested in saving a Union, not in saving a party. Is it not possible that the Chicago *Tribune* might lose more by the breaking of its party than the breaking of the government?"

Writing to a friend a month later, William put the family's position a good deal more succinctly and accurately: "We have helped to build this city by hundreds of thousands & these Editors though strong politically are without body or soul substantially. . . . We are not secessionists by a good deal, but we are for the South having her rights."

The *Tribune* continued to attack; the *Times* continued to defend. In 1864 the battle reached a climax when Cyrus ran for Congress in opposition to the *Tribune's* Union candidate, "Long John" Wentworth. The *Tribune* struck McCormick at a point it thought was weakest. An editorial on September 21 ran as follows:

"The Chicago *Times* is fearful that people will lose sight of the enormous debt which the Northwest owes to C. H. McCormick, and thereby fail to elect him to Congress. The obligation of the Northwest, or of any other section, or country, to Mr. McCormick on account of the patent reaper, is small enough, and has been paid ten times over in cash. We will not go into the early history of the reel of the Virginia reaper, or inquire whether the person who has received all the pay for it really invented it or not. The traditions of Rockbridge County are very conflicting on this point. Probably as many people can be found there to swear that he invented nothing at all as that he invented the reaper which is associated with his name. But we let that pass, and turn to facts which are matters of record within a stone's throw of us.

"Mr. C. H. McCormick, in his efforts to make a reaping machine, pirated the invention of a poor New York mechanic named Obed Hussey. This invention was by far the most ingenious and valuable portion of 'McCormick's Reaper,' viz.: the cutter. Mr. Hussey invented the remarkable arrangement of the zigzag sickle, running within iron fingers, which annually mows down the grain and hay crops of a large portion of the world. Mr. Hussey was poor and perhaps imperfectly acquainted with his own rights in the premises. So Mr. McCormick stole it from him and called it his own. With it he built up an immense fortune, and made himself famous all through Christendom, while Mr. Hussey yet remained poor. By and by, Mr. Hussey became rich enough to assert his rights. He appealed to the laws of his country, and in a suit of almost unexampled length and magnitude, in which Mr. McCormick employed about a dozen of the ablest lawyers of the United States, Obed Hussey established his claim before the world. He proved Mr. McCormick to be an impostor, and a pirate upon other men's toil and brains. He obtained a decree of the United States Circuit Court, Judge McLean presiding, in this city, assessing heavy damages upon McCormick for the use of the cutter, and a percentage upon all future machines which he should make with Mr. Hussey's invention.

"If Mr. McCormick invented anything, he invented the reel which bends the grain over against the cutter. For this he was long ago paid in full, and a balance of some millions has been carried to the credit of the people on account of it. Hussey's cutter is a great and valuable invention without McCormick's reel. McCormick's reel is worthless without Hussey's cutter. Obed Hussey did not live long enough to enjoy the full reward of his great and beneficent invention. He left a name unstained by one dishonorable act, and if the people are called on now to elect anybody to Congress as a reward for the reaping machine, let them find one of the heirs of the New York mechanic who enriched the whole country, but enriched no one so much as the man whom we are now asked to vote for to show our gratitude for the patent reaper."

Most of this story appears to be about as inaccurate as *Tribune* political attacks have always been.

When he first put a reaper together in 1831 Cyrus utilized seven elements essential to all reapers: a straight knife to cut the grain, fingers or guards to prevent the grain from slipping sideways, a revolving reel to hold the grain against the knife, a platform behind the knife to receive the cut grain, a master wheel to carry weight and furnish power, shafts attached in front of this wheel to provide forward draft, and a divider on the left side to separate cut from uncut grain.

At the time, McCormick knew that he was not the original

discoverer of all seven principles. Only the master wheel was original with him, but he worked out the whole seven independently and alone, and by putting them into the proper combination he invented the first reaper, which contained six known principles and one entirely new one.

Three years later, in April 1834, McCormick saw for the first time a description of Obed Hussey's reaper in an issue of *Mechanics Magazine*. Hussey was not a New York mechanic but a Cincinnati candlestick maker and ex-sailor. His machine contained some of the principles used by McCormick in his first machine, so Cyrus wrote to the magazine editor and claimed priority. He also sought a patent immediately. Hussey admitted a few years later that McCormick's machine preceded his, but he went on making his own nonetheless. As a matter of record, the two machines were adapted to different purposes. Hussey's was mounted on two main wheels, which operated the machine, and it had no reel. Its cutting apparatus was the same in principle but different in operation. People came to see that the Hussey reaper was actually better suited to mowing, and mowing machines were henceforth constructed along those lines. McCormick's machine proved its superiority as a reaper time and time again, and those who built reapers thereafter followed his principles. Hussey was never able to meet competition and sold his patents to some rivals of McCormick's in 1858.

Nonetheless, the *Tribune* brazened it out. About a month later it returned to the attack: "Some weeks ago the Chicago *Times* promised to furnish a mess of 'documentary evidence' to prove that Mr. C. H. McCormick is the inventor of the reaping machine, and that he had established his claim in every tribunal where it had ever been denied. We have called for that documentary evidence several times since the promise was made, but it does not come. We have proved that Mr. McCormick took the most valuable part of the reaping machine from Obed Hussey, and that the United States Circuit Court ordered him to pay for it, and enjoined him from robbing Mr. Hussey thereafter. We have proposed to show, from equally authentic records, where Mr. McCormick picked up the remainder of the machine, when the documentary evidence of the *Times* should be given to the public. One might infer that no haste was being exhibited on the other side to bring on the issue. Very well. Least said soonest mended!"

Meanwhile the *Tribune* attacked McCormick's financial support of the war, or the lack of it, a charge which had considerable more truth in it. The *Tribune* fulminated: "In the course of his harangue to the crowd at the Courthouse, night before last, on the subject of cashing county orders, Ald. Comisky charged that John Wentworth and Cyrus H. McCormick, opposing candidates for Congress, had done little or nothing for the war fund. We are confident Mr. Wentworth stands ready to subscribe in proportion to his means. Can as much be said in behalf of McCormick? Mr. Wentworth's property is mainly in the shape of unproductive real estate in the vicinity of Bridgeport, on which he pays heavy taxes and receives little or no income. . . . On the other hand Mr. McCormick is a man of vast wealth. He is reported to be worth from three to five millions. His cash income exceeds $2,000 per day, it is reported. He made in one operation last year by the rise in iron six hundred thousand dollars. He has invested in real estate speculation half a million or more in this city during the present season. His agents in the country are continually on the lookout for opportunities to loan money at high rates on cut-throat mortgages to farmers. No man in Illinois possesses so much ready means as the Copperhead candidate, and no man of means has done so little for the soldiers during the war. It is entirely within McCormick's pecuniary ability to advance to the county the half million dollars required to pay volunteers, and if his love of the Union and the Old Flag was equal to his affection for the rebellion and the slave-holding aristocracy, he would step forward and draw his check for the money and save holders of the scrip from being robbed by sharks and shavers."

The result of all these and other editorial blows was the election in November of "Long John" Wentworth, whom the *Tribune* had never loved until he became by circumstance a weapon in its hands.

McCormick's religious struggle was an absorbing sideshow to the main event. The kernel of the conflict was Old School Presbyterianism, anti-war and more or less sympathetic to the South, as opposed to New School Presbyterianism, the product of vigorous Northern, abolitionist minds.

Cyrus had helped to organize a Presbyterian church (Old School) soon after he came to Chicago. The congregation called it the North Church and it grew rapidly. McCormick was determined to use it as the rock on which the entire national Old School wing of the church could anchor itself, so that it would not break apart politically. It was already a dangerous thing, in his opinion, that there should have been a schism in 1837 which set up the New School as a separate church.

He acquired a powerful ally in Dr. Nathan L. Rice, at the time pastor of a St. Louis church and editor of a Presbyterian journal there. Dr. Rice had twenty years' experience in arguing orthodox Presbyterianism in and out of the public prints. His stand on the slavery question was typical. He was not for slavery, he said, but on the other hand, he could prove by the Bible that Southern slaveholding was not a sin and therefore the Church was not duty-bound to preach against it.

Dr. Rice was debt-ridden and he listened willingly to McCormick's tempting offers to come to Chicago. When Cyrus heard in 1857 that the redoubtable Rice had agreed to move both himself and his paper, he exulted in a letter to William, "It is glorious." The *Tribune* took the news in its own fashion. It flatly accused McCormick of subsidizing the preaching of pro-slavery principles—in, of all places, the *Tribune's* sacred free Northwest.

The St. Louis *Presbyterian*, Dr. Rice's monthly, was set up in Chicago as the *Presbyterian Expositor*. It had never been a going concern financially, and McCormick paid all the bills. It lasted less than two years in Chicago; its new owner put six thousand dollars into the publication, but he did not think of the sum as lost money, because the paper was so strong an advocate of his cause.

Looking about for further weapons, McCormick was not unhappy to learn that a struggling little seminary in New Albany, Indiana, was about to die a financial death. Its board of directors was under the thumb of the Northwest's seven Old School Presbyterian synods. This board, meeting in Chicago with other churchmen, decided to appoint six members of the North and South churches to be trustees of a "Presbyterian Theological Seminary of the Northwest." No provisions were made for location or endowment.

In using his influence and money to get the New Albany School transferred to Chicago, there is no doubt at all as to what was in McCormick's mind. If the seminary came under Old School domination, it would be expected to teach Old School doctrines. Its professors would have pastoral charges in Chicago, and they would contribute sermons and articles to the *Expositor*. The result of all this would be a steady flow of Old School propaganda in the Northwest.

To bring about that happy state McCormick drafted a proposal on May 13, 1859, to endow four seminary professorships with twenty-five thousand dollars each—if the seminary was moved to Chicago and placed under control of the General Assembly of the Old School Presbyterian Church.

When the Assembly met that year there were some who wanted the seminary located in Indianapolis, but it was obvious that there would be no financial support for it if it settled there. It was a case of McCormick and continued existence. Thus the seminary, once the regional representative of Presbyterianism, became the tool of Chicago conservatism.

It quickly became the ground over which plot and counterplot raged as the battle for control of the seminary and of the church itself developed between McCormick and his enemies. The struggle was climaxed with the Chicago Fire, which came at a moment when a fund-raising campaign to finance the institution was drawing to a successful close. Many of the pledges were, of course, instantly worthless. McCormick's unyielding character was never better demonstrated than in that moment. While his own factory burned he wrote out a check for forty-five thousand dollars. The fire reached the edge of the seminary grounds, but nearly all of the buildings were saved. Even the institution's securities, kept in a downtown safe, were found intact when the charred strongbox was opened.

With unexpected suddenness the fire brought final victory to

McCormick. His opponents at the seminary, in the grip of crisis, realized that there was only one man who could pull them through. They turned the reins over to McCormick. A smaller man might have exacted revenge. Cyrus was wise enough to know that the seminary would not succeed in any case unless it had the co-operation of the whole church, and his subsequent moves were made wholly with the intent of bringing about that co-operation.

Cyrus McCormick died in his Rush Street mansion on May 13, 1884. He still believed the Civil War could and should have been avoided. He was still the enemy of Presbyterian liberalism. At his death the family he had established was numbered among the first in Chicago and his business was one of the nation's leaders. These things may have compensated somewhat for the political failures of his life and the stubborn resistance to change for which he paid so heavy a price.

# Chapter 5

## WILLIAM THE UNWILLING

WILLIAM SANDERSON MCCORMICK, Colonel McCormick's grand-father, was overshadowed by his brother Cyrus. His life was a tragedy, a minute cameo of unhappiness in a setting of tremendous events. Yet it is worth examining, because it displays the human side of the McCormick family.

When Cyrus's reaper-building business at Walnut Grove began to expand, Leander departed to conduct his brother's affairs in Cincinnati, while William stayed behind on the farm and helped Cyrus build reapers for the Eastern market. William was not, however, a successful mechanic at the start of his career. The thirty-five machines he completed were unsalable. But William was not too perturbed. He had inherited Walnut Grove by 1847, and he proposed to stay there for the rest of his life and make a home for his mother and for Mary Ann Grigsby, the neighbor girl he married in 1848.

In 1849, however, Cyrus summoned both him and Leander to Chicago, and William sorrowfully held an auction sale of the furnishings at Walnut Grove, bid his mother good-by and took his wife with him to Chicago. His mother, Mary Ann McCormick, died of typhoid fever in 1853 at the home of her daughter, Amanda Adams. Amanda was the last of the McCormick children to live in the Valley of Virginia, and when Mary Ann died Amanda and her husband moved to Chicago too, and the McCormick era in Rockbridge County came to an end. Hugh Adams, using Cyrus's money and reputation as backing, soon established himself in Chicago as a wholesale grocer and commission merchant.

Leander and William discovered that their brother paid only modest salaries. Astutely, they invested what money they could in city houses and lots.

William still owned Walnut Grove and had leased it to a farmer, but he made several efforts to sell it. He tried to persuade his sister Caroline, who had married the Rev. James H. Shields, to settle there. The letter he wrote to his brother-in-law in 1858 was almost pathetically eager:

"Will you and Sister C. remove to Walnut Grove and keep it as long as you live, and let us all occasionally resort to it as a sacred spot? If we enable you to do so, you might help to civilize and Christianize that barbarous people. . . . I ask you this question about W. Grove seriously.

"C. H. ever talks of buying it and keeping it up as a sacred spot even at a loss to him. *He* could afford now to do it. *I* should love to make my home again at Walnut Grove if pecuniary interest were not in the way of it. . . . What says Caroline? You could have Hannah to cook and Anthony to drive your carriage and couldn't you splurge."

It was the second time William had made the offer. It was refused once more. He tried again to sell it for eighteen thousand dollars, without success.

About this time William wrote another letter, which provides an informative picture of business prospects in Chicago. He wrote: "A man of some sprightliness and business tact along with his trade could probably soon work his way up to fifty dollars per month of 26 days, ten hours work. This might take a year or more to acquire. Chicago is getting to be a great City and in it good men can always find employment at fair wages."

At his brother's Chicago plant William soon took on numerous responsibilities, investing much of the company's money and acting in general as a buffer for Cyrus during the hectic war years. He was in general charge of the office, which had to handle a rapidly increasing flow of business.

He enjoyed a happy interlude in England in 1852, when he went there with an expert mechanic, named McKenzie, to push the Virginia reaper. Obed Hussey came over at the same time, and between July and October the rivals contended over the rich English harvest fields. As the summer ended, the McCormick reaper gradually established an edge. One of the most severe trials was a nine-day contest at Circencester Agricultural College, which owned several Hussey machines and was considerably chagrined when William won the contest.

William won in other trials at the Yorkshire Agricultural Society, the Durham County Agricultural Society, and the Driffield Farmers' Club. In early September he moved up to the Scottish border and issued a general challenge to anyone who wanted to contest with him in the fields around Sunderland.

That was nearly the extent of William's happiness after his removal to Chicago. When he came home again, increased business responsibilities kept him inside most of the time. He hated the confinement of an office. In his mind constantly was the thought of the quiet and peace of his boyhood home. He made summer pilgrimages there, breathed deeply of the mountain air and chatted comfortably with his neighbors. Back in Chicago, he could only escape when he was experimenting with some new machine in a nearby harvest field.

Like Cyrus, and many another McCormick before and after him, William could not relax. When he went hunting and fishing up in Wisconsin or Minnesota he took his business with him. After a long day at the office he went on working at home. Many times, after a sleepless night, he rose at dawn and hurried away without breakfast to test a mower while the dew still remained on the grass. He had helped materially to develop a good McCormick mower.

He and Mary Ann were soon accepted by the inner circle of Chicago society, as he quickly accumulated a small fortune, but this recognition brought him no pleasure. He was only Chicagoan enough to acquire the tremendous faith every citizen had in the city's future. Aside from that, he was an unhappy, transplanted Southern farmer who lived mostly for the time he could retire to Virginia again. Mary Ann shared his feelings. In 1857 she wrote naïvely: "What a pity this [Illinois] wasn't a slave state because so easily cultivated." When war came her brother wore a Confederate uniform.

William's fatal illness began in 1856 with dyspepsia. He attributed it to nervous exhaustion and lack of exercise, but he was also a self-confessed "hearty eater of everything eatable almost."

By 1859 he was under a doctor's care, on a diet of stale bread, eggs, milk and vegetables. He also tried riding and exercising in the gymnasium he had built in his new home. It was all in vain.

Only his business judgment did not suffer. With Leander, he made that judgment pay more and more. His efforts to sell Walnut Grove were made mostly to get more money for his real estate speculations, but a long visit to the old farm in the summer of 1859 made him ashamed of this avariciousness. He wondered how he could ever have thought of such sacrilege. In a fit of remorse he planted a new orchard, repaired fences and drained fields. With the war, he nearly lost the property under sequestration proceedings—it then, of course, belonged to an enemy alien—and he saved the spot only by transferring the title to his sister-in-law in the Valley.

Meanwhile the approaching war led to another conflict in William's mind. In May 1861 he wrote to a St. Louis cousin: "Do you clap your Preachers on Sunday? They do it here loud and long. I believe they pray substantially that every devil of you down south shall be killed (not die) in his sins. They don't pray that your eyes shall be opened to see the glorious light of the everlasting patron-saints of the North, but rather that you may in your darkened understanding, plod along up to the cannon's mouth. I never had any sympathy for secession . . . but I fear the remedy is to be far worse than the disease."

William wondered, as did Cyrus, whether the war wasn't political rather than humanitarian. In the summer of 1861 he wrote: "I love the Union of these States as much as any man that lives, but . . . can we save this Union by *blood?*"

In 1862 the Rev. J. B. Stewart, of Ohio, came to preach at North Church, which William attended. On Thanksgiving Day he delivered a sermon which Mary Ann thought was "the worst abolition sermon ever preached in the Church. . . . Thought the proclamation [of Emancipation] did not go far enough and favored arming the negro or in any other way aid them to insurrection, and every other mean thing a devilish heart could devise."

She and William stopped going to church. They could not endure the anti-slavery sermons or the audience's applause when the Rev. Mr. Stewart denounced the South. William wrote to his brother Cyrus, absent on one of his numerous trips: "I do not myself feel like going to Church here and whether I am a skeptic or not I don't know. I have not much confidence in anything I see connected with the Church *here* certainly. I sometimes think I will leave it absolutely and while I conceal these feelings from my family, I know to my sorrow that there are no church influences *here* that are of any service to my family. There has not been a man here that you could even regard as a friend—I mean preacher—and *who* as Elder or Member can you confide in?"

Again Mary Ann was in complete sympathy. She wrote much the same kind of letter to Nettie Fowler McCormick on March 5, 1864. These almost despairing letters represented the culmination of an increasingly impossible situation, as the war crisis deepened and Chicago's Southern sympathizers found themselves more and more unpopular. William put it mildly when he wrote early in the conflict, "A good deal of humility has had to be endured on account of our position."

The pressures on William were many and severe. His political convictions and his nostalgia for the Virginia Valley oppressed his mind. His body suffered from too much desk work. An additional factor, and again a paradoxical one for him, was the heavy responsibility of investing the reaper factory's money. With Leander's help these investments made the family a power in Chicago real estate, but they only added to William's worries.

Cyrus was the conservative member of the family in these matters. As early as 1862 William wanted to invest a million dollars in real estate; his brother said no. By the end of the war McCormick properties in Chicago were valued at nearly that figure and paid off about a hundred thousand dollars a year annually in rents. One of the biggest money-makers was the Revere House, a hotel patronized largely by visiting McCormick agents. The brothers also owned at least two dozen stores. Chicago regarded the three men as the city's biggest landlords, and even their bitterest enemies, the Abolitionists, could not help respecting them for what they had done to push expanding Chicagoland's fortunes.

This expansion was perhaps the only bright spot in William's life, because he believed so profoundly in the future of the city and of the whole Northwest. He wrote in 1863, "Chicago must be a success if any city in this country will be. The best men and capital are here and coming here. There are not enough stores to do the business." Leander, coming home from a trip to London, was more impressed by Chicago than he had been by the world's greatest city.

Mary Ann McCormick, who did not view the scene from a businessman's angle, saw the restless life around her much as returning servicemen were to see New York City in the years of the second World War. She was shocked by "the indifference manifested to the loss of life," as casualty lists continued to fill the pages of the papers. She wrote bitterly: "The idea is with everybody to go ahead and see how much you can swindle out of everybody while this thing lasts."

As the war drew to an end Mary Ann had another cause for concern: her husband's steadily declining health. She wrote to Nettie on January 31, 1865, that William suffered from "nervous headaches, low spirits & general debility—about as he was some years ago."

William tried all the popular remedies of the time to regain his health. He took electrical treatments, spent almost two months at a New York hydropathic institute and tried the famous Dr. Seely "water cure" for ten days in Cleveland. Nothing helped. Physical, religious and business worries continued to gnaw away at his mind.

Something of the desperation which seized William in that summer of 1865 is reflected in a letter from Dr. C. A. Spring, Sr., who was attending him. Dr. Spring wrote to his son that "the patient's mind was intermittently clear, and he was then consulted on matters of business." He wanted to go to Jacksonville because he feared "his mind may be deranged if he does not have the best of treatment."

Jacksonville, Illinois, was the location of the State Hospital for the Insane. William was taken there in late August and put under the personal care of Dr. Andrew McFarland, the institution's

Robert W. Patterson, Captain Patterson's grandfather

...bert W. Patterson, who succeeded
...eph Medill as *Tribune* editor and
...s father of Captain Patterson

Castle on Lake Shore Drive, Chicago, built (allegedly) by John D. Rockefeller to house his daughter Edith and her bridegroom, Harold Fowler McCormick. The mansion became a social center and showplace

superintendent, who took the ailing man into his own home. Dr. McFarland diagnosed his patient's condition as "softening of the brain." He predicted ultimate general paralysis.

At first it appeared that good treatment might postpone, at least, the doctor's prediction. William improved mentally and his dyspepsia responded to treatment. But Cyrus, visiting him two weeks after his arrival, was disturbed to find an epidemic of dysentery in Jacksonville and he tried to persuade Dr. McFarland to send his patient back to Chicago.

By mid-September it was too late. William was stricken by what his doctor called "dysentery of a typhoid character—very little under the control of medical measures." As he lay dying the mistakes of his misspent life were more than ever in William's mind. His brain cleared and he called upon his brothers to realize that money-making was folly. With almost the last breath he drew on September 27, 1865, he urged Cyrus and Leander to "forbear one another in love."

William's death was a blow to Cyrus. They had been closer than any other members of the family. But neither Cyrus nor Leander paid much attention to their brother's dying admonition, and William's last earthly effort ended in futility. The two surviving brothers quarreled sharply over the administration of his estate.

# Chapter 6

## "CHEER UP"

PRINTERS as a class are tough-minded men not likely to be taken in by whatever the type they handle happens to say. The *Tribune* composing room during the Civil War reflected not only the general Northern cynicism about the humanitarian motives for the conflict but also Joseph Medill's own disregard for abolition except as a political weapon. After the Emancipation Proclamation, *Tribune* printers grumbled along with others that they wouldn't have been in such a hurry to enlist if they had known the war was going to degenerate into one of "freedom for the nigger."

But Medill, who had fought the war from the political hustings, emerged from it richer and more of a "realist" than ever, in the manner of the clan today. The war had affected the *Tribune* advantageously, as it had newspapers everywhere. Public anxiety for news had greatly advanced reporting techniques, changed form and make-up in papers, turned weeklies into dailies, and caused the emergence of Sunday editions, hitherto hampered by pious considerations. The greatest effect, of course, was on circulation. In the *Tribune's* case it rose from 18,000 in 1861 to 40,000 in 1864. The paper began to make real money for the first time.

By 1869 Medill was ready to move his property into grander quarters, a new building at the corner of Madison and Dearborn, four stories high. It was built of Joliet marble and cost two hundred and twenty-five thousand dollars.

The following year Medill sought public office unsuccessfully. He was a candidate for congressional nomination in the Republican State Convention, opposing Charles B. Farwell, who beat him by twenty votes. In 1871, however, he was made a member of the first United States Civil Service Commission.

Disaster was Medill's friend. The war had elevated him and the *Tribune* to eminence. The Chicago Fire of 1871 furthered his political fortunes.

His paper had issued a prophetic warning on September 10, only a month before the holocaust occurred: "Chicago is a city of everlasting pine, shingles, sham veneers, stucco and putty. It has miles of fire-traps, pleasing to the eye, looking substantial, but all sham and shingles. Walls have been run up 100 feet high and only a single brick in thickness."

When disaster struck, the *Tribune* was swallowed with the rest of the city. William Bross, back in active partnership with Medill after a term as lieutenant governor of Illinois, jumped on his horse and rode to the *Tribune* office when news of the fire first reached him. He found the paper humming, even though some of its plate-glass windows had cracked from the heat when the blocks fronting it on Dearborn and Madison streets burned.

Medill was on the job. He soon had need to be. The fire seeped across the street, under the wooden pavement and sidewalk, and began to burn in the woodwork of a basement barbershop in the Tribune Building. Medill and the others employed water and a Babcock fire extinguisher to put out the blaze, then went back to work.

Forms for the edition went to the composing room. Bross ordered the men to let the presses roll as soon as the city room sent down a paragraph bringing the spread of the fire up to date.

But even the fireproof Tribune Building, which Bross had thought would "stand a thousand years," was not proof against the intensity of the Great Fire. It went under, while one of the memorable dramas of journalism was enacted in the pressroom. Charles Leavelle, a present-day *Tribune* feature writer, has retold the story:

"In the pressroom of the *Tribune's* building . . . a sweating crew was racing against time. The composing room had delivered type forms for the inside pages—2 and 3—and these were being run off. Meanwhile, the compositors were laboring over the forms of the outside pages—1 and 4—which would contain latest news of the fire.

"Never, probably, in newspaper history has a press crew spent such a night. Above the whir and thump of the Hoe cylinder type presses rose the roar of flames and the unnerving cries from the streets of the stricken city.

"As the last sheet—printed on one side—came off the press, buildings directly opposite the *Tribune* burst into flame. There was a shout that McVicker's Theater was burning. But there was no letup in the mighty effort to get to press. The pressmen vowed they would get the paper out even if the roof over their heads should take fire.

"At that instant, however, their battle was ended by the simultaneous bursting of gas and water mains, depriving the plant of light and of water for the boiler of the steam engine that drove the presses. A few minutes more and the *Tribune's* building was ablaze. In a few hours the physical achievements of 24 years of toil and effort were destroyed."

When Medill saw that the Tribune Building could not be saved, he went down to 15 Canal Street and bought a job printing shop on the spot. The paper's staff drifted down to this shop all through Tuesday, the third day of the fire (the old building had burned the night before), and by Tuesday afternoon the editorial side was functioning in the back part of the room. On Wednesday morning a half-sheet paper emerged from an old press Medill had found stored in a barn. It carried a five-column story about the fire. The business manager got paper for this issue by borrowing sixty-four dollars from his own friends; forty-eight hours before he could have borrowed a hundred thousand dollars on *Tribune* credit.

That first post-fire issue contained perhaps the most famous of *Tribune* editorials, titled "Cheer Up." It began: "In the midst of a calamity without parallel in the world's history, looking upon the ashes of thirty years' accumulations, the people of this once beautiful city have resolved that CHICAGO SHALL RISE AGAIN." And it ended: "Let us all cheer up, save what is yet left, and we shall come out right. The Christian world is coming to our relief. The worst is already over. In a few days more all the dangers will be past, and we can resume the battle of life with Christian faith and Western grit. Let us all cheer up!"

There is no doubt that the editorial helped to inspire the city's magnificent comeback. With that and the *Tribune's* lead in reconstruction work, Joseph Medill swept easily to victory as mayor of Chicago in October 1872, on a "Fire-proof" ticket. In the same month, on the first anniversary of the fire, the *Tribune* returned to its new building at the old location. It was a sandstone structure, five stories high, built at a cost of a quarter of a million dollars. It was fireproof. Medill's term in City Hall was anything but fireproof. He started a conflagration of resentment among his constituents, particularly the foreign-born, so that in a few short months he resigned and fled to Europe for a long rest.

When he resumed active control of the *Tribune* in 1874 he increased his interest to a majority and took over the paper's editorial management, so that it became his voice more than ever before. He made his son-in-law, Robert W. Patterson, managing editor. Robert, son of the eminent minister who had been involved in Cyrus McCormick's church fight, had married Elinor, one of Joseph Medill's two daughters.

Under Medill's direct control the paper became more conservatively Republican than ever. Its circulation—hanging around the 40,000 mark in the seventies but doubling in the eighties—was still small by comparison with the other Chicago papers, but it was prosperous. Advertising revenue continued to increase. The editorial page maintained its Civil War prestige. In general it was one of the country's best newspapers, from the purely professional standpoint.

It must have hurt Medill's old-fashioned, die-hard soul to see Wilbur F. Storey's Chicago *Times* continue to beat the *Tribune* in circulation by use of such lusty devices as lottery drawings, luridly told seduction stories and frequent legitimate beats on page-one stories. It was as though, in our day, the *Tribune* were competing with the New York *Daily News* in the same town.

But the decade of the 1870s was one of victory for Medill. There was only one notable defeat, and that was more sentimental than practical. On June 8, 1876, his daughter Katharine married Robert Sanderson McCormick, son of William and nephew of Medill's personal and political enemy, Cyrus Hall McCormick.

It was a fateful marriage. It united the Medills with the strong, eccentric, dominating McCormick family stream, just as Elinor Medill had earlier blended the Medill blood with that of the religiously powerful Patterson family.

Katharine's second son, born in 1880, was Robert Rutherford McCormick. A year earlier Elinor's first-born had been named Joseph Medill Patterson.

Chapter 7

# THE TRIBUNE VS. THE PEOPLE

IF MEDILL HAD little sympathy with Storey and his sensational *Times* on most points, he saw eye to eye with the rival paper on opposition to labor. The decade of the eighties in Medill history is notable chiefly for the *Tribune's* bitter opposition to labor in any and all disputes. It is a period usually described in the *Tribune's* histories of itself as "prosaic."

The closing years of the seventies had provided a preview of what occurred in the bloody eighties. In the great railroad strike of 1877 Chicago police decided on a policy of not firing the customary warning round over the heads of strikers and of aiming low. The *Tribune* approved this plan editorially and even suggested that vigilante groups be formed to supplement an already militant police and militia. The paper asserted, "Chicago is too far advanced to permit her bad elements to interfere with her interests."

On July 22, 1877, the class struggle broke out in Chicago without hypocrisy on either side. Albert Parsons, at a mass meeting, denounced the capitalist press in general and the *Tribune* in particular. Unemployment was growing, he said, as new machinery was installed, and those who did work labored twelve to fourteen hours a day. Five sixths of the profits went to the bosses.

The *Tribune* counterattacked next morning. It demanded that railway men who refused to take wage cuts and dismissal notices "step out of the way. . . . If they will not step out voluntarily, they must be made to by force." The editorial further referred to strikers as "the scum and filth of the city." Three days later the *Tribune* declared, "Capitalists would offer any sum to see the leaders . . . strung up to a telegraph pole."

On the afternoon this pious hope was expressed there was a battle between police and three thousand workers at Halsted and Sixteenth streets. Two men were killed and many others wounded. The *Tribune's* headline on this story was: RED WAR. DESPERATE CONTEST BETWEEN RIOTERS AND POLICE ON HALSTED STREET. AN ASSEMBLY OF THE COMMUNISTS SWIFTLY SMASHED BY THE POLICE.

The story itself referred to the strikers as thieves and riffraff, cutthroats and bandits, who showed "all the elements of extreme viciousness incident to riots."

It was hardheaded, uncompromising Joe Medill who spoke against labor. He opposed the eight-hour day in his editorial columns on the ground that it would mean the loss of millions of dollars to employers. Of course he and Storey were not alone in the crusade; the New York papers were almost equally vociferous in their arrogant attitude toward any man who dared strike.

The peak of this attack was the almost unbelievable *Tribune* editorial of 1884 which said: "The simplest plan, probably, when one is not a member of the Humane Society, is to put arsenic in the supplies of food furnished the unemployed or the tramp. This produces death in a short time and is a warning to other tramps to keep out of the neighborhood."

In 1886 the fight for the eight-hour day reached a crisis in the historic May Day strikes in Chicago. Most of the city's biggest industries had not accepted the new working time and strikes occurred in those places. Rumors flew through the panting, turbulent city. One story said that the stockyard butchers were marching on the city in a body.

Probably the most important strike occurred at the McCormick Harvesting Machinery Works, where a battle took place between police and strikers. Shots were exchanged. What happened then has never been proved. Conservative historians say some strikers were hit and injured but no one was killed. Labor historians repeat what the strikers charged at the time—that six of their men were killed. A protest meeting was called at Haymarket Square, and there followed the bloody Haymarket riot before labor peace was restored.

In all this trouble Joseph Medill stood solidly with the McCormick plant's management, whom he had once branded as trading under false pretenses. They were Copperheads and impostors no longer, but honest men who had been set upon by anarchists. Thus Medill demonstrated once more that he was concerned not with human issues but only with financial ones. His surface righteousness had reached a high point five years before, on May 21, 1881, when the *Tribune* astonished the newspaper world and its readership by offering, with considerable pious fanfare, a sixteen-page supplement containing the American Revised Edition of the New Testament.

In another labor crisis Medill and the *Tribune* fought workingmen during the Pullman strike of 1894, when even some of management's friends found it difficult to sympathize properly. Carter Harrison, then publisher of the Chicago *Times*, wrote about it later: "Grover Cleveland, Joseph Medill, and John R. Walsh could not have been more thoroughly aligned with the employer side of a labor difficulty like the Pullman strike had they been directors and managers of the interested company. To their way of reasoning an employer was always right, the employee invariably in the wrong. God knows the men involved in the Pullman strike suffered grievously, those discharged threatened with starvation, those at work desperately underpaid, their hours unduly many. No way humanly possible of righting the wrongs except the strike!"

Medill did not hesitate to disown his friends when they harmed his particular interests, and he did it with the utmost hypocrisy, posing as a friend of the common people.

In 1888 the Republican party platform, written for General Benjamin Harrison's campaign, called for an extremely high protective tariff. The *Tribune* fought it because high tariffs, which the paper had previously advocated, were no longer advantageous to the Mississippi Valley. One of its choicer efforts in this turncoat campaign was a poem in which the ironic overtones are painfully obvious.

> *Protection, in a nutshell, means*
> *A right for certain classes;*

*A little law that intervenes*
*To help them rob the masses.*
*The rich may put their prices high;*
*The poor shall be compelled to buy.*

Medill was still a power in politics, though not an active participant, probably because he was becoming increasingly deaf. In 1889, for example, he went to Springfield and saw to it that the State Legislature voted properly to make the Chicago drainage canal possible.

Whenever he could do it profitably, Medill stood on the side of civic virtue. When the nation's cities fought to get the World's Fair in 1893, Medill was one of those who made certain that Chicago's ten-million-dollar bid got the plum. He was one of the Exposition's original stockholders and a director. At the *Tribune* office he supervised the paper's coverage, which was the best in the city. A special bureau in the fair's administration building was the center for a special staff which wired its news direct to the *Tribune*, where it was handled by a special copy desk.

As he gradually relinquished active control of the *Tribune* the aging Medill let it fall more and more into the hands of his managing editor and son-in-law, Robert W. Patterson. Less interested in politics than in newspapering as such, Patterson gave the paper a less violent tone and made it a little more flexible. It was no longer Medill's personal organ.

However, Patterson backed up the old man's long-standing feud with Governor John P. Altgeld, the state's first Democratic governor in forty years, whose election was a major defeat for the paper. Aside from its natural distaste for the governor as a Democrat, the *Tribune* was further offended when in 1893 Altgeld pardoned the three men still in prison as a result of convictions obtained after the Haymarket riot. Four others had been executed. Although the evidence now indicated a possibly too hasty justice, the *Tribune* was incensed by Altgeld's clemency.

In the Pullman strike the following year the *Tribune* took a righteous stand and denounced the governor for not bringing labor peace to Chicago at once. Obviously on the side of the Pull-

## Chapter 8

## THE ERA OF ELEGANCE

WHILE Medill continued to make newspaper and political history in the closing decades of the century, the McCormick side of the dynasty created an era of elegance in Chicago society which persists in our own time. It was a period, too, in which Medill, Patterson and McCormick personalities of the younger generation emerged somewhat from under the shadow of the older clan leaders and took the stage themselves.

Nettie, Cyrus's wife, was one of the city's social leaders—a sweet and gentle woman, who sometimes bewildered her friends by her odd behavior. Young Cyrus, one of her sons, was known as a charming fellow, and his brother Harold had a likable personality, though he also had his erratic moments.

Joseph Medill's wife, Katharine, came from far more proletarian stock than her husband, and she did not acclimate herself to position and wealth with Medill's natural ease. Like many another poor girl who married into money, she lost her sense of proportion. Once she let an enormous bill mount up at the art gallery of William Vincent O'Brien, which was liberally patronized by the Medills, Pattersons and McCormicks. Mr. O'Brien sent her repeated reminders without result, until at last he waited upon Joseph Medill personally to get an explanation. Medill was incensed. He sat down and wrote a note to his wife, to be delivered by Mr. O'Brien. The note said curtly: "Make out check to bearer. And do not, under any circumstances, ever allow such a bill to accumulate again!"

The Medill daughters were like their mother. They took their social position and themselves seriously, and they were at pains to let the world know it. They swept into stores imperiously and expected immediate attention. Elinor Medill Patterson came into the O'Brien Gallery one day and ordered a frame for a portrait of James G. Blaine, then a presidential aspirant. Her husband hoped for a political post if Blaine were elected. Two days after Blaine's defeat the Patterson coachman returned the frame with the excuse that it was "not suited to the portrait."

By this time Chicago had made long strides toward rebuilding the city, a process slowed only slightly by the panic of 1873. The architects followed prefire designs for the most part, modifying them along somewhat feudal lines by building a front entrance with high steps for the master and mistress, with another entrance beneath the steps for underlings. The materials were Lemont limestone, common or Milwaukee cream brick, or local brick of a vivid orange-red shade. The William Sanderson McCormicks lived in a yellow Milwaukee brick house on Huron Street. Mayor Medill occupied a large three-story home in the neighborhood, and the Rush Street houses of Cyrus and Robert Hall McCormick were erected soon after. These houses marked the beginning of the red sandstone era.

Medill's residence stood at the northeast corner of Cass and Ontario streets, on a lot sixty-four feet by seventy-two. Its style was French Renaissance and it was built of Lake Superior brownstone. Like Medill himself, the place was solid and substantial, not ornamental. It cost a hundred thousand dollars. The owner was ahead of his time architecturally. He believed that a house ought to have plenty of sunlight (other householders of those days believed that the sun "faded the carpets," and kept the blinds pulled). Medill instructed his architect to put in ample windows so that every room would have plenty of sunlight. Inside, the house was finished in polished woods. Every room had its own distinctive treatment in design and variety of woods.

At the corner of State and Ontario streets the red brick Ontario Hotel, now a Chicago landmark, began to go up in 1880, to the consternation of neighboring citizenry, to whom apartment hotels were a new thing.

One of the first tenants of the new Ontario was Samuel J. Medill, Joseph's brother. Born in Ohio, Samuel had served for two years in the Union Army, received a medical discharge, studied a year at Beloit College, and then had joined his brother in Chicago. He worked for the *Tribune* first in what was called the "sporting department," later became city editor and finally managing editor. In 1880 he married and later that year was elected president of the Chicago Press Club. He left Chicago in 1882 because of "a serious illness," and died soon after at an early age.

Another early Ontario tenant was Robert Sanderson McCormick and his bride, Katharine Medill. He later entered the diplomatic service and was successively ambassador to Austria, Russia and France.

But the real focal points of McCormick social life were the mansions on Rush and Erie streets which clustered around Cyrus Hall McCormick's patriarchal home. In clannish fashion the aging inventor's family built their stately Victorian dwellings around his place in such numbers that the neighborhood came to be called "McCormickville."

Cyrus's mansion, dominating McCormickville, was one of the great town houses of the Gilded Age. The inventor's son, Harold Fowler, lived in it for a time, and Harold's children by his first marriage occupied it later, thus establishing a three-generation tenure in the fine old three-story home. The house is now on a quiet street, off the beaten path, but it is still one of the city's most famous dwellings, soon to be torn down, however, to make way for a four-million-dollar store and office building.

Although the brownstone façade is darkened by soot, smoke and dust, the luxurious interior is as elegant as when the inventor moved into it in 1879. Remembering his comparatively humble Virginia birthplace, Cyrus determined that the home his wealth would build must be the equal of any built by Chicago tycoons of the seventies. Cudell and Blumenthal, the noted architects he engaged, outdid themselves. Ironically, Cyrus lived to enjoy his hard-won splendor only five years. After he died Nettie stayed on and reared her three children, Harold, Stanley and Cyrus.

Under Nettie's regime the house continued to dominate the city's social life. This was partly due to the widow's charm and wit, and partly to her charities, which were extensive. She had the true missionary spirit. It was her dearest ambition to spread Christianity and Christian education everywhere, to bring medical science to the Far East, and to further the cause of the Presbyterian Church. She was the largest contributor to the Church in America, much of her money going to the McCormick Theological Seminary. The seminary gave a surprise party for her in the old mansion on her eightieth birthday in 1915; she received cablegrams and telegrams of congratulation from personages everywhere in the world.

She died in 1923 at eighty-eight, leaving an estate of about ten million dollars. Harold took over the family home and maintained it for some time. He preserved its palacelike splendor, with its fine tapestried chairs, heavy silken draperies, carved mantels, crystal and gold chandeliers, rare rugs, old masterpieces and family portraits, walnut dressers, panel walls, inlaid ceilings with mahogany beams, and objects of art. The coach house on the north side of the house has since been converted into the library of the McCormick Historical Association, which contains fifteen hundred printed and a million and a half manuscript items about the McCormick family.

Leander Hamilton (he dropped the first name most of the time) was one of the more versatile McCormicks. Born in Chicago in 1859, he graduated from Amherst in 1881 and studied law at Columbia, after which he took up architecture. In his lifetime he dabbled in invention, sculpturing and art collecting. His hundred or so inventions included airplanes, an aerial torpedo, motorcycles and a watch that recorded time all over the world. His art collection contained fine examples of the early English and old Dutch schools.

His greatest love was a somewhat eccentric study he invented himself, called "characterology," or the reading of character through personal appearance. He published a book about it in 1920, and a year later issued a "Student's Course" in the subject. Most of Hamilton's mature years were spent in studying characterology.

He married Constance Plummer, of Canterbury, England, on

February 15, 1887, and the hundred-and-twenty-five-thousand-dollar mansion he built for her became the center of Chicago society. Their dinners were famous events. Hamilton and his wife did not stay long in this luxury. They moved to England about 1900 and did not come back until shortly after the outbreak of the first World War. While they were abroad, living in London for the most part, the two collected pictures, bronzes, enamels, statuary, armor and old furniture, most of which they brought back to Chicago and installed in their residence. Today the Hamilton McCormick home is occupied by the Kungsholm, a restaurant which specializes in Scandinavian cooking.

Hamilton's brother, Robert Hall, lived in still another famed McCormick mansion, at the northwest corner of Rush and Erie streets. It did not have an impressive exterior, like Hamilton's mansion. Inside, however, there was not only the customary luxury but one of the country's largest and most expensive private collections of art, mostly of the English school and including Constable, Van Dyck, Gainsborough, Herring, Hogarth, Holbein, Jannsens, Raeburn, Romney and Watts.

Four years after the Great Fire, Robert moved into his three-and-a-half-story residence, where he lived for forty-two years until he died in 1917 at the age of seventy. The mistress of the place was Sarah Lord Day McCormick, daughter of a noted New York attorney. Like her sister-in-law Constance, Sarah was an outstanding hostess and she entertained an imposing list of great names from Chicago and the nation.

A branch of the McCormick family about which little is known is that of Robert Sanderson McCormick's brother, William Grigsby. The son of William and Eleanor Brooks McCormick, however, Chauncey Brooks McCormick, is a social figure in Chicago today and is sometimes photographed at various functions, notably at Colonel McCormick's wedding in December 1944. Chauncey's wife was mentioned flatteringly in a *Tribune* society column of January 1945 as being among "Chicago's best groomed and most smartly dressed women." On that particular day she was observed wearing "a stunning blue wool dress at a meeting of the Chicago Council on Foreign Relations."

Perhaps the most fascinating members of the McCormick family to contemplate are the seven children of Cyrus Hall and Nettie Fowler. They were, in the order of their birthdays, Cyrus Hall, Jr., Mary Virginia, Robert Fowler, Anita, Alice, Harold Fowler, and Stanley Robert.

The late Harold Fowler is described in the official records as a manufacturer and capitalist. He devoted considerable time, however, to lighter occupations. Harold had no more than graduated from Princeton in 1895 when he married, in November, the amazing Edith Rockefeller, daughter of the financier. Edith had been educated by private tutors, lived abroad and was interested in just about everything. The marriage was unostentatious. It took place in a New York hotel and was followed by a wedding trip to Europe.

Harold and Edith did not come to Chicago until several years after they married, and when they did they settled in a magnificent home at 1000 Lake Shore Drive. It was rumored persistently that the bride's father had bought the place and given it to the couple as a wedding present, but Edith denied it. The residence had been built originally in the eighties by Nathaniel S. Jones, a Chicago millionaire.

Edith ascended to the tottering throne which was slipping away from Mrs. Potter Palmer, long acknowledged as the queen of Chicago society, who was now frequently absent from the city. The new queen reigned until her death in 1932.

Her great house on the Drive was almost a castle, with its turrets, arched entrance and wide stone steps, and a front protected by a highly ornamental grillwork iron gate. In the years before the first World War Edith held court there and raised her three children, Muriel, Mathilde and Fowler. She also installed the objects of art which placed her among the world's foremost collectors. In the huge reception hall, called the Empire Room, she entertained such royal personages as Queen Marie of Rumania in 1926, and Prince William of Sweden in the following year. Royalty walked in this room on the Emperor's carpet, a rug which cost a hundred and twenty-five thousand dollars, made in Persia six hundred years before, and once the property of Peter the Great.

There were art treasures everywhere in the house: gilded chairs given by Napoleon to the Princess Pauline Borghese, a rug internationally known for its beauty, a private library of first editions and other literary rarities, a collection of old lace surpassed only by the Vatican's, and priceless jewels.

Edith had a nervous breakdown in 1913. The illness stimulated an already extraordinary interest in herself, and she went to Switzerland to study psychology under Jung for eight years. When she came back to Chicago a young Swiss architect named Edwin Krenn accompanied her, and shortly afterward, in 1921, she divorced Harold, charging desertion.

When she died at the age of fifty-nine, they opened the great gray stone house on the Drive and placed her body in state in the Empire Room. The coffin was surrounded by Claude Pernet roses. They were her favorite flowers.

She left more than a financial legacy. Edith, for all her eccentricities, had used some of her money for worthy purposes. With her husband she was a founder of the John McCormick Institution for Infectious Diseases, established in memory of their first son, John, who died in infancy of scarlet fever. Antitoxin to treat the disease was developed in this institution. In addition Edith was an original promoter of civic opera in Chicago, a founder of the Chicago Zoological Gardens, and a patroness of opera in English for American audiences.

When the experts got around to cataloguing her possessions at 1000 Lake Shore Drive they were amazed by the endless quantity of antiques and rare porcelains, silver and first editions crammed into every corner of the mansion. But the place was, they agreed, overdone. The dining room was paneled in dark wood and filled with ornately carved furniture. With appalling lack of taste, the owner had priceless Chinese vases made into lamps, surmounted by horrible fringed shades. Edith was not of McCormick blood, but she had one dominant McCormick family characteristic: she loved to collect things.

Meanwhile Harold pursued his rather eccentric way. He married Ganna Walska, the Polish opera star, a year after his divorce. To achieve this union, so the story goes, he resorted to the then popular Steinach operation, a gland rejuvenation process intended to restore sexual vigor to aging men. When word of Harold's strategy got around it delighted his *bon vivant* friends in New York and elsewhere. They paraphrased Longfellow in his honor, and soon this parody was making the rounds of the luncheon clubs and better bars:

> *Under the spreading chestnut tree*
> *The village smithy stands;*
> *The smith a gloomy man is he:*
> *McCormick has his glands.*

But there appeared to be little mutual rejuvenation in the marriage. Mme. Walska never achieved her desire to sing opera in Chicago. She retired to Europe and lived there most of the time until 1931, when Harold divorced her on a charge of desertion. He had one more try at matrimony. In 1938, in his sixty-sixth year, he married Adah Wilson, his nurse and former attendant.

Harold's business career was much more successful than his marital life. He held various executive posts in the International Harvester Company—vice-president, treasurer, president, chairman of the executive committee—and he was also a director of the First National Bank, a trustee of the University of Chicago, the Mc-Cormick Theological Seminary and the Chicago Orchestral Association, and a director of the Chicago Civic Opera Company. He belonged to ten of the right clubs.

Harold died on October 16, 1941, in Beverly Hills, California, of a cerebral hemorrhage. He was sixty-nine. He had been in poor health for several years, and the previous July had traveled to Beverly Hills from Chicago in a private car under the supervision of his doctor. The obituaries noted that he was always annoyed by publicity but was nevertheless good to newspapermen. They revived the memory of his single literary effort, a book about peace called *Via Paci*, published in 1918. The New York *Times* obituary added solemnly that he was "a talented amateur" in music and often entertained his friends by whistling difficult classical pieces. What was left of his seven-and-a-half-million-dollar estate (a comparatively small McCormick fortune), after half of it had been taken by taxes, went to Adah and the three children.

The remaining brothers and sisters of the inventor's clan are not nearly so well known as Harold. One, Robert, died in infancy, as did Alice. Of those remaining, little is said in the family. Mary Virginia, who died a few years ago, leaving an estate estimated at thirteen million dollars, was alleged to be of very eccentric behavior. Anita (Mrs. Emmons Blaine) is a lovely woman who is said to have the habit of giving strange presents. She is also devoted to charity and employs three secretaries to give away her money to worthy causes. She is so selfless in this endeavor that she neglects her own appearance and never dresses in accordance with her wealth and position. Mrs. Blaine is a political enemy of Colonel McCormick.

There remains only one other McCormick worth mention, and because she *is* worth it, she must be mentioned even though she was not a blood relative. That was Colonel McCormick's sister-in-law, Ruth Hanna McCormick Simms, who married Medill McCormick and later rose to political fame on her own account. She was always closely identified with the McCormick family.

Ruth Hanna was a daughter of the distinguished Senator Mark Hanna, of Cleveland. Educated at Dobbs Ferry and Farmington, she married Medill McCormick in 1903, when he was editor of the *Tribune,* and came to Chicago with him. Mark Hanna had bequeathed to her something of his own political genius, and she had already made her first political speech seven years before her marriage. From that point she went on to merit the accolade one observer gave her: "The only woman in America with a political technique." All her political efforts were devoted to the Republican party. In 1918 she became the chairman of the first women's executive committee of the Republican National Committee, and in 1924 she was the first elected Republican national committeewoman for Illinois.

She was in Washington with Medill McCormick when he was senator from Illinois, and after his death in 1925 she became a political power in her own right. Elected congresswoman at large in 1928, she campaigned the following year for her husband's seat in Congress, won the nomination but lost the election.

At the time she was running for the Senate, Mrs. McCormick was involved in a battle which sounds strange in these days of political realignments. Senator Gerald P. Nye headed a campaign funds committee which investigated Mrs. McCormick's expenditures, among others, and did it in a way which made the lady suspicious. She hired private detectives to conduct an inquiry on her behalf of the "methods and affiliations" Senator Nye had used. The results, she said, justified her course and she wondered publicly what Senator Nye would do about it. The senator did not press the matter.

The tall, slender, vivacious woman went into many other fields and was successful in all of them. She was publisher of the Rockford (Illinois) *Register-Republican* and Rockford *Morning Star*, and was Republican national committeewoman from New Mexico when she died, at sixty-four, on the last day of December 1944. She had married Albert G. Simms, former Republican congressman from New Mexico, in 1932.

Ruth's closest approach to the McCormicks was in her politics, because she was unlike them in many other ways. In a less violent fashion she shared the McCormick-Patterson antipathy for Franklin Roosevelt and she used her potent, behind-the-scenes power to work against the Administration wherever and whenever she could. At the Republican Convention of 1944 she was one of the foremost wire-pullers in the maneuvering which gave Thomas Dewey the nomination.

Thus the sons and daughters of the Medills and McCormicks built their Chicago empire in the eighties and nineties and interpenetrated the city's social and business life in the early decades of this century. Even a superficial examination of the histories just related will show that the McCormicks began to overshadow the Medills in the closing years of the last century, and that "McCormickville" was the beginning of the end of the Medill era in Chicago.

Even though McCormick blood more or less absorbed the other family streams, the most important result of this transition was the blending at last of the three lines to create the personalities who are such controversial journalistic phenomena today. All three families bequeathed definite characteristics to the present generation, which is the logical end product of this genealogical process.

Joseph Medill was the mightiest of them all. His death in 1899 ended an era in the history of the dynasty and another in the *Tribune's* history. After an interlude under the great James Keeley, the *Tribune* became a reincarnation of Medill's personal journalism in the new century. Family history gradually focused itself again on a few personalities, as it had during the Civil War, when Medill was in his prime and Cyrus was a reaper king and a Copperhead.

Joseph Medill rose to fame in wartime and he slipped away during another war. In this, the Spanish-American War, the *Tribune* got one of the great beats of journalistic history, even though its coverage of the war front was anything but adequate—a lack of interest traceable to the fact that only one Illinois regiment reached Cuba. The *Tribune* devoted itself to attacks on war scandals at home and began its long campaign for military preparedness.

The beat was Dewey's victory at Manila and, not unlike other news beats, it was the result of a series of accidents. Edward W. Harden, the reporter, had been financial editor of the *Tribune* before he started on a world cruise in 1899. Reaching Hong Kong, he arranged to cover the Pacific front for the New York *World*. He was aboard the flagship U.S.S. *Olympia* at the great battle in Manila Bay.

There was an anxious week of waiting back home after the battle. Dewey had cut the cables, and although it was believed that he must have attacked Manila, there was no way of knowing until the correspondents got back to Hong Kong.

Harden reached Hong Kong with two other correspondents. There was a bitter quarrel at the cable office, which Harden won. He filed his story at the highest rate—$9.90 a word for urgent messages—and paid for it himself out of five hundred dollars in gold that he had in his pocket.

His story reached the *World* office at 4:20 A.M., New York time, on May 7, too late for the paper's editions. Farmer Murphy, *Tribune* correspondent at the *World,* shot the message on to Chicago, where it arrived at 3:25 A.M., Chicago time. The flash from Farmer that the message was coming was received three minutes earlier and caught the paper's staff ready to go home, convinced that there would be no news from Dewey that night. Not even the President had heard an authentic report.

For two hours after that historic flash the *Tribune* boiled with excitement. About twelve thousand copies of the city edition, already out on the streets and in railway stations, were called back and destroyed by hard-riding circulation men who traveled on horseback to the distribution stations and gathered up the papers. Meanwhile the page-one form was cleared and the epic story began to fill it. Managing Editor James Keeley and City Editor E. S. Beck were calling Washington meanwhile to tell McKinley and the Secretaries of Navy and War the good news.

Dewey's own dispatch did not arrive in New York until 9 A.M. that morning, and then it had to be decoded, so that Harden beat even the official communiqué by six hours. It was a high point in *Tribune* history. Oddly enough, Harden did not rejoin the *Tribune* when he came back to Chicago but became editor of the Chicago *Journal,* where he remained until he left the newspaper business in 1905 to be a New York broker.

Joseph Medill missed the Dewey story, which would certainly have delighted him. Three months before, on March 16, he had died during a visit to his ranch near San Antonio, Texas. The deathbed story attributed to him, and considerably less apocryphal than most such stories, is that he died with the classic newspaperman's query on his lips: "What's the news?"

Two days later, back at the *Tribune,* Keeley got a letter from Medill, mailed before his death. It was a packet of clippings intended for the paper and marked in the old man's decisive handwriting, "Must, JM." It was a last tribute to Joseph Medill that the clippings went into the *Tribune* without question—not as a mark of respect for the dead but simply because "Must, JM" meant what it said.

The principle of that curt message had governed the *Tribune* for forty-four years. It still governs today. Only the initials have changed.

Part Two

# TRANSITION

# Chapter 1

# JAMES KEELEY, NEWSPAPERMAN

BETWEEN THE TIME of Joseph Medill's death and the ascendancy of Robert Rutherford McCormick and Joseph Medill Patterson as editors and publishers in 1914, the *Tribune* was in the hands of three men. Two were members of the royal family: Robert W. Patterson and Medill McCormick. The third was James Keeley, one of journalism's greatest figures, who for three years was in absolute editorial control of the paper, the only time it was ever guided by an outsider.

They were years in which the *Tribune* faltered in its self-chosen course as chief exemplifier of personal journalism and became more of a *news*paper than it had ever been before or has been since. It chalked up several of the outstanding news beats in its history, all of which are credited erroneously, and deliberately, in official *Tribune* history, to Patterson.

Robert Patterson did not have his father's dominant personality. Hired on the *Tribune* by his father-in-law, Joseph Medill, he worked his way up quietly through a series of minor jobs until he became business manager. Actually he was in virtual control of the paper for several years before the aging Medill died, and then he was made editor in chief, a position he held officially until 1910. Patterson was interested chiefly in the presentation of news, and in Keeley he had the ideal man to carry out that interest. A background figure, Patterson was nevertheless the *Tribune's* boss; he made policy and stood squarely behind it. That policy was selfish, in its exclusive representation of big business, but it was not hypocritical.

Patterson's reign was a short one. About 1905 he began to fail in health and, after a long-drawn-out struggle, died suddenly in

Philadelphia on April 1, 1910. Almost at the same hour his mother died and their double funeral was one of the most impressive ever seen in Chicago. The service was held in the Second Presbyterian Church, where Patterson's father had been pastor for so many years.

Medill McCormick, old Joseph's grandson, had been made publisher of the *Tribune* when Patterson's health began to fail. He was a most reluctant newspaperman. The business was only an interlude in his political career, and even then he looked upon it primarily as an adjunct. When he was graduated from Yale in 1900 young Medill became a *Tribune* reporter at once, and a year later was assigned to the Philippines, where he got an inside look at the new problems raised by the war and Philippine liberation.

Shortly after his marriage to Ruth Hanna in 1903 he went back to the *Tribune* and remained as the paper's responsible head, more or less, until late in 1910. "More or less," because his influence on the paper was negligible. The *Tribune's* business side was, for all practical purposes, in other hands, particularly after 1909, the year in which Robert McCormick was made treasurer and Joseph Patterson secretary of the Tribune Company. The editorial side, in these years, was in Keeley's hands.

In politics Medill McCormick was a Republican of the die-hard school, although from the viewpoint of the period he was looked upon as an advocate of political reform. He allied himself with the Progressives in 1911 and, as a member of the national campaign committee, worked hard to bring about Theodore Roosevelt's nomination. When the Progressive movement failed, a half-dozen years later, McCormick led the struggle to restore party unity. Illinois Republicans rewarded him by making him first a congressman at large and finally by sending him to the Senate in 1919.

McCormick had a chance to see World War I at first hand in 1917 as a member of Congress on an observation tour. He was even under fire at Verdun. But his Republicanism still came first: he denounced the League of Nations and joined Lodge in the Senate fight against Wilson and the League. It appears probable that McCormick was only a faithful and unthinking follower of the party line in this case. Later he urged anti-lynching legislation and introduced the Child Labor Amendment in the Senate.

Like the rest of his family, McCormick was a rich man and he had a rich man's hobbies. He spent a good many years and a considerable amount of money developing the best Holstein herd in America on his twenty-four-hundred-acre farm near Byron, Illinois, but he did not live long after this accomplishment: he was only forty-eight when he died in Washington, D.C., on February 25, 1925.

Both Robert W. Patterson and Medill McCormick were completely overshadowed in their *Tribune* associations by the remarkable figure of James Keeley. Even in a family history he cannot be ignored, because his influence on family property was great and his personality emphasized, by contrast, all that was unjournalistic in a newspaper dynasty.

Keeley was an English foundling who grew up on the London streets. He came to America at sixteen and served his apprenticeship on the Kansas City *Journal*. At twenty-one he moved to the *Tribune* and in an incredibly short time the rookie reporter became the best man in the shop. His story is told in full in James Weber Linn's excellent book, *James Keeley, Newspaperman,* which should be required reading for anyone who wants to know what makes the newspaper business tick.

Keeley was not quite twenty-eight when he became the *Tribune's* city editor in 1895. He had been in this country only twelve years. His theory of news, which he expressed much later, was: "News is a commodity and for sale like any other commodity." The trait which made Keeley such an outstanding salesman of that commodity was his utter devotion to the news itself. That devotion sometimes made him seem more like a one-purpose machine than a human being, as it has so many other city-room executives, but he made the paper's heart beat with an untiring, efficient steadiness equal to his own.

As an editor Keeley had the instinctive quality of being able to see all sides of a story at once and then to extract every drop of news from it. He was not a writer, like Joseph Medill, or a professional thinker like Greeley, but he knew pre-eminently what news was and how to sell it. He brought a prodigious energy to his job. Before Keeley's day—and after it—city editors on morning papers left the office at 6 P.M., leaving the job of getting the paper to press in the hands of the night city editor. Keeley stayed at the office until midnight in his city-editor days. Even as managing editor he stayed most nights until the first edition was running, about midnight, and then lingered on to lay the groundwork for the next day's labors.

One of the first jobs Keeley did on the *Tribune* was to unify the paper's staff and give it needed morale. He did it by letting the executives under him know that they could depend on him to protect them and back them up under attack, and at the same time he expected them to protect their subordinates. Working newspapermen responded eagerly to that kind of leadership from the top. New men, hired by Keeley, came on the staff, including such memorable figures as James O'Donnell Bennett, Edgar Sisson, Harvey Woodruff, Ring Lardner, John T. McCutcheon and Walter Eckersall. Among all these talents Keeley played no favorites. He gave praise rarely, and then in the form of short congratulatory messages rather than verbally. Philip Kinsley, a *Tribune* veteran and currently its official biographer, says that Keeley thanked him only once in the years he worked under him.

One of the friends Keeley did have, however, was Samuel Insull. The financier enjoyed dropping into the *Tribune* office to discuss European politics with Robert Patterson, and later with Medill McCormick, both of whom he regarded highly. It was Patterson who introduced Insull to Keeley, with the remark, "You two are both Englishmen. You ought to know each other." It was their mutual English point of view that made the two men friends. Insull said later, "I knew *what* Patterson thought and *what* Medill McCormick thought, but I knew *why* Keeley thought as he did. I could understand him without effort."

In 1899 Keeley began one of the *Tribune's* few non-political crusades, the fight for a sane Fourth. Keeley was managing editor of the *Tribune* on the Fourth of July that year, but he was not at his desk. He sat at home beside the bed of his small daughter, who was desperately ill. Outside resounded the customary din of

Cyrus Hall McCormick, the inventor's son. He served as chairman of the board, International Harvester Company

Senator Medill McCormick, briefly *Tribune* editor after Patterson, one of the "irreconcilables" who helped defeat League of Nations

Mrs. Ruth Hanna McCormick, Medill McCormick's wife, in 1930 as she received news of her nomination as Republican candidate for senator from Illinois. At left, her nephew, D. R. Hanna; at right, daughter Katrina

the old-fashioned Fourth, and Keeley gritted his teeth because he thought the noise was making the child worse. Late that afternoon he called his secretary at the office, but there was so much noise at both ends of the line that neither one could hear the other for a time. In the midst of the conversation Keeley had an idea.

"Get reports from thirty cities on the number of killed and injured by this goddamn foolery," he ordered. "Let's see what it looks like."

He called back ten minutes later to dictate the query. "Make it a hundred cities," he added. "Get the figures in shape and we'll print them."

Next morning's *Tribune* devoted a column to holiday casualties. The day after there were three columns of it as more reports came in. The *Tribune* duplicated that performance every year for the next two decades, against opposition from its own readers and other newspapers, until the states began to pass laws limiting or outlawing the use of fireworks.

Even then, so early in his regime, Keeley was developing his basic principle of newspaper management, the principle of personal service. Out of it came one of his most spectacular stunts, the coverage of the Iroquois Theater fire on Wednesday afternoon, December 30, 1903.

The historic fire occurred on a dull afternoon when the *Tribune* city editor, Edgar Sisson, was alone in the office. His reporters were out on assignment, due to call in as usual during the afternoon. The four-eleven alarm had scarcely finished sounding on the city room's fire bell when Sisson had the machinery in motion. Keeley and Edward S. Beck, then city editor on the more important night desk, came in almost together, and Keeley took over the story. Sisson went out to help direct the reporters.

By the time Sisson and his reporters got back to the *Tribune* about ten o'clock that night they had to fight their way into the building through hundreds of people trying to find out the identity of the victims. Inside Keeley and Beck were talking.

"It's names I want," Sisson heard Keeley say. "I'm going to

take all the first page for names, nothing but names of dead and injured."

"I sent in a man to write the lead," Sisson interposed.

"He was only in one spot," Keeley snapped back. "You saw all the spots, the theater, the morgue in the restaurant, and the dead laid out in the hotel rotunda. Write the lead yourself, for the second page. The first page is for names."

Next day, and for years thereafter, hundreds of thousands of words were written about the Iroquois fire. But on the front page of Keeley's *Tribune* the only words were the names of victims— 571 names of the dead and missing. On other pages there were four times as many pictures of the dead as were in all the other Chicago morning papers combined. It was personal service at its highest level, and one of the landmarks in newspaper history.

Three years later Keeley left his managing editor's desk, where he had sat for ten years, and went after a big story himself. It concerned Paul Stensland, an influential Norwegian-American, who was president of the five-million-dollar Milwaukee Avenue State Bank. One day in 1906 Stensland and his cashier suddenly disappeared, leaving the bank short hundreds of thousands of dollars. For three days there was no news in the case, until one of Keeley's tipsters told him where Hering, the cashier, was hiding. Keeley went to the place alone and found Hering in a mood to kill himself, but he persuaded the cashier to go with him to a downtown hotel, extracted a confession from him and then turned him over to the police.

Exclusive publication of the confession was a tremendous story in itself, but Keeley wasn't satisfied. Hering had told him that Stensland planned to hide in North Africa. Keeley put his spies on the trail, particularly to watch Theodore Stensland, the banker's son. One day the tip-off came. It was a business message in Norwegian, sent to Theodore and signed Paul Olson, datelined Tangier. Keeley answered it and nearly lost his quarry by sending the message in English: "Imperative await letters papers Tangier."

With that, Keeley sailed for Africa. But Stensland wasn't in Tangier; he had gone to Gibraltar. Keeley followed him to Gibraltar, and by that time Stensland had gone back to Tangier, where

Keeley finally caught up with him. They talked and Keeley was convinced that the fugitive had been betrayed by his trusted subordinates. "He was a fine, fascinating old chap," Keeley wrote later, "who fell among thieves and fled, foolishly, when his bank was solvent, and who is quite incapable of criminal intent."

Stensland was tried, convicted and sent to prison, but almost immediately he was paroled and worked hard to straighten out the bank's affairs. Keeley asked Insull to help the old man out, and Insull hired Stensland to be an investigator of South American investment projects for him.

For two years after this episode there was comparative quiet in the *Tribune* shop. Keeley had been made general manager and Beck had become managing editor. Then Medill McCormick moved into Robert W. Patterson's office and it became evident that the McCormick family had decided that Medill should run the paper.

The city room murmured with speculation. Everyone wondered how Keeley would take the move, because he had been boss for so long. Of course, they argued, Medill liked Keeley and for that matter the staff members liked Medill—a convivial, agreeable, tall, sandy-haired, nervously quick chap. The staff had only two things against him. He was erratic (a McCormick family characteristic) and he didn't have to work.

For a time the paper's routine went on as usual and Keeley gave the orders. Then one day Keeley disappeared. It was rumored he had gone to Japan for a long vacation. He had left only one order with Beck: "Do whatever Medill McCormick wants."

Again nothing unusual happened for a while except that McCormick devoted some *Tribune* space to promoting his special friends. Presently, however, Medill thought up a crusade of his own. He intended, he said, to make Chicago "a respectable city" and to chase out what he termed "respectable villains." This was to be no ordinary crusade, of the standard varieties which were stock fillers on dull days. Medill proposed nothing less than publication of the names of those respectable citizens who had anything to do financially with the operation of whorehouses. gambling places or established dives of any description.

To compile such a list, comprehensive though it might be, was not a difficult job. The reporters on any paper could have put it together out of everyday experience. There was some hesitation on the city editor's part, but Beck reminded him of Keeley's last order and the research began. It went on for three months. After it was compiled the complete list went into a small red leather book. Between its covers was an impressive list of "leading" and "well-known" citizens, and complete descriptions of the besmirched property they owned.

The city editor was afraid to tell Beck that the list was complete. "What shall I do with this list when I get it hog-tight?" he asked.

"Do what Medill says," Beck told him.

The city editor shuddered and put the little red book back under its Yale lock.

One day, as suddenly as he had departed, Keeley came back from Japan and walked into the city editor's office.

"I hear you have a red book," he remarked.

The city editor gave it to him, without a word.

As Linn tells the denouement in his book: "At midnight that night Medill McCormick went up to the composing room. Keeley was watching an edition being made up on the stones. Medill had on an opera hat, and carried a stick. He laid them both on a table, put his arm over Keeley's shoulders, and laughed. He did not say goodbye, but the next day he went to Europe, and never came back. Of the red book, no more is known."

The *Tribune* in 1909 had already used the slogan "World's Greatest Newspaper" in its advertising copy. Later it was registered in Washington as a trademark, and on August 29, 1911, it began to occupy the spot on the *Tribune* front page where it remains today. Between 1910 and 1913 Keeley gave the slogan all the meaning it was ever to have.

*Tribune* politics in this period strayed from the path of Republican virtue for the only time in its history. In 1910, under Keeley, the paper followed Medill McCormick's lead and seriously considered the Progressive move to renominate Roosevelt. When the Republican party short-circuited this political current in 1912 the

*Tribune's* power lines dangled indecisively, without a connection. As Donald Richberg once remarked, "It stood with one foot on the Republican poopdeck and one in the Progressive lifeboat." The decision to stay in the lifeboat undoubtedly came from *Tribune* ownership, particularly from the influence of young Joseph Patterson, who was already writing socialistic editorials. When the lifeboat sank precipitately in November the *Tribune* did not lose circulation. Keeley had thoughtfully provided life preservers in the form of popular features, thus establishing a pattern which has endured to the present.

Meanwhile the *Tribune* had a political battle at home in 1910. Its intended victim was Mayor Carter Harrison, who had announced that he would run again. The paper's campaign took a form familiar in all phases of its history—a series of articles purporting to be a true history of the candidate from ancestry to malfeasance. This series was titled, "Eight Years of Carter Harrison."

The man assigned to do the job was a veteran *Tribune* reporter, Charles J. Powers, who had been brought up on the city hall beat, where he had been more than friendly with politically unsavory aldermen. There seems to be no doubt that he wrote city hall news with an eye to his own and the aldermen's mutual benefit.

In the first six articles of the series Powers covered Harrison's political career in a rather vague way, deprecating whatever he had done and assuming a cynical tone toward his municipal philosophies. Then came the rabbit punch. It was a story based on the allegations of a small-time lawyer named Arnold Tripp, who described himself as once the attorney for A. W. Friedrichs, the operator of a basement saloon at Madison and Clark streets, whose license Harrison had revoked because he suspected that Friedrichs was allowing prostitutes to operate in his place. Tripp said that he had contributed five hundred dollars to an earlier Harrison mayoralty campaign, had visited Harrison and "discussed" the contribution thoroughly, whereupon Harrison had restored Friedrichs's license.

Powers had overlooked one essential fact in writing this story.

The records showed that the license had never been restored. Harrison decided that he would sue, and engaged as his counsel A. S. Trude, who had been the *Tribune's* special attorney for many years. Trude was so eager to take the case that he took it on a contingent fee.

The suit was instituted for a hundred thousand dollars. Trying to laugh it off, the *Tribune* reprinted attacks on Harrison from the Hearst papers of 1904–05. Harrison responded with another suit for a hundred thousand dollars. Still amused, but laughing a bit hollowly now, the *Tribune* printed another choice set of Hearst items. Harrison slapped back with another hundred-thousand-dollar suit. The *Tribune* dropped the Powers series without another word.

After Harrison was re-elected in 1911 the *Tribune* brazenly began another Powers series on Harrison—complimentary in tone and devoted primarily to his father! Harrison was even more amazed when a *Tribune* reporter appeared at his office one day, expressed the paper's regrets for having published the Friedrichs story, and offered to print a retraction. Harrison advised him to prepare the retraction and submit it. It was done, but Harrison found the apology unsatisfactory and asked for submission of one that was more complete. At the same time he inquired what kind of retraction the *Tribune* intended to make in its editorial columns. He got an answer that startled him: the *Tribune* had never and would never print retractions in its editorial columns. To Harrison's way of thinking the libels had been printed in both news and editorial columns and retractions would have to appear in both places. He called off negotiations.

Meantime the mayor discovered that *Tribune* spies were busy in the Tenderloin district, trying to dig up discrediting stories about him. But the libel suits were still pending, and Trude was opposed to any out-of-court settlement. Friedrichs, now operating a decent hotel in Waukegan, wrote to Harrison and offered to testify that Tripp's story was false, but he was scarcely a lily-white witness.

The *Tribune* fought as long as it was able. It offered cash settlements and they were refused. It pleaded with Harrison to be satisfied with a retraction in the news columns. The mayor insisted on all or nothing. Forced into an impossible position, the *Tribune* gave in at last and published an apology and a retraction in both its news and its editorial columns.

But it never forgave, in accordance with *Tribune* tradition. Nor did Harrison, for that matter. He wrote later in his autobiography, *Stormy Years*, that he wished he had kept the suits hanging over the paper's head for a few years, to "keep the editors in a constant state of nervous tension."

However, this defeat did not hurt the *Tribune*. Even as the Harrison feud went on the paper was involved in a sensational exposé that completely overshadowed its embarrassment. It was a high point in *Tribune* history and the climax of Keeley's career.

The exposé was the result of a change in Keeley's position on the paper. On March 1, 1910, the Tribune Company's directors gave Keeley "absolute control of the *Tribune* property." This might have been an indirect admission that the family thought very little of Robert McCormick and Joe Patterson, its representatives on the paper. They considered McCormick, already twelve years out of college, as promising only in a business way, incapable of handling editorial problems. As for Patterson, he was an out-and-out radical in the family's eyes. He had made speeches advocating municipal ownership of street railways, and he had written tear-jerking plays which satirized respectability and the press with fine impartiality. Worse, he was suspected of being a Socialist. It was obvious, the family concluded, that the *Tribune's* destinies could not rest in such hands. Keeley was the man whose advice and judgment the directors trusted, and so they turned control of the paper over to him.

A week later Keeley was negotiating for a twelve-thousand-word manuscript which he believed would establish him in the driver's seat for good—if it didn't wreck the paper. By April 30 his investigation of the manuscript was ended and he was ready to publish the story. It ran under headlines larger and blacker than the *Tribune* had ever used, the kind of type city-room wisecrackers say is "usually reserved for the Second Coming." The story that ran beneath this head was written by Keeley.

## DEMOCRATIC LEGISLATOR CONFESSES HE WAS BRIBED TO CAST VOTE FOR LORIMER FOR UNITED STATES SENATOR

The Chicago *Tribune* has in its possession and will submit to the proper authorities—Governor Deneen, Attorney-General Stead, and States Attorney Wayman—a sworn statement made by Charles A. White, a member of the lower house of the Illinois Legislature from the 49th district, charging that William Lorimer was elected to the United States Senate last summer by bribery and corruption; that a large number of the members of the last legislature received money for their votes on various bills; that he, White (a Democrat), received $1,000 for voting for Lorimer and that he also received $900 as his share of the "jackpot," a term applied to the general corruption fund distributed at the close of each session.

White admits his criminality—says he accepted money so that he might expose the corruption and rascality of the legislature. He knows he will be charged with attempted blackmail by Senator Lorimer and Lee O'Neil Browne, Democratic leader of the last legislature, because he wrote certain letters to those persons. White denies the blackmail theory, and alleges that the letters were written in furtherance of his plan of exposure.

The *Tribune* is thoroughly conversant with this and other features of the case. White's manuscript has been in the possession of the *Tribune* for a month. A most thorough and searching investigation has been made, the results of which will be given by the *Tribune* to its readers day by day.

Lorimer was one of Chicago's most colorful political figures, called admiringly "the blond boss." He was a contradictory man politically, liked in his city in much the same way that Jimmy Walker is admired in New York. His primary newspaper support came from the Chicago *Inter-Ocean*. Lorimer was a political boss who specialized in the inside track and had come up by way of the transit-franchise grabbers and other exemplars of municipal corruption. Some of the henchmen who were graduated from his school got as far as the United States Senate; others ended in the penitentiary. Oddly enough, he was a pious adherent to the Rev. Robert W. Patterson's staunch faith.

It was Lorimer's bad luck to run afoul of Keeley, whom he had never antagonized, at a time when the *Tribune's* editor needed him for his own career. In spite of the paper's later effort to take moral credit for the exposure, there is nothing in the evidence to indicate that the *Tribune's* interest in the story was anything but political.

The story, as written by White, had a curious history before it reached Keeley. White set it down originally simply because he needed money. First he offered it to Lorimer as blackmail, the price seventy-five thousand dollars. Lorimer was not interested. Then he tried to sell it to *Everybody's Magazine*, but the editor was frightened away by the dangers involved.

White's friends told him to try a Chicago paper, and that was how he happened to come eventually to Keeley. When Keeley heard White's clumsy offer he astutely showed no interest at all but agreed to look the manuscript over with the idea of buying if it appeared to be good enough and could be backed up by an investigation.

As he read the document Keeley realized that this was it. This was the story he needed! He gave White two hundred dollars in expense money and outlined the informer's part in the investigation. Then he organized a staff of reporters and detectives and put them to work. It cost the *Tribune* more than sixteen thousand dollars to verify the story, but it was worth it. As a final step Keeley bludgeoned White down from his original asking price of fifty thousand dollars to thirty-two hundred and fifty.

On the night of April 29 the *Tribune* presses were grinding out extra copies and the story was launched, for better or worse. Keeley went over to the Chicago Athletic Association's clubhouse about four in the morning and played poker until it was time for breakfast.

Next day the follow-up began, with more details from White and new stories based on what the reporters and detectives had turned up. A few days later Keeley drove the final nail in Lorimer's political coffin with a cryptic two-line editorial which he wrote himself. Captioned "Was It Sawdust?" it ran: "Who furnished the 'dust'—to use a colloquialism—to bribe the legislators?"

The purpose of this editorial was to point an accusing finger at Edward Hines and other lumbermen who wanted Lorimer in the Senate to help maintain the duty on imported lumber and wood products. It was this "sawdust" connection, and not White's confession, that eventually led to Lorimer's expulsion from the Senate.

Meanwhile the owners of the paper, particularly R. R. McCormick and Joe Patterson, were probably apprehensive about the outcome of the exposé. If libel suits laid the *Tribune* low Keeley would escape but they would be ruined. However, not a word was said; Keeley was law.

On May 29 Lorimer got up in the Senate and defended himself for six hours. The *Tribune* gave the speech full coverage in page after page of type. In fact the only time the case had been off the front page in the past month occurred when a cosmic event, the arrival of Halley's comet, overshadowed earthly affairs.

In his speech Lorimer told the story of his life in the most flattering terms. He named his enemies one by one. They included President Taft, Theodore Roosevelt, William Jennings Bryan, the Chicago "trust press," and most particularly and especially "the McCormicks and Pattersons." It was the first time that cry was raised, and it is unfortunate for the family's enemies today that it was raised by a crooked politician whom the *Tribune* had exposed. Lorimer also dwelt at length upon the well-worn subject of the *Tribune's* real estate lease from the school board.

Keeley was in his glory as circulation soared, but he got a bad scare on the following March, in 1911, when the Senate voted 46–40 to retain Lorimer in his seat. A piece of new evidence turned up by Herman H. Kohlsaat, of the Chicago *Record-Herald*, involving a hundred-thousand-dollar Lorimer slush fund, caused the Illinois Legislature to appoint a committee of inquiry, whose findings compelled the Senate to reopen the case and unseat Lorimer, by a vote of 55–28.

In the process of testifying before the Senate investigating committee in July 1911 Keeley disclosed some pertinent facts about himself and the *Tribune*. "My authority is absolute," he told the committee, "in all departments." He said that he alone directed the editorial policies. Lorimer had previously evaluated the *Tribune* at three million dollars, but Keeley on the stand said it was worth between seven and a half and ten million dollars. Two thousand shares of Tribune Company stock existed, he said, but not one share had ever been sold, to his knowledge.

His testimony pointed specifically to Edward Hines, the lumber king, and Keeley told with considerable fervor of an incident involving the *Tribune* and Hines, a story designed to put the paper in a pure white light. In the Lincoln Centenary Edition of 1909, he related, Hines had taken a six-hundred-dollar full-page advertisement, and later had remarked that he felt the *Tribune* "owed him something." Keeley sent back the money with the scorn of a man who knows it is costing him nothing to make a grand gesture. He declaimed before the Senate committee: "I told the fellow there was absolutely no connection between the editorial opinions of the *Tribune* and its advertising columns."

The Lorimer case dragged on for three years before the senator was expelled in July 1913. In that time Keeley also reached the peak of his newspaper management practices and was giving *Tribune* readers the kind of "personal service" he had always visualized. His conception of such service is an ideal which could be read with profit not only by the McCormick-Patterson interests today but by the publishers of a good many other American newspapers.

Keeley said: "The big development of the modern newspaper will be along lines of personal service. The newspaper that not only informs and instructs its readers but is of service is the one that commands attention, gets circulation, and also holds its readers after it gets them. . . . It must enter into the everyday life of its readers and, like the parish priest, be guide, counselor and friend. . . . There should be no partisanship in politics, no prejudice in religion, no hostility to organized labor, no antagonism to wealth per se, no color of opinion; in fact, opinion should be barred from the report of every happening, every meeting, every public discussion, everything that goes to make up the daily grist of news. I say it should be; I admit that it is not. . . . But the man in charge of a paper must be impersonal as a judge and his every act must meet the acid test of duty to the people as a whole."

Of course Keeley fell far short of this ideal in several important respects, but he made the effort and that is more than can be said of many newspapers at this moment.

The longest step Keeley took toward the goal was his establishment of departments. He instituted the "How to Keep Well" department, conducted by Dr. William A. Evans, former city health commissioner, and *Tribune* readers learned about mumps, housemaid's knee, first aid and, as they wrote letters of inquiry, about far more obscure troubles. This department was in line with the *Tribune's* long campaign against patent medicines and disreputable medical advertising, which cost it two hundred thousand dollars a year in advertising revenue. At that time some of the best newspapers in the country took all that kind of advertising they could get. The *Tribune* also warred against so-called "medical specialists," who specialized mostly in venereal diseases. Good reporting and the co-operation of the American Medical Association finally cleaned up this situation.

There were other new personal-service departments. Laura Jean Libbey began to write an advice-to-the-lovelorn column. Lillian Russell conducted a department of "beauty hints." A swap column, covering everything from trusses and encyclopedias to at least a dozen orphans, was called "Marion Harland's Helping Hand" department.

The *Tribune* also began to get out booklets, a practice which grew to a small-sized publishing industry in the next fifteen years. One booklet told housewives "One Hundred Ways to Earn Money at Home." Others were titled, "How to Fight the Increased Cost of Living" and "Friend of the People."

But at the zenith of Keeley's career on the *Tribune* disaster overtook him. He left the paper on May 11, 1914, to take over management of the *Record-Herald* from Kohlsaat. His biographer, Linn, asks the pertinent question, "Did he jump or was he pushed?"

The evidence indicates that he was pushed. Apparently he became aware that he was disliked in high places, particularly by Robert Rutherford McCormick. McCormick and Patterson were rising fast in the business, and it was already apparent that they were going to be dominating figures. They were chiefs of the tribe; Keeley was a hired hand. Facing the inevitable, he took the first good opportunity that came his way, before the royal cousins could act.

When Keeley died his obituary ran briefly on an inside page of the *Tribune*, while other papers carried it on page one. The McCormicks and the Pattersons by that time had far transcended the man who made their property, if only for a few years, a newspaper.

# Chapter 2

## THE TRIBUNE VS. HENRY FORD

WHEN THE COUSINS stepped into the *Tribune* throne room in 1914 they inherited a thoroughly sound property. The paper had the prestige built up and bequeathed by Joseph Medill. It had the personal-service connection with its readership established by Keeley and also the political power of which the Lorimer case had been the latest demonstration.

Lorimer had left to the cousins a choice assortment of political enemies. During the paper's fight to unseat him several of the senator's Republican henchmen had organized the Lincoln League to fight back. Members of the League included Len Small, later governor of Illinois; William Hale Thompson, who became mayor of Chicago; and Fred Lundin, boss of the so-called Thompson Republicans.

But the paper was ready to build, and it had acquired the kind of builders it needed for financial success. Patterson began to originate the famed comic strips and other features which so increased *Tribune* circulation. McCormick applied the business pressure necessary to put the paper in the big-money class. Keeley had been no businessman.

In eight years the cousins succeeded in doubling *Tribune* circulation. From 1914 to 1921 daily circulation went from 261,278 to 499,725, and Sunday circulation from 406,556 to 827,028. Advertising, from 1914 to 1921, jumped in columns from 43,503 to 76,703.

Behind these figures lay the instant success of such Patterson-inspired comics as "Andy Gump," "Moon Mullins" and "Little Orphan Annie." Patterson also originated the idea of printing a daily directory of motion picture theaters and their attractions. In line with this he conceived the plan of printing newspaper versions of serial thrillers that were showing concurrently in the local picture houses. Prizes were offered for the best solutions to the mysteries. The first serial printed was *The Adventures of Kathlyn*.

On the business side, McCormick leased the Canadian forest lands and built the Quebec and Ontario paper mills which enabled the *Tribune* to save a paper manufacturer's profit and compete more successfully with Hearst, who got paper for five dollars a ton less than the standard price.

This kind of smart business ended Keeley's and Hearst's dream of Chicago newspaper dominance. Keeley had become publisher of the *Herald*, a merger of the *Record-Herald* and the *Inter-Ocean*. The *Herald* was backed by big Chicago names—Samuel Insull, Julius Rosenwald, Ogden Armour and others. By 1918 the *Herald* had been beaten into submission by the aggressive McCormick-Patterson combination. It merged with Hearst's *Examiner* to become the *Herald-Examiner*. Twenty-one years later the *Tribune* vanquished that rival too. Keeley wound up in the public relations business. By 1918, also, the *Tribune* had eliminated two of its eight Chicago rivals and had jockeyed itself into a position of dominating influence.

In this transition period the *Tribune's cause célèbre* was the Henry Ford libel case, a much-publicized but little understood episode in the lives of McCormick, the World's Greatest Newspaper and the Flivver King.

*Tribune* official histories call the trial a case of "clear thinking against muddled thinking, experience against willful ignorance." It labels the verdict as the first "big, modern vindication of the 'right of comment.'" This is difficult to believe in light of the fact that the jury decided Ford *had* been libeled, and gave him the verdict. The six-cent verdict, which the *Tribune* interpreted as a moral victory, was simply an expression of the jury's opinion that Ford had not been injured financially by the libel.

The case had far wider implications. First of all it was another instance of Joseph Medill repeating himself in Robert McCormick. Under Medill, as illustrated in previous chapters, the *Tribune*, used as a personal political weapon, had not hesitated to turn on those it had once supported, when the alliance was no longer mutually profitable. This was, and is, known as fearless impartiality, or freedom of the press. To the untutored observer, however, it smacks more strongly of the ruthlessness which so characterized Medill as a publisher and now, in the Ford case, reappeared in his grandson.

The *Tribune*, for example, had lauded Ford in 1914 when he announced his "profit-sharing" scheme. That this idea pleased the *Tribune* for its own and not for humanitarian reasons is apparent in its editorial comment: "The action of the Ford Motor Company offers a striking illustration of the new business conscience in action and is the more likely to be heeded, since it is not the act of visionaries and propagandists, but of exceptionally able and successful businessmen."

Later Ford issued his ukase ordering company employees to make their homes more comfortable and maintain "an American standard of living"—all a part of the public relations which established the Ford myth in America. The *Tribune* commented, "The Ford plan of treating the worker is humane, American and modern." As Ford continued to develop his business along lines eminently pleasing to the *Tribune's* essentially hypocritical labor policy, the paper felt moved to commend him on August 7, 1915: "Mr. Ford should be a cheering exhibit to those who are sweeping the country for present day genius that compares with the railroad builders or the consolidators of a steel industry. He is giving the world the day's lesson."

Then Ford made the mistake of disagreeing with a *Tribune* crusade and thereby earned the paper's immediate and undying enmity. The flag-waving section of the American press had been clamoring for war with Mexico in 1916, and the *Tribune* had joined the cry. Here it was solidly in line with the Medill tradition: "We shall permit no nation to abuse Mexico but ourselves." As tension increased on the border between Mexico and Texas, the National Guard was ordered mobilized by President Wilson on June 18, 1916.

This move stirred Henry Ford's pacifism to the boiling point. He blamed the crisis on "the interests," publicly doubted Wilson's sincerity, discouraged enlistment in the Guard and branded the approaching conflict as "organized murder."

That was too much for the *Tribune*. Henry Ford was no longer a "cheering exhibit" who was "giving the world the day's lesson." On June 2 appeared a story from Detroit, with the customary editorialized headline, FLIVVER PATRIOTISM. The story read:

"Ford employees who volunteered to bear arms for the United States will lose their jobs. While most employers have guaranteed not only to give patriotic workmen their old places when they return from fighting their country's battles, but have promised to pay their salaries while they are in service, Henry Ford's workmen will not have a job when they return, much less will they receive pay while fighting for their country. Ford's superintendents refuse to say if there are any guardsmen employed in the plant, but it is known that some seventy-five men of the militia are Ford employees. No provision will be made by Ford for their wives and families."

The *Tribune* next day followed this dispatch with the famous editorial which precipitated Ford's libel suit. The editorial has often been quoted in part, but it is worth reading in full as an example of the paper's complete about-face on the value of Ford as an individual—personal journalism in the best Medill manner. McCormick himself might easily have written it, although it has never been proved that he did. The editorial ran:

## HENRY FORD IS AN ANARCHIST

Inquiry at the Henry Ford offices in Detroit discloses the fact that employees of Ford who are members of or recruits in the National Guard will lose their places. No provision will be made for any one dependent upon them. Their wages will stop, their families may get along in any fashion possible; their positions will be filled, and if they come back safely and apply for their jobs again they will be on the same footing as any other applicants. This is the rule for Ford employees everywhere.

Information was refused as to the number of American soldiers unfortunate enough to have Henry Ford as an employer at this time, but at the Detroit recruiting station it was said that about seventy-five men will pay this price for their services to their country.

Mr. Ford thus proves that he does not believe in service to the nation in the fashion a soldier must serve it. If his factory were on the southern and not on the northern border we presume he would feel the same way.

We do not know precisely what he would do if a Villa band decided that the Ford strong boxes were worth opening and that it would be pleasant to see the Ford factories burn. It is evident that it is possible for a millionaire just south of the Canadian border to be indifferent to what happens just north of the Mexican border.

If Ford allows this rule of his shops to stand he will reveal himself not merely as an ignorant idealist but as an anarchistic enemy of the nation which protects him in his wealth.

A man so ignorant as Henry Ford may not understand the fundamentals of the government under which he lives. That government is permitted to take Henry Ford himself and command his services as a soldier if necessary. It can tax his money for war purposes and will. It can compel him to devote himself to national purposes. The reason it did not take the person of Henry Ford years ago and put it in uniform is, first, that it has not had the common sense to make its theoretical universal service practical, and second, because there have been young men to volunteer for the service which has protected Henry Ford, for which service he now penalizes them.

He takes the men who stand between him and service and punishes them for the service which protects him. The man is so incapable of thought that he cannot see the ignominy of his own performance.

The proper place for so deluded a human being is a region where no government exists except such as he furnishes, where no protection is afforded except such as he affords, where nothing stands between him and the rules of life except such defenses as he puts there.

Such a place, we think, might be found anywhere in the state of Chihuahua, Mexico. Anywhere in Mexico would be a good location for the Ford factories.

The one word in this lengthy and contradictory tirade that stuck in Henry Ford's throat was "anarchist." Ten weeks later he sued for a million dollars, and in the endless litigation which followed it was the word "anarchist" upon which the battle turned.

It was three years before the lawyers got the case into court, but the trial began at last in the summer of 1919 at Mount Clemens, Michigan, a sleepy county seat which is now celebrated as a mineral spa. The stage setting was completely appropriate for the drama which followed. A sign hanging in the corridor of the red brick courthouse advised, "If you spit on the floor in your own house, do it here. We want you to feel at home." Judge James G. Tucker, a sixty-four-year-old jurist, dismissed the jury of eleven farmers and a road inspector every afternoon in time for the men to tend their livestock.

The citizens of Mount Clemens were bemused by the forces which now took over their city. McCormick's counsel had imported more than a score of cattle ranchers and other Texas-border residents to tell the jury of "rape" and "massacre" along the Rio Grande, thus proving that Washington had more than sufficient reason to intervene. The Texans clattered about the little Michigan town in their cowboy dress, which added considerable color to the spectacle. To counteract this coterie of witnesses Ford had brought more than a hundred Mexicans to the trial.

Ford had seven lawyers, the *Tribune* eight. The Flivver King commandeered twenty-five rooms in the Colonial Hotel, and the *Tribune* engaged a rival hotel. These forces were supplemented by squads of private detectives, occupied mostly in shadowing each other. Ford went to get his shoes shined one day and in an instant the shoe-shining parlor was surrounded by *Tribune* strongmen. Meanwhile Ford's counsel accused the *Tribune* of tapping telephone wires.

When it finally opened the case went on for fourteen weeks; more than two million words went into the record. It was the most talkative as well as the most acrimonious case in the history of the Michigan bar. There were some who thought that Judge Tucker was hastened to his grave by the interminable argument. "I have been talked almost to death," the jurist lamented when it was over.

The *Tribune's* attack was based on the establishment of a definition for the word "anarchism" which would be so broad that Ford could be proved a dangerous anarchist if he were shown to be stupid, naïve, uneducated and unpatriotic. Chief counsel in charge of this attack was Elliott K. Stevenson, a brilliant and sophisticated Detroit attorney. He had observed Ford's conduct in a previous trial involving the Dodge interests and knew that Ford's genius was indeed lopsided. Alfred Lucking, Ford's chief attorney, knew it too and anticipated Stevenson's campaign by attempting to give Ford a short course in American history in his hotel room. These daily lessons were a failure. Ford was completely disinterested in American history but intensely interested in a hundred other things; he was always striding away to look at something out the window or abruptly changing the subject, and Lucking was justifiably apprehensive.

For a time it appeared that Stevenson would succeed in his strategy. He began by testing Ford's vocabulary and flunking him on such words as "chili con carne," and "ballyhoo," which Ford defined as "a blackguard or something of that nature." Then he went on to expose Ford's ignorance of American history, during which the manufacturer expressed his much-quoted opinion that "history is bunk." This was a more succinct version of what he had told a reporter before the trial began: "History is more or less the bunk. We want to live in the present, and the only history that is worth a tinker's dam is the history we make today."

But Ford was not the pathetic figure on the stand that the *Tribune* expected him to be. He spoke tartly, in short, succinct sentences that were in sharp contrast to Stevenson's wordy conundrums. In answer to one question he uttered what was probably the most intelligent sentence in the whole trial: "I could find a man in five minutes who could tell me all about it."

In his summation Stevenson declared, "Gentlemen of the jury, they forced us to open the mind of Henry Ford and expose it to you bare . . . to disclose the pitiable condition that he had succeeded in keeping from the view of the public."

By that time, however, most observers present realized, although they could not have defined it, that *Tribune* strategy had turned back upon the paper. Rural America, not Henry Ford, was on trial. The jury knew it. The citizens of Mount Clemens knew it. On the stand Henry Ford was not the already legendary motorcar manufacturer but a typical citizen of the American prairie country, who had come of age in 1884 and was married to a country girl of his own kind. He was virtually illiterate, obviously, and his philosophy was unashamedly out of the cracker barrel. Both these characteristics were common to any number of residents in the American hinterland.

In brief, Henry Ford was exactly the kind of citizen who had been celebrated time and time again by the *Tribune*—the good, Midwestern prairie farmer or small-town store owner, a solidly American type clearly superior, in *Tribune* eyes, to the citizens in any other part of the United States. That was the public philosophy of Joseph Medill; it was the philosophy of McCormick at the time of the trial and right up to the present. This philosophy was expressed in a fierce sectionalism which has taken on the larger form of isolationism in our own time. But although Medill proclaimed this philosophy in one form or another innumerable times in his newspaper, he was an aristocrat who demonstrated often that he had no genuine sympathy for the common man whose cause he exploited when it was profitable. In the Ford case McCormick gave proof that he was cut from the same cloth.

Of course the spectators and participants in the trial did not have the advantage of such perspective. The people who saw or heard about the trial knew only that their good opinion of Henry Ford had been even further enhanced by the man's simplicity and by the disclosure that he was so nearly like themselves. *Tribune* sympathizers were uncomfortably aware that not a few self-made businessmen sitting in Chicago offices and consorting socially with McCormick would have made no better showing than Ford on the witness stand.

When the jury came back after ten hours and announced it had found in favor of Ford, both sides were satisfied. They appeared to believe that the five-hundred-thousand-dollar cost to each litigant was justified. Ford was more popular than ever with the people to whom he wanted to sell cars. Moreover, he had learned a lesson and forthwith hired a staff of writers who in time turned out five books and innumerable smaller compositions under his by-line. The New York *Times's* solemn editorial pronouncement—"Mr. Ford has been submitted to a severe examination of his intellectual qualities. He has not received a pass degree"—only amused the Ford advertising experts. They had been convinced, and correctly, that what the *Times* thought was not an influence on the thinking of Main Street. As for the *Tribune*, the six-cent verdict had removed the only possible source of harm—a costly judgment against it—and the paper began to cash in on the publicity value of the trial.

Chapter 3

# THE GREAT SCHISM

THE COMPARATIVE HISTORIES of McCormick and Patterson during this transition wartime period show clearly the fundamental difference between the two men which led to the division of their interests.

Both cousins became *Tribune* correspondents at the start of the first World War. Patterson, with his proletarian leanings, refused to accept the special privileges to which his position entitled him. McCormick accepted these privileges and enlarged upon them. Patterson was at Vera Cruz in 1914 to cover the trouble there, and later went to Belgium as an observer of the German invasion. McCormick went abroad in 1915, bound for the Eastern Front. In London he had lunch with Prime Minister Asquith and paid a visit to Churchill, then First Lord of the Admiralty. When he completed a round of social calls in London he moved on to Paris and then to Russia. Correct in white tie and tails, he interviewed the Czar. Later, smitten with an idea, he hired a movie cameraman and together they made the first war newsreels ever filmed, which were shipped back to Chicago and shown there with great acclaim. When he got back to Chicago, McCormick also wrote a book about his adventure.

Back home again, the cousins were agreed on German efficiency, mistrust of England, and most of all on the necessity for American isolation from Europe's war. Nonetheless, they were vociferous editorially in advocating invasion of Mexico in 1916, and entered into the affair themselves.

Patterson turned down a commission and enlisted as a buck private in a National Guard artillery unit. McCormick entered the conflict as a cavalry major. Howard Vincent O'Brien, Chicago *Daily News* columnist who was in the Guard with Patterson, says that the authorities tried to make the younger cousin a general, on the basis of his family connections, but that he would have no part of it.

While Patterson sweated it out in the artillery McCormick leased a hacienda and received high-ranking officers. The cousins met by accident one day in a San Antonio hotel, and McCormick was forced to introduce Private Patterson to General Funston as they ascended in an elevator. The general and the private shook hands without embarrassment on either side, to McCormick's amazement.

After the Mexican affair the cousins were united on only one thing and that was their intense opposition to American involvement in the war in Europe. The *Tribune* shouted against American participation in much the same words it used a quarter century later when war came again. It was not until six months before United States entry that the paper yielded to the inevitable. Changing tone abruptly, the *Tribune* became superpatriotic and the cousins again plunged personally into battle, and again each made the plunge in his own fashion.

Patterson worked his way up from the ranks to a second lieutenant's commission, which he held when he was shipped to France. He saw service in five major engagements, was gassed and wounded, and eventually became a captain. McCormick joined Pershing's staff and went to Paris as a member of it, later went to the front with an artillery unit, but by the end of the war was in an executive post as commandant at Fort Sheridan, Illinois.

Much has been made of the fateful meeting in France between the two cousins on a night in 1918 when the New York *Daily News* was conceived. The most bitter opponents of the *News* emphasize the fact that conception occurred on a manure pile, and they see something symbolic in this. More conservative biographers say that the two men met to settle their long-standing differences. The Colonel's own story, told to a group of businessmen, is that the occasion of the meeting was a farewell. Pershing had assigned him to go back to the States and oversee the recruiting of a million more men. (It appeared then that the war would last much longer.) The *Daily News* was a by-product of the session.

However, the tabloid idea was certainly on Captain Patterson's mind when he was called from his battery to meet McCormick, newly a colonel, at the French village of Mareuil-en-Dole. The conversation began in a farmhouse near the Ourcq River, but the noise of operational movement in this field headquarters drove them to climb out a rear window and sit on a manure pile in the back yard, where it was quieter. There they drank scotch and watched the distant flashing of an artillery barrage.

Patterson was full of the interview he had had a short time before with Lord Northcliffe, during a London furlough. Northcliffe had told him the story of his London *Daily Mirror*, and how this tabloid had climbed to an 800,000 circulation at that time. Northcliffe added, Patterson told his cousin, that he believed New York was ripe for a similar tabloid. The story impressed McCormick.

The conversation must also have turned to postwar prospects for the *Tribune*, particularly the taxes which the government would be able to assess on *Tribune* profits. This was a sore point with McCormick, the businessman, and perhaps he saw in Patterson's tabloid aspirations a way to siphon off potential taxable income into a venture which might also turn out eventually to be profitable. Then too there was the undeniable advantage, which cropped out indirectly as the conversation went on, that the cousins would be separated and Patterson would take complete control of the New York paper if it were successful. The diverse characters of the two men made them incompatible, if nothing worse, and separation was welcome to them.

All in all the idea pleased both. They shook hands on the agreement and parted. On June 26, 1919, the *Tribune* launched its tabloid pictorial morning newspaper, the New York *Daily News*. Patterson divided his time between New York and Chicago for about five years, but when the new tabloid showed symptoms of becoming an unprecedented success he moved to New York permanently.

As the decade of the fantastic twenties opened Colonel Robert Rutherford McCormick stood alone at the helm of the Chicago *Tribune*. Once more it was a one-man newspaper.

Part Three

# THE WORLD OF McCORMICK

# Chapter 1

## HOW FIRM A FOUNDATION

THE QUARTER CENTURY from 1920 to 1945 covers the establishment of Colonel McCormick's world. Millions of words have been written about that world—denouncing, defending, explaining, rationalizing—but no final word can be written unless the Colonel chooses to set down his memoirs. Then it will be the job of some future historian, aided by the perspective of years, to weigh, analyze and finally assess. On the basis of existing evidence, however, it is possible to arrive at a conditional estimate and explain *Tribune* history as a prime example of journalistic schizophrenia.

When McCormick re-established the Medill pattern of personal journalism in the *Tribune* immediately after the first World War it was successful for nearly a decade because it suited the times. In the same period the *Tribune* and the *Daily News* were immensely successful in a business way because of the unquestioned executive ability of both McCormick and Patterson. Liberal opponents of these men are prone to forget that the cousins were extremely able businessmen and that the newspaper business is indebted to them for numerous mechanical developments.

But circulation figures and bank balances are not the measure of a newspaper, and despite the contrary protestations of some publishers, a newspaper can be an editorial failure while it remains a business success. This is so obvious as to be a truism, but it still escapes those publishers who are businessmen and not newspapermen. It escaped both Patterson and McCormick.

*Tribune* business history since 1920 is a record of continuous success, but *Tribune* political and editorial history since 1920 is the story of steadily declining influence. The same thing can be said for the New York *Daily News*, except that the *News* never had any considerable editorial influence to lose.

When it began the decade of the twenties the *Tribune* was riding high. Its effect on life in Chicago was tremendous. A striking example of that effect was the circulation war of 1921 between the *Tribune* and the *Herald-Examiner*, which disrupted the city's business routine and momentarily dominated its social life.

Hearst began the fight. His circulation lotteries were already successful in other cities, and he had no reason to suppose that they would meet any serious opposition in Chicago. The scheme was simple—and legally questionable. Early in November 1921 the *Herald-Examiner* began distributing millions of "Smile" coupons. Every day the paper printed a numbers list and the holders of lucky coupons got cash rewards at the office.

The *Tribune* had two alternatives. It could challenge the lottery in federal court or it could counterattack. No one doubted that the Colonel would choose to fight. He did. On November 25 his paper announced its own lottery: "Cheer Checks" would be distributed that day and a public drawing held the next. The day after, 679 prize-winning numbers would be awarded seventeen thousand dollars, "first slice of a $200,000 melon."

For ten days the contest rocked Chicago. More than twenty-five million Cheer Checks were printed and distributed. Banks gave them to depositors. Sunday schools issued them with the morning lesson. *Tribune* delivery trucks were stopped and overturned by money-crazed people. There were riots in the Loop. At the public drawings in different parts of the city great crowds gathered to watch different teams pull out the winning numbers—two street sweepers one day, two Chinese the next, two chorus girls and so on.

Every day the *Tribune* advertised its contest in a full-page display, which included an editorial. One of these editorials, remarkable for its frankness, is also worth reading for the way in which the *Tribune* tied politics to promotion:

## DID WE FALL OR WERE WE PUSHED?

The *Tribune* enters upon its mammoth distribution of cash by lot with strangely mingled emotions. We frankly admit that when our morning contemporary inaugurated this scheme for selling more papers, we looked upon it with disfavor, not to say distaste. Having built our own circulation upon the merits of our newspaper, we felt somehow that the innovation was unethical.

But the judiciary and the officials elected to administer and to enforce our laws co-operated so wholeheartedly in the promotion of this remunerative charity that our scruples seemed actually prudish—a relic of days when skirts trailed below the ankles, and "penny ante" was a mortal sin.

Furthermore, it seemed a shame that an institution which had flourished in such expansive magnificence, even in the piffling banana republics, should receive such niggardly treatment in this rich metropolis. As the dominant newspaper of this community, long supreme both in circulation and in advertising, we were obviously confronted with the duty of seeing that three million people were no longer insulted by being urged to scramble for a share in $500 a day.

The publication of numbers all jumbled up so that holders of tickets could determine only with the greatest difficulty whether or not they had won, was another point not in keeping with the best traditions of this ancient institution, nor with the dignity and fair name of our city.

Having been "pushed" by these factors we "fell"—or rather we "plunged." The reception which the citizens of Chicago have given to our offer of $200,000 and yesterday's split of $17,000 is indeed gratifying. We are also pleased to announce that our contemporary has seen the light (to some extent) and is now "offering" more money.

We must confess that it is difficult to feel so keenly the scruples of past weeks now that circulation is rising in such astounding waves. We could have easily sold a million *Tribunes* yesterday, and we have hardly begun. It seems too good to be true. Such profitable philanthropy.

It *was* too good to be true. Chicago's other newspapers, who were not on the gravy train, complained to Washington, and Postmaster General Hays called in McCormick and Hearst for a conference and told them to cease and desist. Thus McCormick won a battle he hadn't started. The *Tribune* had gained 250,000 readers in ten days, and some of the Cheer Check circulation stuck.

The Colonel was busy in other departments of his paper. He started the chain of development that resulted years later in the wire transmission of news pictures, and he instituted several mechanical improvements. Moreover, a lead story in the *Tribune* of August 4, 1923, written by Harper Leach, veteran Chicago newspaperman who later worked for the Chicago *Daily News*, shows that the Colonel helped to originate the superpower idea, which he later opposed when the TVA put it in practice.

Politically the newspaper had two chief enemies: Governor Len Small and Mayor William Hale ("Big Bill") Thompson. Striking in the style of Medill, the *Tribune* succeeded in indicting Governor Small while that executive still held office. This story is not particularly interesting in itself, but an incident in the campaign is a prime illustration of *Tribune* tenacity and long-range vindictiveness in pursuit of an enemy. Small appointed an unimportant downstate lawyer to an unimportant political job. Avid to "get" anyone who supported Small, the *Tribune* went far out of its way to find out something derogatory about this minor appointee. After considerable research, it was discovered that his grandfather had sold whisky to the Indians the day of the Fort Dearborn massacre. That was enough to discredit him.

It took the *Tribune* longer to get Mayor Thompson. Big Bill was popular in Chicago, despite some controversial eccentricities in his political and personal life, and he was elected to office three times in spite of bitter *Tribune* opposition—in part because of it.

The feud, which eventually encompassed such items as a ten-million-dollar libel suit and public denunciations, began with a relatively trivial matter. One day in a speech Thompson inadvertently poked at the *Tribune's* sore spot—that school board

Harold Fowler McCormick and his second wife, Ganna Walska, Polish singer

Harold Fowler McCormick and his third wife, the former Adah Wilson, who had been his nurse

lease on the Madison and Dearborn corner property. It stirred up the lions. The *Tribune* became Thompson's relentless enemy and hunted him down. Thompson got nowhere legally against the paper. The *Tribune* impugned the mayor's patriotism and Thompson sued for $1,350,000. The case was dismissed. In the name of the city he sued for ten million dollars, charging that the paper's articles on corruption had impaired municipal credit. Again the case was thrown out. Moreover, the *Tribune* filed a return suit as a taxpayer and got a court order which compelled Thompson and other officials to return to the city treasury a million and a half dollars which had been paid in fees to "experts." An appeal reversed the decision but the *Tribune* emerged a clear moral victor in the battle.

A week after the Illinois Supreme Court handed down its reversal decision, on October 31, 1930, a triumphant Mayor Thompson announced that he would denounce the *Tribune* publicly in a noonday speech at the Apollo Theatre. The speech was to be an exposé of the measures used by the *Tribune* to "get its man." But two hours before he was scheduled to deliver the address Thompson was stricken with appendicitis and had to be taken to Passavant Hospital for an immediate operation. The speech was read at the Apollo by Richard W. Wolfe, commissioner of public works, acting as the mayor's proxy.

The speech was a package of crude dynamite, so full of personal venom that it was almost impossible to separate whatever streaks of golden truth there might be in the rough ore, if there were any at all. Naturally it got little publicity. No paper printed it in full, and all of them sensibly refrained from printing the more personal sections of it, which were clearly libelous.

The speech began, after a little preliminary name calling, with a rehearsal of the Lincoln-Medill argument over Chicago's draft quota, with Lincoln's reproof quoted in full. Then Thompson paid tribute to an earlier *Tribune* enemy, Mayor Carter Harrison. He recalled that as a boy he had sat entranced in the Auditorium Theatre and listened to Mayor Harrison denounce the *Tribune*, even as Thompson planned to do many years later. Harrison had wound up by throwing a copy of the *Tribune* on the stage, spitting on it, and jumping up and down on it to express his disgust.

Harrison was assassinated. Thompson did not claim that the *Tribune* had him killed, but in a ludicrous substitute accusation he said that "the deed was charged to a weak-minded newspaper boy" who might have been prompted to the act by reading the *Tribune's* attacks on Harrison.

Then Thompson dealt a punch far below the belt. He quoted from a speech supposedly given by Representative Lee O'Neil Browne before a joint session of the Illinois Legislature. Thompson quoted Browne as making an unfounded and ridiculous attack on Medill's moral character.

He even added more detail to the story. He charged that Representative Browne was attacked shortly after he made his speech and narrowly escaped with his life, and that later he fell or was pushed over a cliff near his home and died.

Big Bill's speech, still quoting from Browne's address, next celebrated Governor Len Small, recounting his accomplishments and winding up with the story of his indictment after the *Tribune's* attack. Small was acquitted by a Waukegan jury after a trial that lasted through weeks of intense summer heat. Small's wife died the day after his acquittal. Browne implied that the *Tribune* was indirectly responsible for her death.

Thompson's speech then returned to his own indictment. In a series of vicious, irresponsible paragraphs he attacked the personal morals of Raymond Patterson, his son Medill Patterson, and charged that Colonel McCormick had followed in Medill's moral as well as journalistic footsteps. The mayor even went beyond the Colonel and assaulted the good names of McCormick's law partners.

The address ended on a note of high melodrama: "And so I am doing today what I conscientiously believe is my duty, and if the Lingle wrecking crew kills your Mayor for telling you the truth for the good of our future generations, I will ask of you citizens with equal courage to see to it that the present editor of the Chicago *Tribune* is properly punished. I leave the matter in your hands and I will accept the consequences of telling the truth and from my nine years' experience on a cow ranch and my ability to handle a gun, I confidently believe that I will not go alone should one of their cowardly attacks be made upon me. . . . I leave this matter in your hands and trust you will join with your Mayor in driving this rotten outfit out of this city as Patterson was driven to the Capital. . . ."

But it was Thompson who was driven out. The driving began next day in the *Tribune's* news story on the mayor's appendectomy. After a straight recital of the news in the lead and second paragraph, the oblique attack began in the third paragraph with a recital of events on the Saturday preceding the mayor's illness. The story related: ". . . on that day the Illinois Supreme Court handed down a decision absolving the mayor of obligation to refund the fees paid to realty experts in his previous administrations, and city hall observers, noting his elation, predicted he was ready to 'play again.'

"That night the mayor, with a party of political friends, sailed on a lake cruise aboard the steam yacht *Mizpah*, skirting the southern shore and remaining out until Monday morning. Next day his purchase of the yacht *Doris* was announced and the following afternoon he was host to another party. At this affair he was ill for a time, but grew better.

"Before the special meeting of the city council on the unemployment question Thursday, the mayor while in his office complained of stomach pain. City Collector Morris Eller rushed to his side with a bottle of stimulant from which the mayor took a copious draught.

"The mayor's condition provoked comment at the council meeting. His face flushed and eyes bright, he escorted his co-defendant in the experts' suit, County Treasurer George F. Harding, to a seat behind him on the rostrum.

" 'The clerk will call the roll and all the wets will answer aye,' the mayor boomed. Next he introduced the county treasurer as the 'Rev. Mr. Harding,' and announced that Harding would pronounce the invocation. The Council moved to the unemployment question with guffaws at the mayor's mood.

"In an aside to Mr. Harding during the session, the mayor was overheard announcing that 'tomorrow, George, I'm scheduled to pull something that will probably land me in jail, but I'm going through with it.' The reference, it developed, was to a projected speech attacking this newspaper. . . ."

It is interesting to note how the *Tribune* and the Chicago *Daily News* reported the same incident. The *News* story said, quoting a friend of the mayor's named Robert Perbohner: " 'The Mayor asked again today how the meeting at the Apollo turned out. I told him fine. Then he asked if any of the papers had printed in full the speech read by Commissioner of Public Works Wolfe. When I told him they hadn't, he said, "I didn't think they would," and he smiled when he said it.' "

This is the *Tribune's* report: "The attendants said the Mayor expressed interest as to the treatment accorded by the press to the speech attacking the *Tribune*, which he had prepared for delivery at the Apollo Theatre on Friday. . . . The Mayor was reported expressing disappointment that the evening papers considered unprintable that portion of his speech in which he dealt with the editors of the *Tribune*."

They were flamboyant, triumphant years for McCormick and Patterson, those years of the twenties. The money poured in so fast that the cousins could scarcely stand it. They dropped fourteen million of it on *Liberty Magazine* before they traded the property to Bernarr MacFadden in 1931 for his ailing tabloid, the Detroit *Mirror*. Patterson ran *Liberty* with one hand while he continued to send his own tabloid's circulation rocketing with the other.

*Liberty Magazine* was a wonderful merry-go-round ride while it lasted. Edward Doherty, a veteran newspaperman, told some of the story in his book, *Gall and Honey*. Doherty was brought East from Hollywood, where he had been *Tribune* correspondent, to join the New York *Daily News* staff in 1924. The star reporters on the *News* staff at the time were Julie Harpman, Westbrook Pegler's wife, and Imogene Stanley.

Doherty didn't stay long. He worked for Hearst's *American* and *Mirror* for a time, then came back to the *News*. Six months later Patterson put him on *Liberty's* staff at $17,500 a year. The magazine's staff included, in 1927 and for some time afterward,

Sidney McNeil Sutherland, Norman S. Hall, Richard Carroll, Grace Robinson and Irene Kuhn. Ronald Miller was executive editor.

Miller told Doherty that *Liberty* expected its editors and writers to dress well, live in the best hotels on out-of-town assignments, ride only in limousines and entertain on a large scale. Doherty took him at his word and spent money lavishly, although always in the pursuit of articles for the magazine. He spent five thousand dollars to get a story about diamonds, from the mine to their sale in Paris and London, and thence by the smuggler's route to America. "We spent Thanksgiving in London, Christmas in Paris, New Year's Day in Amsterdam, and most of January and February in the south of France and the north of Italy," Doherty recalls.

Doherty wrote both articles and fiction. He did the life of Jeanne Eagels and created serial fiction on order. Patterson gave him the kind of assignments a reporter would scarcely dare dream about. He quotes Patterson as saying on one occasion: "Eddie, would you mind going to Europe again? . . . I want to know if they're selling liquor on the United States Lines ships. Suppose you hop the *Leviathan*, drink your way across the Atlantic, and drink it back on the same ship. Thousands of Americans are going abroad on foreign vessels, simply because they know they can get all the drinks they want. They think American boats are as dry as the country. Naturally our lines are losing money. Maybe we can help American shipping."

Doherty helped American shipping with a will—four days and nights of saturation on the water, then thirty-six hours in Paris, and another wet trip home, right up to the twelve-mile limit. Shortly after, Patterson gave him another assignment even more unbelievable.

"Eddie," Doherty says Patterson told him, "I think we ought to have a story showing how the Sicilian Maffia spawned many of our worst gangsters. You can get it out of the New York Public Library, I know. But you'd better go to Sicily, steep yourself in the atmosphere, and get the feel of the story. Make a tour of Sicily. Hire a car and a chauffeur, and an interpreter, and a guide.

You might talk to Mussolini, if you care to. And be sure to drink some of that Lachryma Christi wine."

Doherty carried out his orders to the letter, including an excellent interview with Mussolini, and when he walked into the office on his return Patterson asked him only two questions: "Did you have a good time? Did you like that Lachryma Christi wine?"

The merry-go-round stopped on April Fool's Day, 1931. Patterson called the *Liberty* staff into his office and told them about the deal with Macfadden. "We can't make a go of the magazine," he said. "Bernarr Macfadden can't make a go of his Detroit *Mirror*. I don't know how much it's cost him, but it's plenty. It just shows we're not magazine men, and they are. We're newspapermen, and they aren't."

But the cousins were not newspapermen in Detroit. They were the undertakers who assisted at the interment of the *Mirror*. That sensational little tabloid was no match for the high-quality Detroit *Free Press*, then one of the country's great papers, and the Detroit *News*, always an extremely popular home daily. A three-million-dollar shot in the arm could not save the *Mirror* from quick death.

As for Doherty, Patterson took him on the staff of his New York tabloid at the same salary and assigned him immediately to write the life of Jimmy Walker.

The monument to Doherty's remarkable career is the Medill School of Journalism at Northwestern University, which was his idea. When he was working for the *Tribune* in 1920 as a rewrite man, Doherty was impressed, as many newspapermen have been, with the dead-end character of most newspaper jobs. He saw police reporters who would never write a line of copy and would always be thirty-dollar-a-week men; beat men who would never know how to do anything else; and copyreaders chained to their desks until the last day they were able to work. Why shouldn't the *Tribune* start a school for its reporters, so that they might have a chance to rise in the business?

He wrote a note to Patterson, who answered: "Dear Mr. Doherty. Regarding your idea of a school of journalism for Chicago *Tribune* men. Go and do it."

The idea was modified as it went along. Walter Dill Scott, president of Northwestern University, suggested that the new school should not be limited to *Tribune* men, proposed that it be named in honor of Medill, and outlined a plan of operation which has scarcely been altered in any major particular.

The *Tribune* gave Doherty a thousand-dollar bonus for the idea.

Describing the school's establishment, the Illinois State Historical Society *Journal* observed somewhat tartly: "The original idea was suggested by a *Tribune* rewrite man, Mr. E. J. Doherty. He also carried on most of the preliminary negotiations necessary and brought the thing to a point where its success seems assured. Having done all this and having won our trust and confidence, he now decides to quit us. He is going to Mexico, of all places, to go into the newspaper business."

The *Journal* also described the broad operation of the school as follows: "Full-time university teachers and educators will offer the courses covering economics, literature, and other preparatory studies, while the practical journalistic instruction will not only include part-time instructors on the technical side of journalism, but special lecturers who have made a success of journalism and are now active in that field.

"So far as practicable, an effort will be made to duplicate the conditions in which the student will be employed in actual newspaper work. Probably a newspaper office, in a small way; with typewriters, files, indexes, reference books and other necessary paraphernalia will be provided as a handy journalistic laboratory. . . . There will be inspection trips, through the editorial, business, printing and engraving departments of the Chicago newspapers, so that our students may be familiarized with actual methods."

That is the Medill School's pattern today, and it ranks among the three or four best in the nation. Under Dean Kenneth E. Olson it has won increasing prestige through its faculty and graduates. Although the *Tribune* helped start the school financially, it has never attempted to dictate policy and there are no marks of its influence in the school today, except that it joins with other Chicago dailies in helping to make the place a real newspaper training ground. On the thirteen-man Newspaper Council which helps administer the institution, the *Tribune* is represented by only one man, Clifford Raymond, senior editorial writer. The faculty, studded with names well known in the business, lists only one ex-*Tribune* writer.

# Chapter 2

## RADIO IS HERE TO STAY

ONE OF THE astute moves that Colonel McCormick made in building his empire was to get in on the ground floor of radio, at a time when most publishers scoffed at the idea that it could ever be a serious rival of the newspaper.

McCormick foresaw the future of radio as early as 1921, when he began the negotiations which ended in June 1924 with the purchase of WDAP, then Chicago's most powerful station. Less than a month later the station had its call letters changed to WGN, meaning, of course, "World's Greatest Newspaper." Midwestern listeners and DX fans in other parts of the country were thrilled by the flossy identification, "broadcasting from atop the Drake Hotel." To provincial ears this had a glamorous implication completely unjustified by the facts. The studios were a few bedrooms rented from the hotel; the transmitting equipment was spread out over chairs and tables. Whenever WGN picked up the music from dance bands playing three flights down in the hotel's ballroom, announcers had to hurry down to get the song titles and run back up again to announce them.

WGN was operated by enterprising young men who put it rapidly in the forefront of the growing industry. In 1924 the station broadcast the Memorial Day auto races at Indianapolis, and both national political conventions. Next year its microphones were at the Scopes evolution trial in Dayton, Tennessee; the Kentucky Derby in Louisville; and the World Series in Pittsburgh and Washington.

The station gave Amos and Andy to the world in 1925, as Sam 'n' Henry. Floyd Gibbons, then a *Tribune* reporter, broadcast the first news commentary program in 1926. In that same year WGN outfitted Chicago police squad cars with radio receivers and began broadcasting police calls, which led to adoption of the system now common in all big city police departments. The entertainment field began to benefit too from WGN's activities. Broadcasts from two big Chicago dance palaces, the Aragon and Trianon ballrooms, started such dance orchestras as Ted Weems's and Wayne King's on their way to national fame.

Newspaper publishers began to feel a chill, and even the Colonel must have shivered a little, when, in 1927, WGN accidentally demonstrated how radio could beat newspapers on the news. The excursion boat *Favorite* capsized and sank in Lake Michigan, just off Oak Street beach, in full view of WGN's studios. Many men, women and children were drowned. Announcer Quin Ryan, hanging out a studio window, broadcast the whole tragedy as it occurred. By that time the miracle of radio was beginning to dawn on more and more people. It inspired the most optimistic enthusiasm in Cosmo Hamilton, the eminent playwright and author, when in 1928 he made his first appearance before a microphone in WGN's studios. After the broadcast he wrote out a prophecy and gave it to a staff member.

"What, in Heaven's name, as this is merely the beginning of these [radio] wonders, will be the end of them?" Hamilton wrote. ". . . It goes without saying . . . that anyone with imagination, and not too much of that, can see in the greater perfection of this miracle a series of silent revolutions that will do away with the novel, the newspaper, the theater and the concert room. . . . It isn't to be supposed that the newspaper can live when everyone may hear the voices of Mussolini, Lloyd George, Calvin Coolidge, Baldwin, Herriot, and all the other political world leaders, without waiting for the arrival of the morning edition, with its cables summarizing the speeches of the previous night. Nor will any man read the headlines of the morning news while he bolts his eggs and bacon, when he can get the same news over the radio without making any effort at all."

If these extravagant prophecies were to come true Colonel McCormick was in a position to cash in on them, but he prudently withheld release of Hamilton's statement for sixteen years, until WGN celebrated its twentieth anniversary in July 1944.

The Colonel was well aware of the silent war between press and radio which was then beginning. When the American Newspaper Publishers Association held its annual convention in 1931, radio resolutions were adopted which, according to the *Literary Digest*, boiled down to, "Time to quite coddling radio and treat it as a grown-up rival." Discussing these resolutions, the Colonel told his fellow publishers, many of whom were (and still are) shortsighted on the radio question: "The cheapest advertising anybody can get is to buy an hour of advertising on the air, advertised free in almost every newspaper in the United States. Radio itself is not a good buy, but the material presented in the newspaper in connection with radio programs is a good buy. I suggest that we publishers do not allow radio broadcasters to collect cash for advertising we are giving their clients."

Pending the arrival of that Utopia, the Colonel saw to it that the *Tribune's* interests were properly exploited on WGN. In 1931 he had "Little Orphan Annie," most popular of *Tribune* comic strips, adapted for broadcasting—another "first." The serial is still on the air and shows no sign of losing its grip.

Moreover, when WGN programs first went commercial, only *Tribune* advertisers were allowed to sponsor WGN air. The newspaper tied in this step with full-page ads. But radio grew faster than the station, and in 1934 it was apparent to everyone concerned that chains were going to squeeze out powerful local stations. WGN joined with WOR, Newark, WLW, Cincinnati, and WXYZ, Detroit, in a network which expanded in time to the powerful 268-station (at last count) Mutual Broadcasting System, with WGN and WOR the key outlets. The Colonel owns twenty-five per cent of Mutual stock, and W. E. Macfarlane, *Tribune* business manager, was president of the chain for several years.

Today WGN is a 50,000-watt station operating on a choice clear channel at 720 kilocycles. Its studios are in the Tribune Tower, and they are elaborately air-conditioned, suspended on springs to diminish vibration, and decorated in a vivid red-gray design, with mural paintings.

The omniscient McCormick eye has been focused constantly

on WGN's twenty-odd years of activity, as it is on all parts of the Colonel's world.

In the early days of the station McCormick once asked the staff orchestra to play one of his favorite songs. The request was granted, naturally. Next day came a note from the Colonel saying that he had enjoyed the program, but they had played the wrong melody. The staff orchestra's leader, considerably perturbed, checked up and discovered that the boss had a point—the song had two distinctly different melodies, the popular one played and an obscure version which was the master's favorite.

After the leader had explained the phenomenon McCormick suggested that they play both versions of the song on one program and then ask for letters from listeners so that they could judge which melody was the better known. The program forthwith went on the air, and the announcer requested letters. To this day the Colonel firmly believes that his favorite version is the more popular, because no one has been able to dispute him. Not one listener wrote in to the station.

Sometimes the Colonel dozes over his station's progress. Years after WGN had made a name for itself by broadcasting the music of dance bands, the head of the music department got a note from McCormick with this query: "The term 'swing music' has come to my attention. What is it? Should we have some of it on WGN?"

They let him down as gently as possible.

The Colonel's favorite WGN program is his own, the six-year-old Chicago Theater of the Air, an hour-long show which features condensed versions of favorite operettas and operas, and a short talk by McCormick. It is a network show into which the Colonel has put thousands of dollars, but it has never attracted a sponsor. Probably McCormick doesn't care, because his heart is in the program. During a rehearsal one day he dropped in and listened closely to a song being played by the staff orchestra. He began to hum, cautiously at first, and then he beamed. "That song," he said, "brings back memories of when I used to go to the theater forty years ago." The song was "Ta-ra-ra-boom-de-ay."

The star of Theater of the Air is lovely, titian-haired, temperamental Marion Claire, the Colonel's protégée. Her husband is

Henry Weber, WGN's musical director and conductor of the orchestra on the Theater show. Miss Claire was recently given new duties as director of WGNB, the *Tribune* FM station, and this job—combined with her air appearances and bookings by the Concerts Division of WGN, which the Colonel founded—occupies most of her time.

Even though she is a star, Miss Claire sometimes bows to her husband's musical knowledge. One day at rehearsal her voice wavered in the middle of an aria, and the producer remarked, "You were a trifle flat that time, Miss Claire." The singer's subsequent display of temperament was in the grand tradition. In the midst of it Weber's voice came from the back of the room: "Shut up, you *were* flat." The rehearsal went on quietly.

Although McCormick's second marriage and the *Tribune's* crusades take up more of his time, he still devotes as much attention as possible to the Theater of the Air. The show is always well reviewed in the *Tribune*. A review of *Rio Rita,* for instance, on January 29, 1945, ran:

"The Chicago Theater of the Air gave a gay and vigorous performance of *Rio Rita* in Medinah Temple last night before a huge audience which included several hundred members of the civil air patrol and their friends. . . .

"The tuneful music assigned to Rita—who is half Mexican and half American—was effectively set forth by Marion Claire. She helped notably to create the laughing, Latin quality of the production. . . . Conductor Henry Weber kept the production moving along at an interesting clip. He was able to make the sinuous Latin melodies as effective in their way as the jolly American tunes. . . .

"Col. Robert R. McCormick, editor and publisher of *The Tribune,* spoke on the parallel between Napoleon's and Hitler's Russian campaigns. His remarks will be found on the editorial page."

McCormick's radio addresses are customarily reprinted next day on the *Tribune* editorial page. They are usually as dull as they are informative, and on special occasions reach a peak of reverse effectiveness, as on the night of November 11, 1944, when the Theater began its fifth year on the air.

"Tonight," the Colonel began, "as I look at the capacity audience before me—more than 4700 Americans—and think of the thousands more listening across the country, I am convinced that radio is here to stay. . . ."

Thus convinced, McCormick is still making the most of the medium. On May 11, 1946, the *Tribune* broadcast a facsimile edition, and with characteristic modesty proclaimed itself as the first newspaper to print such a radio-transmitted paper, conveniently ignoring the fact that both the New York *Herald Tribune* and the St. Louis *Post-Dispatch* were years ahead of it.

The McCormick project consisted of four miniature pages containing news, pictures and a special Orr cartoon. The paper was received on a facsimile recorder in the Colonel's home, twenty-nine miles away. Not the first in the field, *Tribune* facsimile transmission was nonetheless asserted to be permanent, and to utilize speedier, larger transmission equipment which therefore made it better than any previous edition. It was certainly, as claimed, "the most exclusive, expensive, privately-printed newspaper edition in the world."

Commenting on the historic occasion, the Colonel remarked, "I do not know what facsimile is any more than I knew what radio was twenty years ago, but we are going to find out all about it. There is no doubt that radio is constantly developing. . . ." Later, on the Theater of the Air program, he elaborated, "At present, facsimile will print a pretty good newspaper. It won't put it the way we are accustomed to it. It is on a roll. But I can get up after 7 A.M. and find a pretty good newspaper: the news, the cartoons, pictures, advertisements; and, of course, facsimile will be very much improved. While it is not immediately a substitute for a newspaper, it is something for a man to look out for. . . ."

Perhaps the most significant thing about the *Tribune's* first facsimile newspaper was the indication that the paper intended to carry over into the new medium the editorializing of news columns which marked the regular edition. One of the two lead stories concerned the proposed loan to Great Britain, which was characterized in both headline and text as the "gift-loan." The story noted further that seventeen Republicans joined twenty-nine "Administration Democrats to put over the financial deal."

Even more frightening to the *Tribune's* enemies, who see in every new development a further spreading of *Tribune* ideas, was the news early in 1946 that short-wave equipment was being installed on the Colonel's estate. Fears were allayed, however, when it was disclosed by the *Tribune* that the installation was receiving, not transmitting, apparatus—a forward-looking move designed to pick up press dispatches from Europe directly and thus avoid congestion and delays in New York. This emancipation from the East was to be achieved by intercepting the overseas messages from Press Wireless, the *Tribune's* own creation, at their receiving point in Baldwin, Long Island, and transmitting them directly to the Colonel's Cantigny farm.

In reporting this news, the *Tribune* made no effort to refrain from reminding its readers that Press Wireless had grown out of the paper's initiative in 1919, when the flood of news from the Versailles Conference choked the Atlantic cables and the *Tribune* solved the problem by arranging with the French government to use its wireless facilities.

Reviewing WGN history on the station's twentieth birthday, *Newsweek* magazine might well have been at a loss for a headline after it had encompassed Cosmo Hamilton's WGN prediction, WGN progress, WGN firsts, WGN and Mutual, WGN's Theater of the Air, and WGN's future, which includes construction of a ten-story building to house present facilities, FM station and television studios, and a two-thousand-seat radio theater—the whole termed by WGN "the most modern and spacious radio structure in the world."

*Newsweek* hit upon an apt, McCormick-like headline: WORLD'S GREATEST EVERYTHING.

# Chapter 3

## "TREES TO TRIBUNES"

ONE OF THE lesser-known aspects of Colonel McCormick's world is the complex mechanical operation of paper supply, which the *Tribune* promotion department aptly terms "Trees to Tribunes."

As noted, the Colonel originated this operation in the early days of his control by leasing Canadian forest lands and building paper mills in Quebec and Ontario so that the *Tribune* could compete with Hearst's cut-rate paper supply. It was a smart business move which has paid off many times over.

*Tribune* timberlands cover about 2,700,000 acres, some far up on the rocky north shore of the Gulf of St. Lawrence, others in Ontario, including the more recently acquired 448,000-acre tract on Heron Bay, at the north end of Lake Superior. As late as 1943, when most lumbering operations and newspaper offices were hard hit by the manpower shortage, the *Tribune* employed about six thousand people in its timberlands, paper mills, boats, and in Tribune Tower itself. All these people were involved in the complicated procedure by which Canadian trees were translated into 964,778 weekday and 1,339,368 Sunday copies of the *Tribune* (January 1945 figures).

When it first went in search of paper in 1915 the *Tribune* knew it had to have spruce and balsam forests located on waterways suitable for transportation to shipping points. McCormick sent a veteran Canadian explorer, William Carter, on an expedition to find such lands. Carter embarked in a little sailboat and covered hundreds of miles of dangerous coast before he found what McCormick wanted.

He found it at the mouth of Rocky River, and on December 4, 1915, the *Tribune* concluded a deal with the Province of Quebec

by which the paper acquired control of 300 square miles in this
territory. These holdings were increased later to 500 square miles.
Here, initially, were 192,000 acres of trees, ready to become
*Tribunes*. Around them, in the Shelter Bay area, the *Tribune*
built a town, a wharf, a loading plant, a powerhouse and numerous roads.

It was a pioneering adventure, the building of Shelter Bay.
Land had to be cleared before the town's first log cabins could
be built, and the inhabitants endured all the rigors of wilderness
life. Shelter Bay is now the largest town on the St. Lawrence's
north shore, except for the new town of Baie Comeau, built recently by the *Tribune* a hundred miles southwest.

Shelter Bay is the perfect company town, familiar to anybody
who has ever lived in one. A man who wants to build a home
submits his design to the *Tribune*, if he has a design. If he hasn't,
the *Tribune* will give him one. The *Tribune* gives him the site
and the rough lumber, and provides other material and labor at
cost. This money is repaid by the employee in monthly install-
ments prorated according to wages. He gets, also at cost, elec-
tricity, hot and cold water, and heat from the company's own
utilities. The company has a church and a hospital; *Tribune* efficiency has been able to combine the hospital, a school, and a
doctor's office in a single building. These institutions minister to
the needs of about a thousand inhabitants.

In this Canadian wilderness, however, the company's organizing
ability had a long, tough struggle with rampaging nature. The first
wharf built there in 1916 was swept away in a few months by a
raging southeaster. The war interrupted further construction
until 1919, and then the second try was destroyed by another
gale. In the end the *Tribune's* engineers sank their teeth into the
problem and put up a superwharf which stands against gales that
send waves over the wharf as high as the loading conveyor's platform, fifty feet above.

The company went through a nearly identical experience when
it began to build a powerhouse in 1917 on the Hay River falls. A
difficult job at best, it was finished in a year, but in the following
spring above-normal floods swept it into the river. Again the en-

gineers refused to give up. They salvaged the machinery and set it up in a new location, where it withstood the floods of the next twenty years. The plant lights the town, provides power for the mills and for the loading system. This system can put two hundred thousand logs on a boat in twenty-six hours. Between June and October more than sixteen million logs can be shipped from Shelter Bay to the *Tribune's* mills.

*Tribune* management extends even to the most primary operation, that of sawing the trees. A *Tribune* lumberjack invented a special saw, with an instantly replaceable blade, which is manufactured in another *Tribune* town, Franquelin, ninety miles west of Shelter Bay. In 1930 McCormick modernized lumbering even further by installing three transmitting and receiving radio stations in its timberlands, the first such installations in the industry's history.

When the logs are ready for transportation in the spring they are taken to *Tribune* paper mills at Thorold, Ontario, between Lakes Ontario and Erie, on a fleet including the paper's own three steamers—M.S. *Franquelin*, S.S. *Outarde* and *Shelter Bay*—and several chartered vessels. The *Tribune's* boats were designed and built by company engineers. The fleet takes eleven boatloads every two weeks from Shelter Bay. Its flagship is the *Chicago Tribune*, a Diesel-engined craft which carries newsprint from Thorold to Chicago, three thousand tons of it at once. This fleet is supplemented by schooners, yachts, launches, scows and barges, and two fast small craft, the *Trib* and the *Vamp*, used by *Tribune* executives.

At Thorold, and at Baie Comeau, *Tribune* timber is turned into *Tribune* paper by two of the best paper mills in the world. The Thorold plant alone turns out about 140,000 pounds of newsprint annually. This is shipped in *Tribune* boats through the Great Lakes to the *Tribune's* warehouses on the Chicago River, only a few hundred yards away from Tribune Tower. There the paper rolls are loaded on pint-size freight cars called "dollies," which operate by gravity and carry the paper over narrow-gauge tracks into storage. During the winter, when ice stops Great Lakes navigation, these warehouses carry as much as thirty-eight thousand tons of paper, with five or six thousand tons more stored on docked *Tribune* ships.

The paper moves from warehouse to Tribune Tower on another gravity-operated railroad, which runs underground. Stored as deep as six floors underground, it is taken to the press reels in the second subbasement and fed directly to the presses on the floor above.

Few papers are as well equipped mechanically as the *Tribune*. At last count, it had 101 news-printing units, sixteen of them designed for high-speed color work, printing four four-color pages at once. Seven high-speed press units in combination can print fifty thousand fifty-six-page papers in an hour. Besides these 101 news-printing units, there are sixteen others used for printing the four-color, twelve- to sixteen-page Sunday *Tribune* comics section. From the mechanical standpoint the chain from trees to *Tribunes* is as near perfection as any publishing operation anywhere.

McCormick links the far parts of his world together, so that each can see how the other lives, by sponsoring periodic trips to Shelter Bay for *Tribune* executives, members of the WGN staff and the station's symphony orchestra. These good-will junkets are enjoyed equally by the visitors and by the mill hands at Shelter Bay. The visitors stay at a hotel which is as well appointed as any in the city.

In the spring of 1944 the entire WGN symphony orchestra performed for the Shelter Bay natives, who appeared to be greatly impressed. After the concert, however, the natives surprised the Chicago musicians by getting out their fiddles, accordions and other instruments, and serenading them.

WGN people who have made the trip say that the "*Tribune* protective feeling" prevails in the Shelter Bay settlement. Colonel McCormick's paternalism is thus international, extending to the farthest corner of his world.

# Chapter 4

## PERSONAL SERVICE

THE "personal service" idea instituted at the *Tribune* by Keeley was transmuted under McCormick into a promotional rather than an editorial conception. The paper soon owned one of the most comprehensive collections of promotion ideas ever possessed by any newspaper.

Chief among the items in the personal service gallery were the paper's features. Today these features account for perhaps a major portion of *Tribune* readership. Nearly every newspaper to some extent depends for readership on the popularity of its comics and other features, but the *Tribune* is unique in its virtual monopoly of extraordinary features which undoubtedly keep many readers buying the paper who would otherwise desert it for political reasons.

After McCormick took it over the *Tribune* was departmentalized more than ever before. For instance in 1926 the paper had twenty different departments, of which fourteen were *Tribune* developments. Attesting to the popularity of these departments, they received collectively about seven hundred thousand letters in that year.

In the year before, the *Tribune* published a booklet about its women workers, who were largely responsible for the paper's features. The paper was the first metropolitan newspaper to employ a woman Sunday editor, and the roster of females had jumped from 16 in 1896 to 369 in 1925. The Sunday editor, Mary King, later married Captain Patterson. During her regime she bought the immensely popular Blue Ribbon fiction, which the Tribune Syndicate circulated to more than sixty newspapers. She paid Booth Tarkington $3500 for a short story, and $13,500 to E. Phillips Oppenheim for a serial.

On that 1926 pay roll were such women feature writers and editors as Doris Blake, Mae Tinee, Antoinette Donnelly, Fanny Butcher, Sally Joy Brown, Loretta King, Inez Cunningham, Genevieve Forbes Herrick, Kathleen McLaughlin and Sigrid Schultz. Many of these are still familiar names to newspaper readers.

Today's *Tribune* features include a health column; the famed contributors' column begun by Bert Leston Taylor, "A Line O' Type or Two"; a "law department," quiz questions, Voice of the People, cartoons, radio listings, almost every kind of woman's-page feature, complete amusement coverage, a day-by-day report of doings on the *Tribune's* experimental farm, and a picture page. Nothing that other papers do not have, but *all* the others have.

The *Tribune* touches its readers most closely with the annual public events which it sponsors. Most of these are spectacular outdoor shows, like the giant Chicagoland Music Festival, held in Soldiers' Field, the Golden Gloves bouts, the All-Star football game, and the Silver Skates Derby.

Golden Gloves is representative of all these. It began in 1923, stemming from a *Tribune* crusade. Boxing had been banned in the state for nearly twenty years, but the *Tribune* did not take notice of it until a band of reformers who happened to be enemies of the paper succeeded in closing a Navy boxing show. The *Tribune* attacked the reformers in a strong editorial, which announced that the paper would put on an amateur boxing show of its own as a test of the legislation.

The show was held in the Ashland Boulevard auditorium, under the direction of Walter Eckersall. A total of 424 boxers entered, drawn from universities, gymnasiums, parks, playgrounds and YMCAs. Knute Rockne lent his support, and one of his noted Seven Mules, Rip Miller, competed in the heavyweight class, where he was runner-up to the winner. The show netted six thousand dollars and the *Tribune* turned over the money to the fund for disabled war veterans.

The National Reform Association and the Law and Order League sought to stop the show, but the *Tribune* got an injunction restraining them and held the event. Having routed the reform element, the *Tribune* went to work on the prohibiting legislation.

While the tournament stood suspended, the paper used its political power to get the law repealed, which it accomplished in April 1926. Meanwhile, however, Patterson had picked up the idea as a *Daily News* promotion stunt, named it Golden Gloves, and put on the first show under that name in New York in 1927. Next year the *Tribune* held a Golden Gloves tournament of its own.

From that beginning the Golden Gloves idea blossomed into an international event from 1931 to 1935, with boxers from France, Germany, Poland, Ireland and Italy represented. Arch Ward, *Tribune* sports editor, succeeded in getting the tournament recognized as the national tryouts for the boxing team to represent the United States in the Olympics. After that, until 1940, American Golden Glovers fought all-European teams—probably the only international activity which the isolationist *Tribune* ever promoted.

Golden Gloves is one of the *Tribune's* numerous charity events. All its sports events and other public shows are actually ventures to promote the paper, but the money goes to charity. In 1944 these events yielded a total of $783,550 which was distributed among 82 charities. From 1928 to that date, they produced more than two million dollars.

*Tribune* enterprises reach out to all classes of its readership. In the month of January 1945, for example, the paper was operating two contests designed to scoop in a large selection of non-political readers. One was an American history essay contest open to all Chicago high school students, instituted with the purpose of encouraging "the boy and girl of today to obtain the knowledge of American history that will help the man or woman of tomorrow to keep their bearings in a confused world." The prize was a five-hundred-dollar war bond. Subjects for the essays were listed as follows:

THE PILGRIMS
THE CAUSES OF THE AMERICAN REVOLUTION
THE DECLARATION OF INDEPENDENCE
THE CONSTITUTION OF THE UNITED STATES
THE SETTLEMENT OF THE MIDDLE WEST

ABRAHAM LINCOLN
THE EMANCIPATION PROCLAMATION
ULYSSES S. GRANT
AMERICA'S PART IN THE FIRST WORLD WAR
AMERICAN NEUTRALITY, 1939–41

At the same time the *Tribune* appealed to women with its sixth fashion contest and, in announcing it, put the contest on a frank political basis, the basis of nationalism. The announcement story said:

"For 150 years the American people, freed from the old world tradition of obeisance to an all-powerful authority, have been amazing the world by such talents, ingenuity, and progress as had not been recorded before in 6,000 years of world history. It is paradoxical that not until only five years ago did America step forward to take her rightful place in another field that had long been neglected in this country.

"Since the satiny, swirling days of Marie Antoinette, Paris had been the world arbiter of fashions—until five years ago. America's smart set slithered and strutted in imported labels. That is, until five years ago.

"It took a war to free American women and American designers from another old world tradition: to be fashionable it must be from Paris.

"But they have been freed. And in five short years America has made fashion history of the kind that comes only when creative genius must no longer bow down to any pre-supposed authority. Today the American woman wears an American label on her back and wears it proudly.

"Today the slogan *American designs for American women* is taken for granted, the same as bathtubs, hot dogs, moderately priced automobiles, and all the other things that are typically and uniquely American.

"The Chicago *Tribune* is proud of the role it has taken in boosting America to top spot in the fashion world."

This contest for fashion designs brought nearly fifteen thousand entries in 1940, its first year, and the total now is much higher.

*Tribune* female readers, from schoolgirls to veteran seamstresses, compete—and of course buy the *Tribune*.

Another *Tribune* project, not a contest, is aimed at a large segment of *Tribune* readership—the farmers in the five states within the paper's circulation zone. It is the *Tribune's* Fox River farm, whose activities are related in the daily "farm diary" feature. On this farm of 1332 acres, the *Tribune* tests new farming methods and reports on them to rural readers. The farm has 539 acres of pasture and woodland, while the rest of it is divided into plantings of corn and oats, and into hay land and farmstead.

*Tribune* activities extend all the way from the big projects outlined above to such relatively small but significant gestures as the annual awarding of a Chicago *Tribune* gold medal to the outstanding R.O.T.C. student at Roosevelt Military Academy, at Aledo, in Mercer County.

*Tribune* enterprises, including charities, are overwhelmingly publicized as part of the *Tribune's* perennial campaign to glorify itself. Some Chicagoans assert facetiously that the paper has a bureau called the Glorifying-the-*Tribune* Department. Probably no other American newspaper has published more books, pamphlets and promotional material about itself.

An example of routine glorification is the exhibit of *Tribune* color photos which opened early in 1945. The paper's own story on this event ran:

"One of the most interesting and brilliant exhibitions of the new year is the Chicago *Tribune* color photo exhibit which opens at the Chicago Historical Society tomorrow with a formal preview. . . .

"The *Tribune* color studio has scored numerous firsts since its 1939 opening, the first newspaper studio of its kind in the country. Among the imposing figures are the first Paris fashion in color, the first wire photos in color of the British king and queen visiting Washington, D.C., and the first bombing picture of England in color. *Tribune* color cameras have toured army camps, naval stations, Hollywood, New York, Washington and Europe. . . ."

A more unusual glorification was the *Tribune's* beat in being the first American newspaper to publish on Luzon Island after American liberation, and later the first in Tokyo. The *Tribune's* Luzon edition was published on captured Japanese paper, and the first copy was presented to General MacArthur, who in turn inscribed it to Colonel McCormick. *Tribune* correspondents gathered some excellent promotional quotes from Chicago GIs. A few samples:

"It certainly warms a fellow's heart to know the *Tribune* hasn't forgotten us fellows out here."

"I'm not from Chicago, but my dad is a *Tribune* subscriber and reads it all the time. I'd sure like to get in on this."

"Hey, Mac, how's about my morning *Tribune?*"

Thus the "*Tribune* protective feeling" in the world's far corners.

Often glorification takes the form of an editorial. On November 26, 1945, the *Tribune* was moved to extol itself as "A World Newspaper." It declaimed:

"Readers of the Voice of the People are becoming increasingly aware that The *Tribune*, altho a Chicago newspaper which is proud to proclaim itself as 'An American Paper for Americans,' has a world audience. Our correspondents write from far away lands. Some strange datelines appear on the views they submit to The *Tribune* Forum of opinion. The other day there was one from Durban, Natal, in the Union of South Africa. The writer wished to record his agreement with *Tribune* policy.

"The great attractive force of The *Tribune* is that it is the voice of liberty. It has resisted with all its strength the designs of government to circumscribe the liberties of Americans. It has spoken against oppression everywhere, whether the victims are the Indonese, the Annamites, the people of Malaya, Burma, India, the African colonies, the helots of the new communist imperialism in eastern Europe, or the peoples of former enemy countries suffering under an occupation that is partly American.

"Our readers know that The *Tribune* will never be silent where there is injustice. They know that we are in no one's debt; that there are no favors which, offered, could tempt us, and no coercion which, threatened, could divert us from our course. In these columns no punches are pulled and no double-talk indulged. We say what we mean, and mean what we say. That is why *The Tribune*, already the most quoted newspaper of its time, is continually extending its influence and winning attention and respect wherever its voice is heard."

But glorification, sporting events and other features are overshadowed by the collection of comic strips which have attracted and held so large a part of the newspaper's readers.

*Tribune* comics are scattered through the paper, with the idea of distributing reader interest among the advertising pages. The line-up begins with Dick Tracy, the square-jawed detective, whose duels with a choice collection of exotic underworld characters have been publicized in a *Life Magazine* layout and on the network radio shows of the nation's most popular comedians.

Antedating Tracy is Harold Teen, the perennial high school lad, whose appeal is a cross between Booth Tarkington and a college humor magazine. Another favorite of ancient vintage is Winnie Winkle, whose comic-strip career began as the personification of the white collar girl's life struggle but wound up as a soap opera. A veteran soap opera in comics, which began long ago as a really "comic" strip, is "The Gumps," whose principal character, Andy Gump, was once as well known to Americans as the President. Other long-established strips include "Moon Mullins," which celebrates the pratt-fall, low-comedy type of humor; "Smitty," a glorification of the office boy; and "Gasoline Alley," a drama of Main Street life, the only strip in which the characters grow up and have children and in general behave like real people.

These strips, developed by the *Tribune* and its syndicate, have long been national favorites. Keeping up with the times, however, the paper also prints "Smilin' Jack," an aviation adventure strip, and for some time—until the Chicago Sun Syndicate hired him away—carried Milton Caniff's enormously successful "Terry and the Pirates," a sex-war-adventure comic which is one of the most popular strips ever developed, as well as one of the most publicized. The Tribune Syndicate still owns the strip's characters and title. A paper combining all these old and new favorites, whose names are as familiar to most people as those of their next-door neighbors, cannot help acquiring a large and faithful following, no matter what its politics.

This was one of the obvious facts emerging from the battle fronts when Marshall Field started the Chicago *Sun* in opposition to the *Tribune*. The *Sun* started its comics page with several completely new strips, apparently with the idea that *Tribune*-haters, swinging gratefully over to a new morning paper, would not mind so much what comic strips they read. But *Sun* comics were, for the most part, a dismal failure.

Although some newspaper people pooh-pooh the idea that a reader will stick to a paper for its comic strips alone, there are astute circulation men who believe that the *Sun* would be able to hurt the *Tribune* seriously if it only had its rival's comics.

The ace *Tribune* comic, however, surpasses all its companions; it is unique in its field. "Little Orphan Annie," born in the *Tribune's* art room in 1924, enjoys top readership everywhere it appears. This is a phenomenon difficult to understand. Annie could not be considered funny, even by her most ardent admirers. As soap opera, her adventures are far inferior to other cartoon serials because they are devoid of sex and are exceedingly repetitious. A hollow-eyed perpetual orphan, this obnoxious child is the heroine of a continuous cartoonized political speech—an editorial column of tremendous influence.

Little Orphan Annie is the Westbrook Pegler of the comic strips. Sometimes she anticipates her real-life counterpart, as in 1935, when Annie established herself as an ardent critic of labor, well in advance of the establishment of Pegler's similar reputation. In that year she so irritated the Communist *Daily Worker* that the party organ counterattacked with an even more humorless strip called "Little Lefty."

Annie reaches a far wider audience than Pegler's—approximately twice as large. She appears in 250 papers with a combined circulation of twenty million, while Pegler's column runs in 179 papers whose combined circulation is ten million. Both labor in the same vineyard—a day-after-day attack on the New Deal and on organized labor, and a continued nostalgic appeal for the "good old days," meaning *laissez-faire* capitalism.

In the deeps of the depression, when publishers were dropping every possible feature, Annie remained one of the best-selling properties owned by the Chicago Tribune-Daily News Syndicate. She sniped away steadily at the government, while her creator, Harold Gray, was making as much as sixteen hundred dollars a week.

Probably more than any other comic-strip character, Annie has become a real person to her followers. When her dog Sandy was missing Gray got this amazing wire, which was later authenticated:

> PLEASE DO ALL YOU CAN TO HELP ANNIE FIND SANDY. WE ARE
> ALL INTERESTED.
>
> HENRY FORD

That was only one of many such incidents. Other *Tribune* comics provoke similar reactions. When Dick Tracy was wounded in a gun battle thousands of sympathetic letters poured in and a Brooklyn man offered a pint of his blood for transfusion. When Lady Plushbottom, a character in "Moon Mullins," had twins, she got such gifts as a perambulator and a complete layette. Harold Teen once refused to marry a lovely adventuress and a dozen bachelors wrote in offering to take his place.

These are tangible evidences of what syndicate men well know —that Americans read comic strips more than any other form of literature, and that many of them half believe in the characters as real people, if their belief is not even more complete.

A public of sixty-five million people reads comic strips, more than half of the nation's adults and two-thirds of children over six. Only fourteen per cent of men and women in the United States have favorite columnists, but fifty-one per cent have a favorite comic-strip character. The point of these statistics is that comic strips are not to be taken lightly in their effect on newspaper readers, a chilling thought when one surveys the opinions transmitted to the twenty million followers, more or less, of "Little Orphan Annie."

A prime example, and an apt summary of Annie's sentiments, can be derived from the recent supposed death of her Daddy Warbucks, the venerable financier who adopted the orphan early in her history and then left her in the hands of others most of the time while he led big business in remaking the world. Daddy was believed dead many times, but always before he had turned up, usually at Christmastime, to rescue Annie from some hard fate into which his negligence or her stupidity had precipitated the unfortunate child.

In August 1944, however, Daddy Warbucks came home to die, apparently for good, and even in the midst of real wartime grief many Americans found room in their hearts to mourn for Daddy. Thousands of letters were received in newspaper offices all over the country. The 76th Division Sergeants' Club, of Tomah, Wisconsin, sent a huge funeral wreath which was delivered to the syndicate's office with this message: "We regret very much the passing of a great American and a very rugged individualist."

Some of the great American's philosophy was expressed in the closing scenes of his life. This was the dialogue in one strip:

> ANNIE: What do you mean, it's *time* for you to go?
> DADDY: I've been what's called a capitalist. Some have called me "*dirty* capitalist"—but I've merely used the imagination and common sense and energy that kind Providence gave me. It made me wealthy—powerful—hated by some—admired by others. But now? Well, Annie—times have changed and I'm old and tired. I guess it's time to go!

The final strip in the episode pulled out all the stops. A box in the first frame mourned: "Rich or poor, he was the same—a really great American. Let us not weep, but be as brave as he who recognizes Death as a friend." Then the dialogue went on:

> ANNIE (*musing to herself*): Daddy! My Daddy. They're taking him away forever. Across the inlet to a hospital, where they say he may get well. But it's no good! I know it's the end.
> (*Scene shifts to Daddy's bedside.*)
> DADDY: Ha! Ha! Don't look so gloomy, Annie! *I'm* not worried—and after all——
> ANNIE: Oh, my Daddy—Daddy—Daddy!
> DADDY: Death worries only cowards! Why, Death's been at my shoulder for years. We're old pals. Cheer up!

ANNIE: B-b-but I'll n-n-never see you again.

DADDY: Ha! Ha! Sure you will, if you live right. Because *that's* where *I'm* going. Be brave, Annie, always! Honest, decent and *brave!*

ANNIE: Oh, I *will*, Daddy. I'll always try to be just like you taught me!

DADDY: Yes! And independent! Keep your ideals, Annie, no matter what. Ideals are the only verities!

(*Scene shifts to a dock and a waiting boat.*)

DADDY: Ho! *My* River Styx, eh? Well, boys, let's go! Good-by, Annie, my darling. Until we meet again!

ANNIE (*as boat moves*): G-g-gee! He's so doggoned b-b-brave!

COMPANION (*an elderly lady character*): Why not? He's a *man!* He's lived a good life—an honest and courageous life—to the end.

ANNIE: He's waving—and he's smiling! Oh, if only I can smile back!

COMPANION: You must! He's only going away on a little trip.

ANNIE: But he won't be back from *this* trip!

COMPANION: True—but in time we all will follow him. For me, it won't be long now.

ANNIE: But why—why must he have to go *now?*

COMPANION: Hm-m-m. I wonder, too. This country made him great. But his kind made this country great! Let's never forget that! We are seeing, not only the passing of a man, but also the passing of an era—of a way of life—in this land we love!

Daddy's passing got what the theater calls a mixed press. Typical were two letters in the New York *Daily News* Vox Pop column:

## DADDY STILL AROUND?

Westchester: I have good news for these mourners over Daddy Warbucks' seeming kickoff out of the Little Orphan Annie comic strip. My overpowering hunch is that Daddy is not dead, but has merely gone on a secret mission for the Government, and that he will turn up in time to "die" again in a few months.

OZZIE

## DADDY'S DEPARTURE

Manhattan: Farewell, Daddy Warbucks, beloved Dutch uncle, or whatever it was, of Little Orphan Annie. May your soul rest in peace, after a life of ambition, hard work and thoughtfulness for others. We'll try not to feel too badly about your passing, but we will miss you very much.

MRS. G. K.

It remained for the Philadelphia *Record* to give Daddy an unsympathetic obituary which represented the thoughts of the anti-Annie element. An editorial on August 19, 1944, read:

## LITTLE DELINQUENT ANNIE

Little Orphan Annie is back in politics.

Annie is the precocious juvenile delinquent of the unfunny comic strip. A year ago she was smearing OPA, sneering in her childish way at wartime rationing. Last April she made a deal to get around the child labor laws and the Social Security Act to get a job as a delivery girl—the implication being that these were New Deal laws and not to be obeyed. Then she handled "payoffs" to politicians, and now——

Well, this week the rich Daddy Warbucks (who neglects Annie 90 per cent of the time) came home to "die." . . . *Poor* Daddy Warbucks! Giving up at a time when the National City Bank statistics show that capitalists are doing better than ever before, with corporation profits 11 per cent higher than in 1943. And the Treasury's figures show that in 1943 corporations made an all-time high of $9,580,000,000 after taxes.

Maybe if Daddy Warbucks had not been blinded by his hatred of the New Deal he could see that times *had* changed—*for the better*. Maybe if he had paid decent wages to a tutor-chaperone, Annie wouldn't have become a juvenile delinquent.

We know now that the real problem is delinquent parents.

Annie's delinquent parent is named Daddy Warbucks in the comic strip, but his name in real life is Captain Joseph Patterson, of the New York *Daily News*.

Though the strip is drawn by Harold Gray, it is Patterson who is credited with being its originator and who controls the syndicate which distributes the strip. Though the figure in the strip is that of Annie, the voice, with its childish hatred of the Government, is really the voice of the editor of the New York *Daily News*.

After Annie's last venture into politics, the Louisville *Courier-Journal* threw the strip out of its columns, and Gray was quoted as saying he had made a mistake in letting Annie lug his private political banner.

But now, with election coming on, Gray, and his mentor, Captain Patterson, apparently have decided to risk further losses to spread what poison they can in the minds of the youngsters and parents who read this strip. It is rather slimy politics. But not surprising when you consider the source.

As 1944 closed, Annie summarized the year on December 31 in a pageful of color-comic philosophizing. For a lone orphan it had been a rather successful year by ordinary accounting. She had kicked the child labor laws and the Social Security Act in their respective backsides, discredited the OPA, aided and abetted crooked politicians. But as Annie plodded through the page—first washing dishes, then scrubbing laundry, finally shoveling coal into the furnace of her oppressive employer—she minimized her accomplishments while striking another blow for Daddy's philosophy.

"Gee," Annie remarked, "what a lous . . . er . . . what a bum year it's been! Still, it could have been worse. . . . I'm still alive an' healthy and pretty chipper. . . . Poor, dear, kind, honest, old Daddy . . . Gone! I can't believe that anyone with Daddy's ideals and hope and ambition and honesty is out o' fashion in this country . . . or ever will be."

Poor, dear, etc., Daddy was not really "gone," as it turned out. To the consternation of those who had not mourned his passing, he reappeared once more, as he had so many times in the past. He explained that his "death" had been staged deliberately so that foreign agents would think he was out of the way, enabling him to go on a highly secret mission which, the reader was given to understand, put the war in the bag for the Allies.

Gray did not miss the opportunity to slap back at those who

Cyrus McCormick, the inventor's grandson, in 1931 when he was vice-president of International Harvester, shown at Havana where he was honeymooning with the former Mrs. Florence Sittenham Davey, ex-wife of the noted artist, Randall Davey

wler McCormick, Harold's , shown in 1931 with his de, the former Fifi Stillman, ently divorced after a sen-ional courtroom drama

Leander McCormick, son of Leander J., in 1933, shortly before his marriage to the
Countess de Fleuriau, a Parisian beauty

had rejoiced over Daddy's demise, and he did it in a most characteristic way. In the strip for August 31, 1945, the dialogue ran:

> ANNIE: Gee! They said some awful nasty things 'bout you, Daddy, when they thought you were dead.
>
> DADDY: Ha, Ha! Yes—I got quite a kick reading my obituaries!
>
> ANNIE: But *why* did some papers and com'tators say such terrible things?
>
> DADDY: Oh, I guess it was fashionable to sneer at "big incomes"—they fail to mention that most of those big incomes go to pay everybody's bills, and make the load lighter for everyone else! I believe that the more a man makes honestly, the more he helps this country and everybody in it. What I think we need is a lot *more* million-a-year men! Mighty little *they* can *keep*, anyway.

These words were reassuring proof that Daddy was back, and that all was right again in the McCormick-Patterson world.

# Chapter 5

## THE TRIBUNE METHOD

THE *Tribune* today is wealthy and independent. Its circulation is great. Its reporters and investigators are highly competent. In spite of its innumerable faults it is never dull. Yet it is not an outstanding newspaper in the opinion of appraisers who make a business of evaluating journals. It has never been given the Pulitzer prize for disinterested and meritorious public service, nor has it been honored by the Pulitzer jury in any other way, except for John T. McCutcheon's winning of the cartoon award in 1932.

Nor has the *Tribune*, in spite of its power, self-righteousness and crusading editorial force, been successful as a reformer in recent years, although its history as already recounted shows that its influence was great right up to the middle twenties. It was still the same newspaper in those days, the personal Medill kind of newspaper it had always been, but the times were beginning to catch up with it. Arrogance, omniscience and the everlasting fitting of the news into the *Tribune* pattern began to irritate readers.

Some students of the subject place the real turning point in *Tribune* influence at June 1930, when Alfred ("Jake") Lingle, a *Tribune* reporter, was assassinated.

Lingle was a police reporter at a time when holding that job for a Chicago newspaper involved at least some degree of association with the underworld. He had been a *Tribune* man for eighteen years, but according to the publisher's friends McCormick was so remote from his employees that he was never aware of Lingle's extracurricular activities. These activities, as outlined by the hint-and-rumor circuit in common talk that was never proved, consisted of racketeering and fixing, growing out of Lingle's too intimate associations with underworld figures.

When Lingle was shot one afternoon in typical gangland style the *Tribune* was nearly hysterical with rage and humiliation. A twenty-five-thousand-dollar reward was posted for apprehension of the assassin. An editorial asserted that Lingle was murdered because he was on the verge of a tremendous exposure of gangdom. He was a martyr, the paper said, and righteous citizens were called upon to rally around the flag of civic decency, which the *Tribune* had flaunted so proudly since its founding.

But other newspapers, seeing the *Tribune* vulnerable for once, closed in for a possible kill. The St. Louis sheets sent reporters who wrote into their stories strong hints that Lingle had double-crossed someone and paid the usual gangster penalty for it. The *Tribune* called these reporters "coyotes." McCormick appeared at an emergency meeting of the Chicago Newspaper Publishers Association and tried to inspire his fellow publishers to accept the Lingle murder as a challenge from the underworld to a free press— the old battle cry. His colleagues, however, were not impressed. Walter Strong, then publisher of the Chicago *Daily News*, made some blunt remarks about Lingle's reputation, and added that he thought it was strange that only the *Tribune* didn't know about him. This precipitated an explosive quarrel. At the height of it McCormick walked out of the room. He never appeared again at a meeting of the association, but the *Tribune* has remained a member and is represented at its sessions by the business manager or some other executive.

The *Tribune* insisted on finding the murderer of Lingle, and a member of the paper's law firm was made a special assistant by the state's attorney. Later came the indictment of an obscure St. Louis small-timer named Leo Brothers. This man went to jail as the assassin of Lingle. Before that event, however, the *Tribune* had been forced to listen to the evidence and to modify its high opinion of the deceased police reporter.

There were two by-products of the Lingle case. The assistant state's attorney who conducted the prosecution of Brothers was C. Wayland ("Curly") Brooks, who became a United States senator largely through the campaigning of the *Tribune*, which always rewards its friends and never forgets an enemy.

The other by-product was less pleasing to McCormick. When the Lingle killing was being investigated a young police reporter named John Boettiger did most of the leg work. In appreciation the Colonel assigned him to cover the Roosevelt inauguration in 1932. Boettiger went to Washington and met Anna Dahl, the President's daughter, divorced his wife and married her. Presumably he was excommunicated forthwith by the *Tribune*.

From 1930 onward the *Tribune* began to lose its influence in Chicago and elsewhere. However, it continued to gain in circulation. Probably the major reason for *Tribune* circulation success is its unorthodox methods in this department. These methods began in 1910, when the paper hired Max Annenberg from the Hearst papers to run its circulation department. Annenberg, who had helped make Hearst's Chicago *Examiner* stronger than the *Tribune*, applied his talents to reversing this situation, and he did it in a long battle which rose to a bloody climax in the violent circulation wars of the twenties when circulation crews were adept at street fighting and the use of small arms.

Louis Rose, who succeeded Annenberg as circulation manager, became a unique figure in his field. Rose decided whether extras would be printed. He conferred with McCormick at least once a week, and with the city editor every day. Defending his unusual participation in editorial affairs, he once remarked, "After all, I have to sell the paper. It's merchandise, like anything else."

Equally unusual is the way the merchandise is made. J. Loy Maloney, the managing editor, installed a unique system for running the city room, shortly after he took charge at the close of the first World War. To newspapermen coming from orthodox city rooms, the Maloney system looks incredibly involved—but it works.

Maloney does the thinking for every man on his staff. He comes in at eight o'clock each morning, and instead of making assignments personally he dictates them to a stenographer, producing pages of questions which must be answered by the reporter while he is on a particular assignment. If a reporter is smart enough to think up questions that slipped Maloney's mind he deserves whatever commendation he may get.

There are separate copy desks for day and night staffs. The day city editor works from eight to five and gives out assignments only. He sees no copy. That is the job of the night city editor.

Maloney is excessively devoted to McCormick journalism. "If the Colonel asks for a pound Maloney gives him a ton," a *Tribune* reporter once complained. But he felt compelled to add, "One thing about it, though: Maloney always backs up his boys."

An incident which may have inspired the reporter's complaint was the garden-hose campaign. It originated in one of the memos typed out and attached to clippings by Genevieve Burke, McCormick's secretary. Miss Burke gets the clippings, often illegibly scribbled upon by her boss, when McCormick reaches the office after his trip from home in the bulletproof car which is so heavy, it is said, that the chassis must be replaced every two years. The Colonel spends the time on his trip to the office tearing items out of the newspapers and starting the memo chain.

These memos, with clippings attached, eventually reach the city room. A typical one read: "Too many garden hoses being stolen in Chicago. Too hard to replace during wartime." A reporter was assigned to the story and reported that only one garden hose had been stolen in the city during the previous six weeks. Nonetheless, Maloney did not at once stop the campaign against stealing garden hoses because no one dares tell the Colonel that he is wrong.

A fair share of the *Tribune's* rank and file—reporters, copyreaders and subeditors—are said to have no sympathy with *Tribune* policies, but they stay with the paper because it is a good place to work from a professional point of view. McCormick's paternalism, suffocating though it may be to some rebellious souls, offers comparative security and material comfort to the paper's employees.

As they write and edit for the *Tribune* these employees are not unique in fitting the facts to the publisher's views. It is, of course, one of the commonest boasts among nearly all publishers that they never dictate the handling of news, and indignant, rhetorical pronouncements are made on that subject. Yet working newspapermen accept as commonplace the fact that no one in the "front office" has to tell them: they write and edit according to the paper's particular pattern without question.

McCormick is sincere, even though he is speaking only for himself and not for his employees, when he says, "In discharging its fundamental responsibility as a newspaper the *Tribune* has no political, financial or social tie-ups which compromise its freedom to report the truth."

One wonders by what process of reasoning the Colonel would square his pronouncement with a story which he tells himself. When Ira Nelson Morris, a prominent Chicagoan, was advised that he would be appointed minister to Sweden, he called on McCormick and asked as a favor that the *Tribune* not refer to him as a "packer," because he was not active in the packing business which bore his name.

McCormick, who has so often proclaimed in and out of print that his newspaper grants no favors or privilege to anyone, instructed the managing editor to have the Morris story written in advance, set in type, and okayed by him before it was used. A story was then prepared in which there was no reference to "packer" or "packing family."

This piece of business, not unusual in any newspaper, would have been carried out successfully except that someone forgot to pass the orders to the headline writer, and somehow a page-one banner slipped through and confronted the Colonel at breakfast one morning with the flat statement: PACKER MADE MINISTER.

Greer Williams, an ex-*Tribune* reporter, disclosed several instances of McCormick's brand of domination in a *Nation* article on October 10, 1942. He reported: "It took me six months to answer the question [from RRMc], 'What is known of the relation between syphilis and unemployment?' I first tried writing a story giving the known facts, but this was not what was wanted. I was expected to prove that syphilis was more prevalent among Chicago relief clients than among the unemployed which I finally did, after hounding four government agencies into making a joint survey."

The Colonel's whims, according to Williams, are translated into stories of every variety. One day his car nearly ran into several stray dogs on his morning trip downtown, and next day the paper was busy advocating the removal of stray dogs. Another time he conceived the theory that sap rises in trees because the wind in the branches causes a pumping action, and Williams's accurate story on the process of sap rising, which ignored the ridiculous idea of wind action, brought only a note from the Colonel: "Our sap expert missed a trick."

Williams says that the funniest RRMc assignment he ever saw read: "Everyone should be interested to know how hard a lobster pinches. Crabs, clams, oysters. This information should be easy to get, I suppose."

In the process of making the facts fit, the *Tribune* occasionally is embarrassed, as in the case of the late Governor Henry Horner, who was elected to office on the Democratic ticket. The paper had been friendly to Horner before that event, then suddenly turned against him, and when Horner wanted to know why, McCormick replied that his paper would ride "roughshod" over anyone who supported the New Deal. One phase of riding over Henry Horner was the *Tribune's* discovery that a state policeman accused of fixing a jury had been a convict. The paper began asking this daily question: "How is it that the Governor can appoint an ex-convict to the state police force?"

After searching his files, Horner discovered that McCormick had nagged him into making one of the Colonel's chauffeurs a state policeman without pay so that the man could carry a gun. Imparting this information to the publisher, Governor Horner added that this chauffeur was also an ex-convict, "and that is how the Governor can appoint an ex-convict as state policeman." The *Tribune* appeared to feel that its question was answered.

In the less spectacular phases of their work, *Tribune* men are given front-office chores to do of about the same kind as those allotted to workers on other papers. Once, according to Williams, an editor assigned a reporter to look into the status, social and economic, of the students in a private school his daughter intended to enter. Another time Williams was sent to the railroad station to help McCormick find his wife when she arrived on a train.

The *Tribune* is guilty of producing distorted news, and it also suppresses news, in the sense that it denies evidence of truth if this evidence is contrary to its editorial policies. After the 1937 Memorial Day massacre in Chicago it was well established that the Chicago police were responsible for the deaths of ten strikers, who had been shot in the back. The truth of the affair was forced into the open, first by the St. Louis *Post-Dispatch*, which compelled a Paramount newsreel to be introduced as evidence after attempts had been made to suppress it, and later by competent newspapermen who testified before a congressional investigating committee.

But the *Tribune* did not print the facts about the newsreel, although many other papers did, and after the investigation it continued to assert editorially that the massacre was justified because property had to be protected, and that the strikers were "Reds."

In this the paper was repeating its action in accepting the Ku Klux Klan in 1921, despite overwhelming evidence of the Klan's lawless viciousness. On April 16, 1921, the *Tribune* carried a full-page ad for the Klan, signed by Imperial Wizard Simmons. The ad read: "The Knights of the K.K.K. is a law-abiding, legally chartered, standard, fraternal order, designed to teach and inculcate the purest ideals of American citizenship, with malice towards none and justice to every citizen regardless of race, color, or creed."

Three days later a dispatch from London quoted Bernard Shaw on the subject of his canceled visit to America as follows: "I have no intention of going to prison with Debs or taking my wife to Texas, where Ku Klux Klan mobs snatch white women from out of hotel verandas and tar and feather them." The *Tribune* edited out the name of the Klan in its printed version.

A few months later, on August 27, the *Tribune* defended the Klan editorially. The old Klan, it said, created under the "danger of Negro domination," may have had some black marks to its discredit but it contributed "one of the romantic episodes in our history." As for the new Klan, "All the great fraternal orders which accomplish so much quiet good . . . make use of this natural liking for mysterious rites and secret ties, and the new Klan will hardly be denied the right to adopt the same policy." Although this great fraternal order had already been accused of such crimes as murder and terrorism, the *Tribune* replied blandly, "The head of the order repudiates them."

In its crusade against organized labor and against the New Deal the *Tribune* has not hesitated to print what seem to be outright lies. One is compelled to admit, with shame, that this has also been true of several other American newspapers, but few were more unabashed in their apparent lying than the *Tribune*.

On November 27, 1938, the paper carried a front-page "exposé" in its news columns to the effect that CIO auto workers in San Francisco were strangling that city's industry to the extent that the Chevrolet plant had moved away to Los Angeles. A. L. Kennedy, manager of the industrial department of the Oakland Chamber of Commerce, wrote to the *Tribune*, "In the first place, the Chevrolet automobile assembly plant is not located in San Francisco; it is located in Oakland. In the second place and most important, it did not move to Los Angeles; it is still here. Furthermore, it has never had to operate under strike conditions. . . . In fairness to this community a retraction is in order." The protest was carried as a letter to the editor—on January 4, 1939, more than a month later.

Throughout the thirties the *Tribune* attacked WPA, as did most of the nation's richest, largest newspapers. None of these attacks is a credit to American journalism, but among the blackest pages of that record are those written by the *Tribune*. The worst was a two-week concentrated anti-WPA campaign, under such headlines as these: GRAFT, FRAUDS, THEFT: WPA REEKS WITH CORRUPTION.

In response Howard O. Hunter, assistant WPA administrator, prepared a twenty-five-page statement which he gave to nineteen Chicago newspapermen in his office. This statement proved that all of the *Tribune's* fourteen stories had been untrue, and the denial was categorical. Hunter wrote, in part: "Every statement published by the *Tribune* was found to be false. Ordinarily we would not dignify such accusations made by the Chicago *Tribune* by going to the trouble of answering them, because any intelligent person in Chicago knows that such charges have been faked and trumped up by the *Tribune* for years.

"But when column after column is pawned off on the public as news, none of which has any foundation, when columns are used to falsely attack individual unemployed citizens and to misrepresent to the public the work they are doing, it is time that the public is acquainted with the truth surrounding the publication of these articles."

The *Tribune* did not carry a word of Hunter's statement.

Cartoons have been another indiscriminately wielded *Tribune* weapon. Orr, Parrish and McCutcheon take turns belaboring McCormick's enemies. These are samples:

An Orr cartoon shows a mother talking to her little boy: "You want to grow up to be President, don't you? So your little boy can be a General; don't you? And his little doggie can ride airplanes; don't you? Well, then, be nice."

A Parrish cartoon (they are usually more complicated than Orr's) shows a nearly denuded "Private Enterprise" being held up by a swinish-looking, grinning figure labeled "Burocrats," while President Roosevelt throws dice captioned "Loaded Gov't Competition." Roosevelt says:

> *My fellow countrymen! Hear ye*
> *Th' eternal President's decree:*
> *Not one but seven there shall be—*
> *Seven valleys of the Tennessee.*
> *New hosts of T. V. Burocrats*
> *In striped pants and shiny hats*
> *And dainty gloves and spotless spats*
> *(They're all deserving Democrats).*
> *I vowed (before Election Day)*
> *That I would furnish jobs and pay*
> *For sixty million; hence I say*
> *We need a super TVA.*

*At first we'll take the one we've got*
*And multiply by seven,*
*Which may suffice. If it does* not—
*Well, seven come eleven!*

A typical McCutcheon cartoon is in two panels. The first shows a brutal, cigar-smoking Churchill calling from Britain, "Give us the tools and we will finish the job!" His call reaches Uncle Sam, who sits under a sign reading: "A Pledge to American Fathers and Mothers: Your sons are not going to be sent to foreign wars." The caption under this panel says, "We all remember those broken pledges." Under the panel below it is a line reading, "And here is another one to be remembered." The picture above shows John Bull megaphoning from England: "Give us your men and we'll show them how to finish our job." Uncle Sam, standing under a sign saying, "Pledge suspended for the duration," shouts back, "Great Scot, isn't that enough?" On John Bull's right is an insignia over Europe: "Four million American men to bear the brunt of a European war."

These are of a piece with some of the *Tribune's* foreign reporting, although its correspondents have numbered many of the ablest now practicing. These men, however, were not able to endure the kind of editorial direction they were expected to accept and left the paper, leaving behind them a trail of almost unbelievable anecdotes of life abroad in the *Tribune* foreign service.

The most amazing of *Tribune* correspondents was Donald Day, who filed *Tribune* party-line stories for more than twenty years from northern Europe. Day covered Russia from Riga, Latvia. His stories dealing with Russia were published in Chicago under the most fantastic headlines, the whole being a strictly *Tribune* depiction of international events. Day was the most consistent of correspondents: not one of his stories was pro-Russian.

On August 8, 1936, a Donald Day dispatch asserted that "Moscow has ordered Reds in the United States to back Roosevelt against Landon." The Chicago *Times,* on August 28, offered five thousand dollars if the *Tribune* or any other newspaper could prove, to the satisfaction of the ASNE and the ANPA, that this story was true. No paper accepted the challenge; most were too busy backing Landon themselves. But four years later, in a radio speech on February 15, 1940, Colonel McCormick repeated this story.

One of the last dispatches by Day was filed from Stockholm, datelined March 8, 1942. The lead read: "There are persistent rumors in Stockholm about negotiations between the Soviet and German governments which may lead to a truce on the eastern front."

On March 30, 1945, the Department of Justice asked United States Army authorities to arrest Day, whenever they found him in Germany, and bring him back home to face charges of treason, which would be lodged against him. In the summer of 1944 Day had made several broadcasts over the Berlin radio in which he glorified Hitler and called upon Americans to fight Roosevelt, Churchill, Stalin and the Jews. One of Day's later broadcasts, recorded by the FCC on January 8, 1945, began: "Hello, Americans! This is Donald Day, correspondent for the Chicago *Tribune* for twenty years in northern Europe, reporting to you from Berlin."

Yet even while it was printing Day's dispatches the *Tribune's* foreign staff could produce such outstanding news beats as Floyd Gibbons's 1921 story on the famine in Russia, an oft-told newspaper tale in which Gibbons scooped three other reporters, after walking with them through the heart of the famine zone, by striding into the post office of a deserted town and nonchalantly asking an emaciated telegraph operator to send his copy. The other correspondents went back to Moscow to file their stories and, when they got there four days later, learned that Gibbons's exclusive was already a sensation in America.

Innumerable stories are told of McCormick's attempts to run the world from a desk in Chicago. Some of these stories have been related by George Seldes, who was in the *Tribune's* foreign news service from 1919 to 1928. Seldes was supposed to be head of the Berlin bureau, but he spent two years in Italy, two more in Russia, a year with French armies in Syria and another year in the Balkans.

In that period McCormick demanded a weekly letter from each

of his men abroad. Two or three times a year he held a conference in some European capital, where, as Seldes says, he "impressed us all by his willingness to listen to the views of his correspondents. He was modest, friendly, easy to get along with. . . ."

After this early impression Seldes ran into trouble when he got an order to produce a story on the failure of government-owned and -operated railroads. Not knowing that McCormick was compiling a case against government operation of American railroads, Seldes sent a story about the success of German government railroads. Next day he got a long set of instructions from the Paris office telling him exactly what to put in his story. Irked, Seldes made a complete inquiry and proved his point. He cabled a long story, complete with facts and figures, but it was never printed.

Near the close of his *Tribune* career Seldes encountered a more serious example of McCormick suppression. Sent to Mexico to make an investigation, he approached his assignment with a completely open mind on what was a controversial subject. At that time all the stories coming out of Mexico were anti-Mexican, based on the thesis that the country was becoming a subsidiary of Moscow since President Calles had altered Mexico's feudal system, and there were hints that perhaps the United States should take steps to restore the old system, or else take over the country.

This kind of talk was *Tribune* talk, along the lines laid down by Joseph Medill in his stated belief that only America should have the privilege of pushing Mexico around. Thus, when Seldes submitted a series of twenty articles, ten pro and ten con, on the question of whether the United States should seize Mexico, the *Tribune* printed three for and three against; after that, only the anti-Mexican side of the debate was printed.

The real reason for Seldes's Mexican assignment turned up years later, when it was disclosed in Congress that an attempt had been made by special interests in America to provoke war with Mexico in 1927, and McCormick, anticipating the conflict, had wanted to have a *Tribune* man on the spot when war came. The plot was exposed by liberals in Congress and by the New York *World*, the St. Louis *Post-Dispatch*, the *Nation* and the *New Republic*.

In the thirties McCormick stripped his foreign staff of most of its veterans. After a series of conflicts with the McCormick theory of foreign coverage William L. Shirer was fired summarily by cable, for work "unsatisfactory to the management." At that moment the *Tribune* had in proof a promotion piece lauding him as a great correspondent. Even more puzzling, Shirer got a letter from the Colonel six weeks after he was fired, reading:

DEAR SHIRER,
    You did some excellent work in India, but since then you have almost vanished from the picture as a European correspondent. Is it that your health is so bad, or do you think that your field is non-productive? We might transfer you elsewhere, if that is so. . . .

Edmond Taylor, head of the Paris bureau, got the ax in a different way, eliciting one of the Colonel's most-quoted messages. Taylor cabled a story in December 1939 predicting that German-Russian collaboration would end in an attack on Rumania. McCormick cabled: "What do you mean, sending bedtime stories by cable?" Taylor defended himself in a dispatch and got the famous reply: "Your fantastic Rumanian story, hysterical tone, and your recent cable and other vagaries indicate you, along with Knickerbocker, Mowrer and others, are victims of mass psychosis and are hysterically trying to drag U.S. into war. Suggest you join Foreign Legion or else take rest cure in sanitarium in neutral country until you regain control of your nerves and recover confidence in yourself. Until then file no more."

By considerable maneuvering, Taylor was able to retire with three months' pay. The Colonel is often considerate when he fires an employee.

## Chapter 6

# McCORMICK VS. THE UNITED STATES

THE Chicago *Tribune's* conduct throughout the second World War was one of the bitterest, most hotly debated subjects in the American press. There is no need here to add to the tremendous mountain of words hurled at the *Tribune* for its conduct, but it is perhaps time to summarize the story and let the words and actions of the McCormick-Patterson world, this American dynasty, speak for themselves.

Before the war began the *Tribune* was die-hard Republican, fanatically against the New Deal and all its works; as always, its attacks were extreme but they were worse only in degree from the antics of a considerable section of the American press.

In the quarter century between World Wars, McCormick and Patterson agreed on only one thing: the need for a big navy. By 1940 the cousins had found another area of agreement. They advocated appeasing Japan and urged Britain to settle with Germany on "the best terms possible."

Early in 1941, when the Lend-Lease Bill came before Congress, Patterson and McCormick found a third bond in common. Their respective isolationisms merged and united into one screaming voice. While the isolationist debate raged on street corners, in homes and in Congress, the *Daily News* called for "a new Declaration of Independence from Britain" and the bill, HR 1776, was always referred to as the "Dictatorship Bill." Meanwhile the *Tribune* denounced Wendell Willkie's "treachery" and termed him the "Republican Quisling." At hearings on Lend-Lease in Washington the Colonel pronounced, "I am very willing to let Britain have whatever she needs, and I think she doesn't need anything."

During the tense, emotional summer of 1941 this kind of talk brought Chicago's anti-*Tribune* sentiment to a head. Three thousand people gathered in the Chicago Opera House one August night, nominally to voice support for the President's foreign policy but actually to denounce *Tribune* isolationism.

The meeting was in the best tradition of *Tribune* denunciation, as fiery as the public meetings addressed by Mayors Harrison and (by proxy) Thompson. Five years before, the *Tribune* had been attacked in a violent recapitulation of stormy Civil War days: on 1936 election night irate crowds, irked by the bitterness of the McCormick attack on Roosevelt, had burned *Tribunes* in State Street and thrown rotten eggs at Tribune Tower.

Feeling in the Opera House, stimulated by the long isolationist-interventionist debate, ran almost as high that hot August evening, three months before Pearl Harbor, as Edmond Taylor, one of the *Tribune's* ex-foreign staff veterans, delivered the principal address, titled "What Is Wrong with the Chicago *Tribune?*"

The audience adopted a resolution which denounced the *Tribune* officially and at the same time proposed a movement to "end the un-American monopoly now enjoyed by the Chicago *Tribune* and in the interests of freedom of enterprise, freedom of speech, truth, fairness and justice, give positive encouragement and co-operation to those individuals who are . . . now contemplating to provide Chicago and the Middle West with another morning newspaper." After the meeting the crowd bought early editions of the *Tribune* and burned them in the streets.

Colonel McCormick's response to this attack followed the familiar *Tribune* pattern. He composed a full-page advertisement headed: THE TRIBUNE ACCEPTS THE CHALLENGE. Four anti-*Tribune* leaflets and petitions were reproduced in the ad and the moral of the layout appeared in a single sentence: "The *Tribune* welcomes the attacks of Communists and all others who object to publication of the truth."

At the same time Patterson and the *News* reached new heights of isolationist fury at the President and accused the Administration of "keeping the war scare pumped up to frightful proportions in order that it may quietly and under pretext of wartime emergency transform our democracy into some sort of totalitarian state, before many of us know what is happening."

These were the peaks of an attack which the *Tribune* had begun early in the days of the Roosevelt Administration. Some of these first *Tribune* slurs were strongly reminiscent of Medill and the Civil War *Tribune*. For instance the paper indicted the President's whole ancestry as "un-American." "Great-grandfather James was a Tory. . . . A Southern connection, James Bulloch, would have destroyed the Union. . . . He comes of stock which never fought for the country and now betrays it."

On another occasion the *Tribune* asserted, "His purpose is to confuse and frighten the American people into the belief that they are confronted by stupendous dangers. He will make this his excuse to impose new totalitarian restraints—his aim is dictatorship which will be the destruction of the Republic."

The *Tribune* had endorsed America First editorially, but it was careful to stay away from the more violent manifestations of the movement. This caution was rewarded when Lindbergh made his famous speech at Des Moines, which apparently offended even the *Tribune*. A full page in color, showing the flier's decorations and medals, was already off the presses. Caught short, the paper had to say, "We are confident that none of our readers will assume that the publication of this page at this time is to be regarded as in any sense an evidence of approval of the Des Moines speech."

The real climax came on the morning of December 4, 1941, when the *Tribune* faced the advent of Marshall Field's Chicago *Sun* in the morning field, which the *Tribune* had monopolized. Chicagoans were startled that morning to find unusually large black headlines on the *Tribune* front page announcing F.D.R.'S WAR PLANS! The story, widely publicized since, quoted in detail a joint staff report to the President, dated September 11, 1941, and signed by General Marshall and Admiral Stark. The story began: "A confidential report prepared by the joint Army and Navy high command by direction of President Roosevelt calls for American expeditionary forces aggregating 5,000,000 men for a final land offensive against Germany and her satellites. It contemplates total armed forces of 10,045,658 men.

"One of the few existing copies of this astounding document, which represents decisions and commitments affecting the destinies of peoples throughout the civilized world, became available to the Washington *Times-Herald* and the Chicago *Tribune* yesterday."

The phrase "became available" was a giveaway to newspapermen as to how the *Tribune* had secured its story about these secret plans, one of several sets prepared by the general staff in preparation for inevitable conflict.

All but the most isolationist newspaper friends of the McCormick-Patterson papers refused to stomach the disclosure, and Secretary of War Stimson voiced a national revulsion of feeling when he asked, "What would you think of an American General Staff which in the present condition of the world did not investigate and study every conceivable type of emergency which may confront this country and every possible method of meeting the emergency? What do you think of the patriotism of a man or a newspaper that would take those confidential studies and make them public to the enemies of this country?"

Meanwhile the shock of Pearl Harbor three days after publication of the *Tribune's* story prevented any further exploitation of it. But the detailed contents of the article had already been disseminated and exploited for propaganda purposes by the Berlin, Rome and Tokyo radios. By the time Hitler went on the air to declare war on December 11 he was able to scream, "A plan prepared by President Roosevelt has been revealed in the United States, according to which his intention was to attack Germany by 1943 with all the resources at the disposal of the United States. Thus our patience has come to the breaking point. . . ."

McCormick's patience was apparently no greater than Hitler's. The *Tribune* supported the Administration's war effort for almost exactly a month after Pearl Harbor, when it had pledged to let bygones be bygones for the sake of unity. Then it declared that "the nation would have been spared much of the bitter news of recent days" if it had followed the paper's isolationist ideas.

In reply the Chicago *Daily News* tried to embarrass the *Tribune* by quoting a few gems from these ideas:

"There has been no menacing word or act by any of the enemies our alarmists see on the horizon. . . ." (March 2, 1941.)

"Japan already has her hands full against China." (March 16, 1941.)

"What vital interests of the United States can Japan threaten? She cannot attack us. That is a military impossibility. Even our base at Hawaii is beyond the effective striking power of her fleet." (October 27, 1941.)

The *Tribune* paid no attention to this evidence. It roared back: "The isolationists were not heeded. The attempt to put the blame for Pearl Harbor on them is an attempt to cover up for the men whose dereliction caused that disaster."

By February 1942 the paper was back in pre-Pearl Harbor form. A headline over a story on Democratic Chairman Edward J. Flynn's demand for a Democratic Congress termed it, A SCHEME TO WRECK THE REPUBLIC. Four days later the *Tribune* used the death of an ex-employee in the Philippines to demand editorially, "It is time that those who willed the war were driven from their hiding places and sent to the front where they can share some of the agony they have created."

Within the next three months the *Tribune* unabashedly produced another of its "became available" stories from Washington. Simultaneously with the Washington *Times-Herald* the paper attacked as "Communists" the Union for Democratic Action, the *New Republic*, and Freda Kirchwey, editor of the *Nation*. The object of the attack was an admirable *New Republic* supplement on the coming congressional elections, which summarized man by man the position of congressmen on all major issues. This survey naturally threw a sharply unfavorable light on the isolationist congressmen, and the *Tribune* followed its usual line in pinning the Communist tag on the originators of the survey.

But as Miss Kirchwey pointed out in the *Nation*, the disturbing thing in the *Tribune's* attack was the quotation of an alleged report on the UDA supposed to have come from State Department files. The *Nation's* editor posed a not unfamiliar question: "How did this collection of false statements get into the department files, and once there, how did it get out? . . . How did it come into the possession of a Chicago *Tribune* reporter—a man who, incidentally, has been the medium of at least one other major leak?"

The reporter was Chesly Manly, who had written the "war plans" story. Manly insisted that the report was in the "Communistic activities" file at the State Department, but I. F. Stone, writing in the *Nation's* Washington column, reported: "Michael J. McDermott, chief of the department's Division of Current Information, said that he was unable to find any trace of such a document in the department, but hesitated to issue a denial until he was sure."

In June 1942 the *Tribune* congratulated itself profusely on its ninety-fifth birthday, meanwhile looking toward its centennial. Its march onward and upward, the *Tribune* said, had "left the bones of our contemporaries bleaching by the trailside of Chicago." To commemorate that march the paper announced its projected three-volume *Tribune* history to be written by Phillip Kinsley, a *Tribune* veteran. Characteristically the announcement described this tome as "the most ambitious and comprehensive project ever attempted in newspaper history. It is not to be a dead history, or a eulogy, but the march of living men, like the march of an army whose banners were often shot down but always raised aloft again, an army with captains whose voices ring like silver trumpets, counseling in peace, assembling courage in war."

One volume of the history has already appeared under the imprint of Alfred A. Knopf, another under that of the *Tribune* itself, and the third was still to come at this writing.

In commissioning the history, Colonel McCormick told Kinsley to devote himself to the job, to make full use of the *Tribune* files, and to tell the paper's story without fear or favor. As the announcement promised, it is not a "dead history," because no history of the *Tribune* could be dead. It is, however, a long and eloquent eulogy and the silver trumpets ring in virtually every other paragraph. Nonetheless, it *is* ambitous and comprehensive in its own company way, and the *Tribune* is right in its assertion that no other newspaper has attempted anything like it. No other paper would think of it.

Even while the *Tribune* celebrated its birthday the McCormick-Patterson newspapers shocked the nation for the second time in less than a year. This time it was not the outright disclosure of a secret document, as the "war plans" story had been, but a far more involved piece of work.

The controversial story was published simultaneously on June 7 in the *Tribune*, *Daily News* and *Times-Herald*. Datelined Washington, it was written by Stanley Johnston, *Tribune* reporter whose dispatches and book about the aircraft carrier *Lexington* and the Battle of the Coral Sea were already war classics.

Johnston's story concerned "confidential information" he was supposed to have gathered during his Pacific assignment, particularly at the Battle of Midway Island. It carried specific names of Japanese ships involved in that battle and described Navy strategy in a manner not hitherto permitted by censorship, with the whole story attributed to Navy officials. The *Times-Herald's* headline read: U.S. NAVY KNEW IN ADVANCE ALL ABOUT JAP FLEET. GUESSED THERE WOULD BE FEINT ON ONE BASE, REAL ATTACK ON ANOTHER.

The story was actually written in Chicago, and the information it contained was as true as it was confidential, for the most part. In the subsequent controversy about it, however, both sides lost sight of the facts and the story itself became a major issue.

Most upset, of course, was the Navy Department, whose censors enjoyed the reputation among newspapers generally as being the most backward and arbitrary in the armed services. For once, according to some observers, they appeared to have a valid point in claiming that the *Tribune* story had violated the voluntary censorship code and had tipped off the Japs to sources of Navy information which would now be useless.

Under the first blasting attack the *Tribune* retreated slightly. The story did not come from Washington and its source was Mr. Johnston, not "naval intelligence," the paper admitted. But these were comparatively small matters. More important was the admission that Johnston had arrived at his accurate list of Japanese warships by "deduction," presumably aided by Jane's *Fighting Ships*. Much of Johnston's information, however, was too secret to be in Jane's and could have been derived only from knowledge which had now been disclosed in clear violation of censorship and possibly of national security. This story was a tip-off to the Japs that we had broken their communications code.

In defense of all this the *Tribune* brought down the wrath of other newspapers by asserting that the kind of faking in its story was "common practice, and newspapermen all over the United States follow it." There was enough truth in this too sweeping statement to bring forth the righteous indignation of McCormick's fellow publishers, who had adhered to the censorship code at the risk of just such news beats as the *Tribune* had demonstrated an unco-operative newspaper could obtain.

The voluntary nature of censorship made it obvious that the government could do nothing about the *Tribune's* violation and Washington admitted as much. But the Navy refused to give in. One irate admiral threatened to send Marines to take over Tribune Tower. The Navy Department brought pressure to bear on Attorney General Francis Biddle, who announced two months after the story's publication that a federal grand-jury investigation was under way in Chicago to ascertain whether the *Tribune* had violated the amended Espionage Act by unlawfully communicating documents or information concerning national defense.

The *Tribune's* reply to the investigation surprised no one. It called the charges "outrageous and ridiculous." The investigation, it said, was inspired by Secretary of the Navy Frank Knox, and many saw in this editorial the implication that Knox had used his official position to strike a blow for his Chicago *Daily News,* the *Tribune's* rival. The other big guns of the *Tribune* counterattack were much more familiar: the Administration was after any newspaper which "demanded an all-out war effort and removal of high officials who have been fumbling the war at home." The *Tribune* shouted its perennial battle cry when attacked, "freedom of the press," and it summoned the always convenient shade of Jefferson to provide it with an appropriate slogan: "Our liberty depends upon the freedom of the press and cannot be limited without being lost."

There were simultaneous repercussions of the incident in Congress. Representative Elmer R. Holland, of Pennsylvania, denounced the McCormick-Patterson empire in the House as "America's No. 1 and No. 2 exponents of the Nazi propaganda line," charged them with impeding the war effort, and of "doing their best to bring about a Fascist victory."

Captain Patterson's response was as characteristic as his cousin's had been. His signed editorial was headed: YOU'RE A LIAR, CONGRESSMAN HOLLAND. Holland, in another speech, listed all the news stories, editorials and cartoons in the McCormick-Patterson press which he deemed fascist and defeatist, and asserted, "Daily these publishers rub at the morale of the American people. Daily they sow suspicion. Daily they preach that we are in a hopeless struggle. Daily they wear at the moral fiber of the people, softening it, rotting it, preparing us for defeat."

The chief and almost the only congressional voice raised in defense was that of an old *Tribune* friend, Senator C. Wayland Brooks, of Lingle memory, who echoed his favorite newspaper's editorial columns by denouncing the grand-jury investigation as a "vicious, malicious and constant attack" by members of a "purge and smear campaign."

Whatever justification the investigation had to begin with, any attempt to get at the truth was quickly lost in a maze of legal complications, Navy censorship rigidity and politics. William D. Mitchell, Attorney General under Hoover, who conducted the investigation, pointed out the legal whatnot in the case. The government would have to prove willful intent to aid the enemy, as the Supreme Court had interpreted the Espionage Act, and Biddle readily agreed that it would be virtually impossible to establish such intent. This in spite of the fact that Mitchell conceded the Japs could have been aided by the story.

The Navy then sank its own case, after insisting that both sides be presented to the grand jury. The intelligence officer assigned to present the Navy's case refused to tell the jury why the story could have been useful to the Japanese because this information was still a Navy secret.

At that point politics added the final crushing blow to the investigation. Anti-Administration newspapers and magazines had lined up with the *Tribune*, for the most part, and the indirect sniping characteristic of their support was aptly illustrated by *Newsweek Magazine's* comment that the Navy's "secret" had been "bandied about for weeks in Washington clubs, pressrooms and cocktail bars." *Newsweek*, however, was as obdurate as the Navy in refusing to bandy the secret in its columns. The real political stinger in the *Newsweek* story came at the end, when an anonymous "Justice Department partisan" was quoted as saying, "Knox pushed Biddle out on a limb, followed him there, then sawed them both off."

The grand jury refused to indict and the Colonel made his triumph the occasion for a paternalistic gesture, undoubtedly sincere and natural under the circumstances. He strode into the city room when the news was announced and a cheering staff surrounded him. McCormick told them, "I had no fear of this investigation. I had the utmost confidence in Pat Maloney and Stanley Johnston. There never has been a bunch like the *Tribune* bunch. As I have told you before, every member of the *Tribune* is a member of my family."

This historic incident was reported by the *Tribune* in full. Almost in the same triumphal hour the Chicago branch of the Union for Democratic Action was busy organizing Chicagoans against the paper. In August 1942 it published a seventy-two-page pamphlet titled *The People vs. the Chicago Tribune*, an extraordinarily able piece of pamphleteering. Readers noted that the executive board of the UDA's Chicago branch, printed on the back cover, listed a defection from the McCormick clan's ranks: Anita McCormick Blaine (Mrs. Emmons Blaine) was vice-chairman.

The pamphlet was presented as an indictment. It began with a rehearsal of the "war plans" and the Johnston stories. Then it offered an unflattering word picture of Colonel McCormick. A third section was devoted to a discussion of the *Tribune's* propaganda line, and here there was a telling page on the paper's attitude toward Marshall Field III, who had so recently become a competitor.

A facsimile of a *Tribune* layout for February 21, 1919, showed Field in uniform with his wife, under the caption: "Back with

Laurels of War. Capt. Marshall Field III, Who Won Way up from Ranks, and His Wife Return to Chicago."

Paired with this was a facsimile of the *Tribune's* lead editorial for July 26, 1942. This editorial, so reminiscent of Joseph Medill, is worth reproduction here because it represents a low point even in personal journalism. It read:

### THE WORD IS COWARD

Ralph Ingersoll, editor of *PM*, has been shamed into entering the army as a volunteer after his draft board had refused to grant him a deferment requested by his boss. It remains to be seen whether Ingersoll's friends in Washington will obtain a commission and a safe berth for him. Whatever his value as an editor, and it isn't much, he has had a real value to his owner. The publicity given to Ingersoll as a draft dodger has detracted attention from Marshall Field as a slacker. Field is of age to volunteer. He cried for war before it came. Now that it has come, he lets men like MacNider and O'Hare do the fighting while he skulks in his clubs, night and otherwise. No one would suggest that he is indispensable to *PM* or to anything else. The term to fit to him and to all the herd of hysterical effeminates is coward.

Even the most broad-minded, objective student of *Tribune* history could find no better word to fit this editorial than inexcusable. Field did not dignify it by making a reply. It may be added as a footnote that Ralph Ingersoll, whose induction was not the brightest page in the history of Selective Service, worked himself up from the ranks and had become a lieutenant colonel by 1945.

The UDA pamphlet concluded with a section on what it cited as the *Tribune's* parallels with native fascism and "the vermin press," another on its political maneuverings, and a final exhortation to fight the *Tribune* in every way. Yet the call to arms fell on apparently deaf ears because there is no evidence that people stopped buying *Tribunes* in any considerable quantity.

In fact McCormick went off on a new tangent in December 1942 and momentarily had both his friends and his enemies baffled. He came out editorially for the "American Century," a form of apparent imperialism previously advanced under exactly that title by Henry Luce, whose publications had been frequent objects of *Tribune* scorn.

It was not a meeting of minds, however, nor was it a breathtaking repudiation of isolationism. Puzzled readers absorbed whole sentences of praise for our naval victories in the Southwest Pacific before the meat of the argument was exposed to them. Our victories, the *Tribune* said, showed that America had become the guardian of Australia, New Zealand, "perhaps South Africa," and all of the Americas including Canada. Therefore, it concluded, "the military power of the United States, which is now beginning to make itself manifest in many parts of the world, is destined to be the determining factor in the organization of the postwar world. . . . This is the American Century."

The readers, no longer puzzled, sighed with relief. It was obvious that the *Tribune*, unable to conceive of our participation in a world organization, had vaulted to the other extreme—American world rule. The point of this particular exposition of postwar philosophy was that America would preside over the dissolution of the British Empire, if Churchill would not, and would take unto itself all the sundered lands which were now "dependent" on it.

That was the *Tribune's* thinking as the first year of war closed for the United States. Peering into 1943 on New Year's Day, the Colonel editorially endowed the American people with seven resolutions, which he said they had already "taken." They were:

That dictatorship, however masked, is not for Americans.

That the three coordinate branches of government—executive, judicial, and legislative—are to be restored to their just proportion and constitutional balance.

That the citizenry is not to be commanded by those who forget that they have been accepted as servants, not raised up as masters.

That the will of the people, as expressed thru their representatives, henceforth will control.

That waste and extravagance must end.

That incompetence must no longer be condoned.

That the American way of life must be preserved, the victory sped, and the republic saved.


Up to that point the *Tribune's* contributions to preserving the American way of life in wartime had been to maintain a ceaseless barrage directed against every phase of the war effort. It had never advanced any alternative plans of its own.

Colonel McCormick remedied this omission in April 1943 with an astounding deadpan editorial titled "States Across the Sea." It led off with the reminder that new states could be admitted to the Union by Congress, and then it set forth this proposition:

"If the British Commonwealth and the nations of West Europe wish to enjoy close association with us, and if for our part we wish similarly to link ourselves with them, the way . . . is clear. All that they need to do is adopt written constitutions and apply for membership, and all we need to do is accept them. . . . Great Britain could come into the Union, for example, as four states . . . Canada could constitute another state. . . . Australia, New Zealand and the contiguous island might form still another. . . .

"For the people of Britain, particularly, statehood would have many advantages. American manpower . . . and wealth would be instantly and automatically available if Britain . . . were threatened with invasion. . . . Britain would have to give up its king, but as his constitutional powers are said to be merely nominal . . . the change to a republican form of government could be made without difficulty. . . . The hand-kissers in this country should welcome the close relationship if only because it strengthens their representation in Congress. . . . The more advanced states of Western Europe that show aptitude for constitutional government might also be included."

Opinion on the editorial was divided sharply. The school believing in McCormick's sincerity thought he meant it; others said he was either trying to discredit plans for world co-operation or else was engaging in his favorite sport of Britain-baiting.

The British did not rise. For once they were only amused. The London *Observer* wrote: ". . . The Colonel's brave new thought is far from original. In his play, *The Apple Cart*, produced over fourteen years ago, Bernard Shaw made exactly this suggestion. *The Apple Cart* was voted quite good comedy."

As political maneuvering began in the summer of 1943 the Colonel turned his attention to domestic affairs, and he did not like what he saw—the attempt of liberal Republicans to inject internationalism into the party at the Mackinac Conference. The attempt was only partly successful for the moment, but the Colonel felt it necessary to rally the isolationist forces. He held a "Constitution Day" dinner in one of Chicago's best hotels, the Palmer House. More than a thousand guests heard McCormick celebrate Illinois and the Midwest, concluding with this peroration: "When the most brilliantly conceived and executed coup was sprung upon the Republican meeting at Mackinac, to bring to a successful conclusion the conspiracy so unsuccessfully begun by Major André and General Arnold a hundred and sixty-three years ago, it was Governor Green of Illinois who stood like Washington at Valley Forge and prevented the contemplated stampede of the excited delegates."

Thus the Colonel foreshadowed the Republican split which was to lay the groundwork for Thomas E. Dewey's defeat.

Norman Cousins summarized the case against the McCormick-Patterson papers in the *Saturday Review of Literature* on January 22, 1944, with an editorial titled "The Poison Gas Boys." His three-point indictment charged the papers with:

(1) Splitting up of the United Nations—by provoking suspicion in America against her Allies and vice versa.

(2) Weakening American morale—by merchandising in distrust against our civil and military leaders, and by trafficking in casualty speculation in advance of military operations.

(3) Jeopardizing the success of military operations—either by disclosing of secret plans or by loose talk that might force the enemy's hand.

Cousins went on to attack specifically an editorial in all three papers advocating the use of poison gas in the Pacific Theater. "Can anyone imagine anything more incredibly irresponsible and potent, more incendiary than an editorial advocating the use of poison gas?" Cousins inquired. "We fail to see how the offending newspapers can hide behind the issue of freedom of the press here. . . ."

The *News* kept up the poison-gas campaign, while McCormick devoted his attention to domestic politics and the approaching election. A fantastic episode in his attempt to control the party came as an aftermath of the presidential primary in Wisconsin in April 1944, at which the state's voters rejected the internationalism of Willkie in favor of Dewey's more orthodox Republicanism. These voters were presumably astounded at Colonel McCormick's interpretation of the results. He asserted solemnly that the Wisconsin GOP had voted for the *Tribune* as against Willkie, the Milwaukee *Journal* and other state newspapers that had supported Willkie.

Blandly the Colonel proposed to enlighten Wisconsin by establishing a *Tribune*-owned Milwaukee newspaper, for which he asked paper from the WPB. The *Tribune's* Milwaukee edition already had a circulation of 35,089 daily and 58,639 Sunday, but this figure was far behind the Milwaukee *Journal's* 282,509. The Colonel asserted, "The recent primaries in . . . Wisconsin have amply demonstrated that the people of that state have repudiated many . . . Wisconsin newspapers," and he cited specifically the *Journal*, the (Madison) *Wisconsin State Journal*, and the Sheboygan *Press*. He did not mention Hearst's Milwaukee *Sentinel*, which had supported Dewey.

As in his proposal to make states of the British Empire, and similar startling propositions, it was difficult to determine whether McCormick spoke seriously or with an ulterior purpose. In any case the Wisconsin papers remained unruffled, the WPB quietly sidetracked the *Tribune's* paper request, and other publishers finally concluded that it was McCormick's way of putting the WPB on the spot, so that if it granted the Chicago *Sun's* appeal for extra newsprint the *Tribune* would have more anti-New Deal ammunition.

That the fight against the Administration was uppermost in the Colonel's mind could be seen from the speech he prepared for delivery to a conference of Rotarians (179th District) on April 18, in which he charged that "Communists and their abettors not only dominate the Democratic party, but are actively trying to control the Republican National Convention as the New Deal did in 1940. . . . Communists dominate our government because four hundred odd thousand of them . . . have held the balance of power in New York State and New York State has the largest vote in the Electoral College. . . . My friend Winston Churchill suggested to the Republican Conference at Mackinac, with the approval of President Conant, of Harvard, and apparently of President Roosevelt, that we repeal our Declaration of Independence and re-enter the British Empire as lower-class subjects of the British crown. Some of our millionaires favor this plan so that they may buy for themselves the titles that they can now only purchase for their sisters and daughters."

That was the McCormick-*Tribune* approach to the crucial election of 1944. Even after that election's repudiation of Mc-Cormick philosophy, penetrating to the heart of his empire, the *Tribune* pattern did not change in the least, as it has never changed in any similar situation. Taking an example at random, consider the paper's editorial page for December 17, 1944.

The lead editorial, a column and a quarter long, discussed "A Pertinent Question." The question: "Is it the policy of the state department to follow the British lead in Europe completely and depend on the British lead in the far east?" Answering this query, the editorial distorted American diplomatic history in attempting to prove that our foreign policy had always been "Anglophile" and under the spell of Britain in one way or another. "Why," the essay inquired rhetorically, "have American diplomats, one after another, been so easily manipulated by the British? Why the adulation bestowed on titled foreigners?"

This editorial was followed by a *Tribune* excursion into economics, based on the history of Teddy, the prize Hereford steer, brought from Bryant, Iowa, by a young 4-H stockman to win the grand championship of the Chicago market fat stock show. The point of Teddy's history was that he would have been a more profitable beast if it were not for such people as a "consecrated young nitwit in the war food administration, a professor, at that," who believed that in wartime it would not be unreasonable to expect "less profits for farmers, less meat for city folk."

The editorial columns, however, would have been incomplete without a sample of *Tribune* philosophy, and this was provided in an editorial:

## MIDWESTERN CRUCIBLE

A long time reader of *The Tribune* makes a significant contribution to the Voice of the People today. His letter, entitled, "We Said It 40 Years Ago," quotes a *Tribune* editorial of 1904. That editorial is representative of more than the consistency of *The Tribune's* outlook. It describes a distinctive temper and character that set the middle west apart from the eastern seaboard. These distinctions are as valid today as when the editorial was written.

We were not wrong in saying then, and we are not wrong in repeating now, that the middle west is "the crucible in which national issues are being distilled." It is as true now as then that the windows of the east, with its traditions of colonial dependence and its emphasis on social caste, look out upon Europe, and that only after the Alleghenies are crossed and a descent made into the midlands does the American discover the roots of his heritage.

These facts are remembered by too few aspirants in politics and leaders in government. The candidates who have succeeded at the polls have disregarded the counsels and desires of the people in this great midland country. They have held America cheaply, sought to devote themselves and their country slavishly to the interests of Europe, and as a reward have been patronized with a second class regard from over the sea. Those who have contended with them for office have too often been easterners or the creatures of eastern interests, which is to say of European interests, and as such have not been able to make themselves acceptable in the middle west. Neither camp has been able to command the faith of this section, with its dedication to Americanism.

The middle west is still the crucible. Men and issues are tested in it. When its belief in an America independent of the discredited old world is recognized and its aspirations on behalf of our own people are espoused, it will lead this country back upon the road which its faithless leaders have deserted.

The editorial of 1904 that was the inspiration for this pronouncement was indeed a proof of *Tribune* consistency. It began: "Why is it that Chicago prefers democracy and honesty to any amount of efficiency secured by subservience to traction companies and by acquiescence in corruption? Because it is the main city of that great tract of prairie west of the Allegheny mountains in which democracy was given its first trial.

"The nations of Europe, tho many of them have adopted a measure of political democracy, still have to work with material drawn from the ruins of the old aristocratic social structure. And the American colonies along the Atlantic seaboard were founded with distinctions of class. These distinctions survived the Revolution. It was only when the Alleghenies were crossed that a pure democracy appeared in the world."

The letters column contained other communications in the spirit of the 1904 and 1944 editorials. Several missives were in answer to a previous Vox Pop letter titled, "Soldiers Say Foreign Wives Best." All these replies reflected the *Tribune's* propaganda line. These are sample excerpts:

"Perhaps if European women would step on their men once in a while and start demanding instead of submitting like meek little lambs, we wouldn't have to go over there every 20 years to fight their wars."

"The reasons these prize foreigners don't demand luxuries are that they wouldn't know a luxury if they saw one, inasmuch as they've never had any, and that they are very hard up for men, any men."

"The first thing our boys will give their foreign wives when they reach America is the American Joneses' way of life, because they themselves will want it."

As the United States entered its fourth year of war in 1945 the *Tribune* did not waver in its pattern. It was opposing the movement in Illinois to write a new state constitution, a movement

Colonel Robert R. McCormick and his first wife as they returned on the S.S. Paris after a three-month honeymoon abroad

The clan gathers for Colonel McCormick's second marriage, December 21, 1944. Left to right: Captain Joseph Patterson, Mrs. Chauncey McCormick, Colonel McCormick; his bride, the former Mrs. Maryland Mathison Hooper; Chauncey McCor-

backed by the other Chicago newspapers and by such conservative bodies as the League of Women Voters. The *Tribune* called the movement a Red plot. "Communists and fellow travelers," it shrieked editorially, would take away the state's "republican form of government" and "make Illinois the first of the soviet states of America."

In this manner the McCormick empire fought the second World War, fought by following its perennial line of isolationism to a logical conclusion in which, according to its own admission, it interpreted events by the same standards it had used forty years before. The dynasty's empire had grown mightily in those four decades, but the thinking of its owners had grown not at all. The *Tribune's* boasted consistency was simply a naïve confession that it had not changed its mind for nearly a half century. At a time in world history when America deserved leadership from its newspapers, the *Tribune* stood where it had always stood—selfishly alone.

# CHAPTER 7

# THE PATTERN

A CLOSER STUDY of the McCormick-*Tribune* pattern indicates how its consistency is reflected in repetitive attacks on hate objects. An analysis of the paper's contents for November and December 1944 shows this clearly. In that sixty-one-day period totals were compiled from the editorials, the news columns on page one, editorial-page cartoons and page-one cartoons. The results show that there were 105 attacks on the Administration in these four places combined, 69 pieces opposing wartime controls, 61 others designed to discredit the peace, 58 anti-British, 49 anti-Russian, 35 nationalistic, and 20 anti-labor.

Those who believe that a newspaper's right to comment is unlimited will say that such statistics are meaningless. One would agree that a paper has every right to express its opinions, but at the same time there must be a point where good taste and public responsibility draw the line, and the statistics cited are derived from instances where that line has been crossed in force. Though it is true that newspapers, almost without exception, have used their news columns for political purposes at one time or another in some degree, the *Tribune's* transgressions in this respect have been consistently flagrant.

To illuminate the pattern by actual examples, let us examine the *Tribune's* anti-Administration record. A good place to begin is 1936, when Roosevelt was nominated for a second term. At that time Colonel McCormick wrote a letter to Managing Editor Beck which was posted so that the whole staff could read it. The letter called for strict impartiality during the campaign, "complete unbiased reports with an effort toward equal coverage subject to news value." Admirable. But the letter then went on to say that in his first term Roosevelt had "tried to control the [Washington] correspondents," and it concluded with the prophecy that "there will be so much Roosevelt news created by his commissars that it will be necessary to see that Landon gets a fair share of the total. But the Roosevelt stories must be adequate and must be written without any animus against him."

What followed on the editorial page was exactly what could be expected: a daily attack on the President under the heading, "Turn the Rascals Out." What happened in the news columns was inexcusable.

A prime example of *Tribune* impartiality was the picture it printed after Roosevelt's campaign visit to Chicago. The picture showed a street filled with Roosevelt buttons, apparently thrown away by people who opposed the President. The picture caption read: "Roosevelt buttons intended for coat lapels land on ground. A rag picker helping himself to Roosevelt buttons on a street near the Loop yesterday. Apparently the buttons were tossed aside by pedestrians to whom they were handed by women members of Young Democrats of Cook County, who made wholesale distribution."

The Chicago *Times* exposed the picture and its caption as faked. The man in the picture signed a statement confessing that he had been paid twenty-five cents to pose, and a witness confirmed his story. The *Times* added that the *Tribune* photographer had thrown the buttons on the street himself. The *Tribune* did not even deny it.

After the election, and right up to the day of President Roosevelt's death, Colonel McCormick continued an attack which ranks with the most vicious in newspaper history. Here are some examples of the language and methods used:

*On Churchill's support of Russian Polish claims* (December 18, 1944): "Many of those in this country who are now expending their indignation on Mr. Churchill are themselves not wholly blameless. They should have known that Mr. Roosevelt's word is not good, and, in particular, they should have known that if ever he promised to oppose a British policy he could be expected to dishonor his pledge. To any one who has followed Mr. Roosevelt's foreign policy it is obvious that his great love is Britain, with Russia holding a good second place in his affections. That's about all there is to his foreign policy."

*On taxation* (December 23, 1944): "The federal taxing machinery today is becoming as oppressive as the feudal system. The lord of the manor is again claiming the right to take first and to take as much as he wants without leaving much more than a bare subsistence to those who produce the wealth."

*On manpower* (December 28, 1944): "The truth about the manpower situation is that the Roosevelt administration bit off more than the country could chew. It undertook to fight two major enemies in distant theaters of war, one without effective allies and the other with allies who, in recent months, have dogged it and left the United States to carry an unfair proportion of the burden. . . ."

*On labor draft proposals* (January 8, 1945): "The plea for a labor draft is typical. Instead of seeking ways to increase the efficiency of the war plants and his procurement organization, Mr. Roosevelt aims to make a slave of every American citizen. It is the same old song. If he were only given more power, he wouldn't fall down on the job."

*On peace plans* (January 12, 1945): "Experience has taught the country that he [Roosevelt] cannot be trusted with any grant of power, since he will invariably disregard any limitations placed upon it. Give him authority to use troops without consent of Congress and he would keep a permanent army in Europe, interfering in the affairs of other nations wherever and whenever the whim seized him."

*On obsolete tanks* (January 15, 1945): "The reason, then, that new American tanks have been developed—Mr. Roosevelt doesn't say that they are in combat or even in production—is that we have been fighting the Nazis with obsolete equipment. . . . The President has a great advantage in concealing shortcomings, for all the facts are at his disposal, and censorship and a policy of secrecy contrive to keep them his personal property. Not until deficiencies are disclosed on the field of battle does the public hear about such matters, and by then Mr. Roosevelt is able to advance to the microphone and assert that he has had something done about it, so there is no reason to worry. Altogether, it works out very nicely for him, altho perhaps not to the liking of our tank crews and infantrymen."

*On Wallace's appointment* (January 23, 1945): "As a business man, Secretary Wallace is a fit companion for Mr. Roosevelt, the speculator in worthless German marks; Mr. Morgenthau, the gentleman farmer made a financier by fiat; Honest Harold Ickes, the stock market sucker, who had to be bailed out by his wife; and those two professional spenders of other people's money, Harry Hopkins and Madam Perkins. . . . It is impossible to recall in American history an appointee so completely incompetent to perform the duties of his office, or one whose appointment was more brazenly in discharge of a political debt. The debt is primarily to Sidney Hillman and those of his followers who are bent upon destroying the American government and substituting for it the slavery of communism, rather than to Wallace himself."

*On "White House Standards"* (February 3, 1945): "Self-gratification rather than self-denial has been a characteristic of White House life. Quite naturally one son thought he had prerogative to fly a dog from England and send it as government air freight to the west coast. . . . Quite naturally another son holds a train in Chicago that he, as if a high official on imperative business, might make connections. Mr. Roosevelt, with sons in the service, is, as commander in chief, conceivably in a difficult position. He might have to withhold from one or more of the young men rewards and promotions well deserved and deny them because he and they must be above suspicion of father to son favoritism. Mr. Roosevelt, it need not be remarked, found no dilemma at all. Nothing Spartan occurred to him. There is no self-denying ordinance in the White House. The motto is: 'You can't take it with you.' "

On the week in April 1945 that President Roosevelt died the *Tribune* attack was aimed along its customary lines. A Parrish cartoon displayed Pandora and a box tagged "Confidential! F.D.R." Out of its seams burgeoned foul insects and odors labeled "Internationalist Schemes for America," "Divulged Commitments" and "The World's Woes Brought to America." A poem enscrolled above this touching scene concluded:

> *Pandora, must you also break* this *chest*
> *Wherein New Dealia's secret pacts are hid?*
> *It's true a few have been revealed. The rest*
> *We do not know. What sorrow if we did!*

The editorial columns fulminated as usual. On April 10 one titled "So Red the Rose" asserted: "Over a period of twelve years there has been speculation whether Mr. Roosevelt knew what he was doing or merely abounded in other people's ideas, which he issued because they made good rhetoric. . . . Experience with Mr. Roosevelt would suggest that he would take very kindly to a system which gave him and his administrators control of capital and labor."

On the day before the President died an Orr cartoon depicted Liberty rocking the cradle of an infant labeled "Future America," while behind stood a female nurse, a caricature of the President. The nurse's apron said "New Deal Planners," and her left hand carried a book half behind her back, a book titled *Dr. Karl Marx. Red Doctrines.* The nurse was saying: "Madam, p-le-a-s-e! Kindly step aside!! I'm taking complete charge, heah!"

Next day the *Tribune* shed its crocodile tears in a brief, black-bordered editorial:

### A NATION MOURNS

President Roosevelt is dead and the whole nation is plunged into mourning, those who opposed him in politics no less than those who followed him.

History will appraise his work. For the moment we can only express the deep sorrow which all Americans feel at the passing of their chosen leader.

President Roosevelt did not live to see the victory for which he strove but he died in the certainty that the hour of triumph could not long be postponed. He earned his rest.

To his widow and to his children, the people of this nation extend their deepest sympathy. His successor, President Truman,

inherits an immense task at a difficult hour. He will receive the
loyal support of all of us.

To many, the editorial seemed almost indecent in its *"nil nisi
bonum"* tone. No one could possibly believe, in the light of the
*Tribune's* record, that any such tribute had the least sincerity. It
was no more convincing than the pious and patriotic expressions of
support for President Truman which were forthcoming next
day from the *Tribune* and other bitterly anti-Administration
newspapers, many of them adroitly worded to cover the relief
that the publishers felt at having their hate object removed and
replaced by a figure who, they were convinced, would be far
more malleable.

If these are harsh words, if apologists insist that the *Tribune* and
newspapers of its ilk proved by their editorial words after the
event that what they wrote before about the President was only
"politics" and "freedom of the press"—let it be said that the black
borders and the fine rhetoric do not conceal the facts. The record
is clear, and it does no credit to American journalism.

These editorial quotations from the *Tribune* have been chosen
deliberately to represent the commonplace, not the extreme examples. By and large they are worse only in degree than the
editorials in the Hearst and Scripps-Howard papers. But no other
paper has so consistently slanted headlines and news stories under
Washington datelines as the *Tribune*.

A characteristic of *Tribune* Washington stories, which has not
changed since Roosevelt's death, is their playing up of the anti-
Administration angle completely out of proportion to its importance. This is done not only in headlines but in the wording of
stories. A headline reading, CAPITOL ANGRY AT PLANE
RIDE BY ELLIOTT'S DOG, was followed by this lead paragraph: "The halls of congress resounded today to indignant demands that members of the Roosevelt family stop 'playing at
war.'" The resounding, it appears, issued entirely from the mouth
of Representative Clare Hoffman, of Michigan, who used the
phrase "playing at war" in a typical windy speech. But this fact
is buried on page five, in the runover from page one. The front-

page headline and lead create an impression completely unjustified by the facts.

Hoffman and Representative John Rankin, of Mississippi, have been mouthpieces for the *Tribune* in Congress, and their every remark gets prominent display in the paper. These speeches by Hoffman and Rankin, as printed in the *Congressional Record* and recorded at least in part by the McCormick-Patterson papers, deserve a consideration of their own, because their unrestrained, irresponsible vituperation has seldom, if ever, been equaled in the Congress of the United States. Only congressional immunity protects these men.

When either representative speaks in the House the *Tribune* stories invariably imply or assert outright that he speaks the sentiments of his colleagues. Representatives who make speeches in opposition are said to "bellow" or "yell." Ex-Senators Burton K. Wheeler and Gerald Nye have been the other *Tribune* favorites. They were used as loudspeakers for isolationism; Hoffman and Rankin are the criers against "Communism" and "subversive activities"—the stereotypes of the pattern that came to be known as anti-Rooseveltism.

Reporting a radio speech by Wheeler on January 5, 1945, his second after America entered the war, the *Tribune* story was headlined: POWER POLITICS WILL BEAT US IN WAR: WHEELER. The slanted lead said, "In a caustically incisive analysis of the state of the war, Sen. Wheeler (D., Mont.) tonight cautioned America will lose the war unless power politics is halted at once and a working federation is established in Europe as the basis of permanent peace." The second paragraph read: "Warning that 'truth is the first casualty of war' and noting that 'the opiates that have been poured down the throats of American people by propaganda peddlers are now wearing off,' the senator urged abandonment of the 'brutal and costly' slogan of unconditional surrender and any thought of a peace of vengeance."

Another choice example is the farewell speech made by Senator Nye on December 19, 1944, before he left the Senate on January 3, after twenty years of tenure. The speech was headlined: NYE ASSERTS U.S. FACES NEW WAR IN 10 OR 20 YEARS.

BRITAIN PREPARED TO COAX US IN, HE WARNS. The story began: "Charging the allies of the United States are fighting a political war, Sen. Nye (R., N.D.) warned the senate in his farewell address today against American entanglement in world politics which he said threatens to lead us into a third world war 10 or 20 years from now. Nye will leave the senate Jan. 3 after 20 years of service in that body, marked by consistent efforts to keep the United States from entering Europe's wars and to insure that this country's involvement in the present conflict will not result in the sacrifice of American interests."

A sample of the Hoffman line is contained in a story datelined December 13, 1944, headlined: SAYS U.S. PICKS ON WARD'S AS LABOR "PAYOFF." WLB ACTIONS LINKED TO 4TH TERM VOTES. The piece begins: "Charges that the national war labor board is paying off the CIO-PAC for fourth term votes by ordering Montgomery Ward & Co. of Chicago to appear at a hearing in Washington tomorrow were made today by Rep. Hoffman (R., Mich.) in a speech inserted in the house record."

An able lieutenant of the Rankin-Hoffman team was the *Tribune's* man, Senator Brooks, of Illinois. His line of attack is best illustrated by this lead on a Washington story, written by the *Tribune's* veteran correspondent, Arthur Sears Henning: "Depicting American boys fighting and dying to make Europe safe for the new British and Russian spheres of influence that Churchill and Stalin are carving out in defiance of the Atlantic Charter, Sen. Brooks (R., Ill.) arose in the senate today and challenged President Roosevelt to use our preponderant power, resources, and influence to get an agreement on a just peace."

A prime example of distortion in *Tribune* news stories is this lead, written by Walter Trohan, on the nomination of Elliott Roosevelt to the rank of brigadier general: "A sharp senate engagement was anticipated today over the belated third wedding present President Roosevelt gave to his 34-year-old son, Col. Elliott Roosevelt, by nominating him to be a brigadier general."

The next three paragraphs in this story are an example of the *Tribune* at its worst, and thus merit reprinting:

"Confirmation of this nomination by the senate would give

the President's second son the most meteoric rise in the army for a man without previous military experience and without a college education. He entered the army four years ago as a captain.

"It would also give the Hyde Park line of the Roosevelt family its first general and put Elliott well ahead of his three tall brothers in the race for military honors which has brought the four brothers 12 promotions in three and a half years of war.

"Until the present war none of the Hyde Park Roosevelts had ever served in the American army. In the Revolution the family members were Tories. Neither the President, his father, his grandfather, nor great-grandfather had borne arms in war."

This, of course, is not reporting. It is political attack purporting to be news.

In its local stories the *Tribune* political line takes the form of using its news columns to oppose and discredit any governmental ruling. When more farmers were needed in the draft, the *Tribune* news story of January 8, 1945, began: "A sharp drop in food production in Illinois and the nation was predicted yesterday by Illinois farm leaders and officials as a result of the selective service order for examination as to physical condition and reason for deferment for all deferred agricultural workers. . . ."

·When excessive use of heating was ordered stopped to save fuel, the *Tribune* headline read: CHICAGO COOL TO 68° EDICT. NEW DEAL RADIATORS SIZZLE.

Opposing enforcement of OPA rules, a *Tribune* news story said: "Charging that the office of price administration has discarded its policy of co-operative education pledged prior to the November election and is embarking on a program of harassing enforcement, Joseph T. Meek, executive secretary of the Illinois Federation of Retail Associations, yesterday predicted chaos in the retail field unless OPA officials seek 'friendly co-operation' with retail merchants."

Speeches like Mr. Meek's, and like others reproduced here, must be printed by a newspaper as part of the flow of news, but the prominent display of news favorable to a paper's policy, the slanted headline over it, and the distortion of news in the story itself cannot be condoned.

This slanting was carried over into news from the war front. Here is the beginning of a story by Henry Wales, datelined Marseille, France, December 27, 1944: "To understand the friction and dissatisfaction existing between the local populace and the Yanks in these areas one must examine the French point of view; and the simplest explanation is that the French accepted the flamboyant American propaganda that the United States entered the war solely from altruistic purposes."

In its constant anti-British barrage the *Tribune* sometimes goes to absurd lengths to clear its own skirts at the expense of England, as for instance this editorial, printed January 7, 1945:

## IMMIGRANT WORDS

Mrs. Luce, upon her return from Europe, told reporters in Washington that in her opinion a great many of the soldiers are America firsters, but few of them are isolationists.

What she meant by that is her secret. In truth, isolationism is a political catchword that was emigrant from England and never was naturalized in America. No American political leader of consequence and no American political party that amounted to anything ever advocated the kind of living behind a Chinese wall that the term implies. In that sense there never were any isolationists in this country and there probably never will be as long as we continue to be a leading importer and exporter, the leading lender to the world, the leading almoner to the world, the most traveled people in the world, and a nation maintaining diplomatic relations with the nations of the world.

We don't know when the word "isolation" first was used as descriptive of a political attitude. We had a notion that it appeared in English politics about a century ago, when England had decided to have nothing to do with the Holy Alliance that was trying to run the continent, but if so the Oxford dictionary doesn't support the theory. The first use noted was in 1896. Early in February of that year, Sir Wilfrid Laurier, the Canadian leader, seems to have said:

"Whether splendidly isolated or dangerously isolated, I will not now debate, but for my part I think splendidly isolated because the isolation of England comes from her superiority."

Within a few weeks George Joachim Goschen, then Britain's first lord of the admiralty, picked up the phrase in the following sentence: "We have stood alone in that which is called isolation—our splendid isolation as one of our colonial friends was good enough to call it."

The first use of the word in this country is credited to a Philadelphia newspaper in 1899, three years later. The new American historical dictionary doesn't include "isolation." As an import from abroad, it has a companion in "appeasement," another word that has no native roots. Both of them came into use here—thanks to the efforts of British propagandists and their American collaborators. People who talk about "isolationists" and "appeasers" thereby reveal that they are the tools, conscious or unconscious, of British propaganda. . . .

Such exercises in etymology are among the milder examples of the *Tribune's* anti-British line. More often the paper attacks, as it did on January 16, 1945, when *Collier's Magazine* advocated postwar Lend-Lease extension to help rebuild Britain and British trade. This is the *Tribune* on *Collier's:*

"Collier's waxes lyrical in praise of the British for holding out 'as an advance base for allied operations against Germany until American, British, and Canadian strength could be massed for the smash into France.' Collier's ought to stop pretending that it is an American publication. It is an English mouthpiece, and, as was revealed some years ago in a senate investigation, is allied with an international banking firm whose present head formerly was active in the magazine. He sometimes wrote for it, once a six-part serial about a diminutive figure who was one of his partners. The international firm which plays a prominent part in Collier's has financed the British government since the Boer war. It referred to Germany as 'our enemy' early in 1916, altho President Wilson was then and later calling upon all good Americans to be strictly neutral. Partners of the London branch are high in British government councils."

An ideal anti-British story until Mr. Roosevelt's death was one which linked the President with any movement, real or imagined, to help Britain. Thus Joseph Cerutti reported from London on

January 14, 1945: "President Roosevelt's budget message which called for the setting up of an international bank, was interpreted in London as implying the United States was eager to aid its war torn allies of Europe, particularly Britain, with dollar loans. It was suggested that the postwar international credits policy would clear the way for the United States to help finance British exports to Russia."

If this kind of story came from Washington, so much the better. Here is a Walter Trohan masterpiece, dated January 7, 1945, and headlined: CUT U.S. FILMS TO FEED BRITISH AND RED MOVIES. The lead read, "Americans at home and on the world's fighting fronts will get fewer and shorter motion pictures for their entertainment for the duration of the war in order to enable Britain and Russia to make propaganda pictures for distribution in the spheres of influence they are hacking out of war torn Europe."

The *Tribune's* attitude toward Russia is cut from the same pattern. Its reporting of Russian news shows the same distortion that appears in some of its other campaigns. The record is a shabby one.

On August 2, 1921, the *Tribune* printed a picture allegedly showing Soviet soldiers machine-gunning men, women and children. Investigation showed that the picture had appeared in the *Tribune* four years before as a World War scene.

In October 1925 *Tribune* headlines reported: SOVIET FIGHTS FAMINE AS GRAIN MYTH EXPLODES; DOOM OF SOVIET; and the revolt of Siberia. On March 20, 1926, the headline collapse began again: SECRET REPORT SHOWS RUSSIA NEAR COLLAPSE. Later: ROUMANIA HEARS OF WIDESPREAD RUSSIAN REVOLT—proved to be a Rumanian propaganda story. And still later: ODESSA TROOPS MUTINY AGAINST MOSCOW REGIME. TRADE, INDUSTRY TOTTER. By August 10 the breathless and fictitious headline revolution reported: RED FACTIONS GRASP FOR POWER. Three days later: REINFORCE KREMLIN FORT AS MUTINY GROWS.

The *Tribune* revolt went on through 1927. April 9: REVOLT AGAINST SOVIET BEGINS. April 19: the Red Army was fighting against South Russia. April 21: the troops were called home "as revolt rises." July: a new famine. October: INDUSTRY FACES SWIFT DISASTER. November: hundreds died IN UKRAINE RIOTS, ROUMANIA HEARS.

In the thirties, when Russian aviators flew over the North Pole from Moscow to the United States, the *Tribune* scented a "Red plot," at first "timed to lend the greatest support to the waning C.I.O. movement," and later editorially as timed to "land in America when Lewis and his C.I.O. needed something to distract the public attention from their violent activities and take some of the curses off the Red purges which filled the world press. . . ."

On November 13, 1937, a *Tribune* London story reported "discovery of a plot by German agents to assassinate Soviet Dictator Josef Stalin. . . . Confessions of two alleged German spies arrested in Leningrad early in the fall are said to have compromised Litvinoff, Soviet Commissar of Foreign Affairs, and to have been the real reason for the reputed arrest of three Soviet ambassadors."

Of all the anti-Russian stories up to this point, the kindest thing that could be said of them journalistically was that they were completely unsubstantiated rumors printed as news. Of more recent anti-Soviet stories, the best that can be said is that they follow the *Tribune* policy of shaping the news to suit the publisher's viewpoint, an aggravation in the *Tribune's* case of a disease that afflicts other newspapers as well.

Anti-Administration, anti-British and anti-Russian campaigns are all well-known facets of the McCormick-*Tribune* empire. Much less familiar are the *Tribune's* specialized attacks, particularly those on New York and on American magazines.

The New York assault, by far the more curious of the two, began on December 30, 1944, on column one, page one. It was introduced this way: "After roving the world nearly 20 years as a *Tribune* foreign correspondent, Alex Small has come home and written his impressions of life in America's biggest city. His engrossing analysis of the New York melting pot is from the fresh perspective of an expert observer of the metropolises of the world. . . ."

The expert observer's first article was devoted to a comparatively calm over-all picture of New York's present constitution and its history, except that near the beginning of his story, in picturing the extremes of attack and defense concerning the city, he cited the "superlatives" which "are not spared by its critics." Since the *Tribune* could be cited legitimately as New York's severest critic, it appeared to be the Colonel himself who was calling it "the modern Babylon; it is a Sodom and Gomorrah of sin; it is the octopus which battens on the rest of the United States and strangles the free enterprise of competitors. Further, its slums are just behind its palaces—the sordid reality behind the pretentious facade. . . . Its young people are immoral and its mature people burned out. It is the reservoir of evil from which disintegrating revolutionary doctrine spreads over the country."

By January 4, Mr. Small was in his stride. His piece for that day was headlined: CUBISTIC ALIENS PUZZLE HOOSIER VISITORS IN N.Y. FURTIVE FACES IN CROWDS AROUSE DISTRUST. The story began:

"The very sight of the New York crowd antagonizes the visitor who has come into New York from his farm or small town on the western plains. These frizzy heads, these broad, brutish cheekbones, these furtive, piggy eyes, these slack mouths—the whole 'muffin-faced race' which he sees in the New York subway—how different from the well-marked features of his neighbors back in Iowa or Kansas.

"So comes the conclusion that New York is an alien force inside the United States. The westerner finds a new reason for distrusting and loathing the city, if he did not have plenty of reasons already. Then comes the corollary when he hears of some novel political or social idea, which obviously was launched from New York. It is the fault of New York's foreign colonies, importing old world ideas."

Next day the series was devoted to New York's magazines, newspapers and book-publishing houses. Mr. Small was willing to concede that the city led the nation with its magazines and books, but he was concerned about "what Westbrook Pegler calls the butcher paper weeklies. . . . They go into schools and libraries, where each copy may reach hundreds and they have their bands of devoted zealots. These are precisely the ones who make their numbers count. They talk in clubs. They write to newspapers and congressmen. Each week the nation's cosmic busybodies get a fresh dose of 'liberalism' and 'leftism' from the professional thinkers of Manhattan."

As for the New York newspapers, Mr. Small dismissed them as "purely local." In this tone he brushed aside the New York *Times* in words indirectly uncomplimentary to his own paper: "At present the New York *Times* has some aspirations to being national, and is taken seriously by many people. How many of them, however, would read it exclusively and disregard the local press? On international events, certainly it is the only newspaper of ours which attempts to give the sort of coverage that might be approved by a future historian."

The subject of the following day's sermon was education in New York, headlined: NEW YORK LACKS UNIVERSITIES OF A REAL CALIBER. JOKE ABOUT DEGREES GIVEN BY COLUMBIA. Mr. Small, a Harvard man himself and an ex-English instructor at the University of Wisconsin, wrote:

"New York is the great gathering point in the United States for people who take their own thinking capacity seriously. Such often gather in or around educational institutions; yet in this respect New York has no such preeminence as in finance or the theater.

". . . As American institutions became Germanized in the closing decades of the century, they founded graduate schools and went into the Ph.D. business for themselves. Columbia, in its great expansion under the presidency of the restless Nicholas Murray Butler, put the Ph.D. degree on a mass production basis.

". . . Despite its showing of professors concerned only with their business or who have a positively conservative point of view, the prevailing tone of Teachers' college (Columbia) is 'radical,' 'liberal,' 'leftist.' You probably know what that means in these times. It has nothing to do with liberalism, as the word was once used, nor with 'radicalism' in the sense of opposition to orthodoxy. Instead, it is concerned with keeping to the orthodox line in its special religion, Marxism, with allowances for new revelations which come out of Moscow."

The final article in Mr. Small's New York series reiterated a familiar McCormick theme, indicated in its headline: A SUBSERVIENT NEW YORK BREWS AMERICA'S WARS. BRITAIN INFLUENCES EVEN ITS EDUCATION. It began: "The wars—or better the world saving crusades—of the United States are to a great extent brewed in New York. Here we confront intangibles like emotions and states of mind, which are translated into policy, or better into action. Again, on analysis, this intangible is something not special to New York, but New York is the decisive factor because it is a focal point.

"This intangible may be briefly called colonial mindedness. Impolitely, but accurately, it could be called subserviency to the British."

After a long development of this theme the article and the series closed with a comparatively mild speculation on New York's future. Mr. Small believed there was "good reason to think it may lose its overshadowing position in American life. Already much of it looks like a hangover from the horse and buggy or early automobile ages."

Mr. Small followed this daily series a month later with some Sunday articles on "The Periodicals America Reads." Concealed amid the verbiage were the poison darts which the *Tribune* never fails to throw. The articles were obvious propaganda pieces, as these samples will indicate:

*Of* Time: "The *Collier's* reader will like *Time* as being more systematically devoted to his intellectual uplift than a periodical which is largely fiction. The highbrows find in it the material on which their superior spirits can work and enable them to be earnest about the world."

*Of the "slick" magazines:* "So I should confidently expect if Roosevelt ever founded a formal dynasty to find nice little articles on the advantages of monarchy, and cute little anecdotes about royal eccentricities. Likewise if we ever go the whole way into communism, and these periodicals can still publish, there will be some snappy writing on the wisdom and energy of the ruling commissars, but not too snappy."

*In praise of the* Saturday Evening Post: "In those same years the *Post* also braved the ravings of our vociferous 'leftists' by pointing out some of the consequences of the orgy at Washington."

*On Mr. Small's boredom with magazine fiction:* "The advertisements seem to me more interesting than the fiction . . . and they probably are a more accurate picture of American ideals." (Probably a reference to Nash-Kelvinator's "don't-let-them-change-anything" series.)

*On Henry Luce:* "In the agitation which preceded the entry of the United States into the war Luce was on the side he was bound to take as a result of his early influences. He was born and spent his formative years in a missionary colony in China, exactly the sort of environment where the idea of the Anglo-Saxon community is taken for granted. His schooling at Hotchkiss, Yale, and Oxford was bound only to strengthen this assumption. *Time*, to be sure, by its policy could not come out openly for American participation in the war. But it did everything it could to make such a course acceptable to our public opinion, both by its slant on the presentation of news and its insinuations about the motives of any one who questioned the righteousness of either the western allies or of Russia."

*In defense of the* Reader's Digest: "More harsh words are undoubtedly coming the *Digest's* way for its recent condensation of the book 'Report on the Russians,' by William L. White. This Mr. White appears to give the Russians a perfectly fair deal, but in some passages he shows that life in Russia is far from being any carnival; in fact, it's just plain awful. That will never do; what the professional friends of Russia in America want is not a fair deal."

There was a polite fiction at the head of Mr. Small's articles: "The opinions stated in the following article are Mr. Small's and do not necessarily coincide with those of *The Tribune*."

Oddly, Mr. Small's opinions appeared to coincide neatly with the *Tribune's* in every respect. The Colonel moves in mysterious ways his mission to perform.

# Chapter 8

## SPHERE OF INFLUENCE

IN THE DAYS of America First and the battle over intervention, the *Tribune* became the idol of all the fly-by-night chauvinistic publications in America. They quoted the *Tribune* frequently and with admiration. McCormick may have been embarrassed by this unsought-for support, just as some liberals are embarrassed when the *Daily Worker* has kind words for them. A newspaper cannot be judged solely by the people or publications who quote it, of course, but in the *Tribune's* case its editorial pronouncements provided ammunition for the campaign against the war effort conducted by persons eventually indicted for sedition by the government.

The Republican Nationalist Revival Committee, operated by such notorious isolationist figures as Elizabeth Dilling and Joe McWilliams, once urged McCormick to run for President. He did not think it necessary to acknowledge the proposition one way or the other. Edward James Smythe organized a Republican Nationalist party which also proposed McCormick for President. John Roy Carlson, in *Under Cover*, said of Smythe that he had "committed every political vice permitted under the slogan 'Christian-American-Patriotism.'" Small wonder that McCormick took no notice of Smythe or his nomination. Harry Jung, founder of the American Vigilant Intelligence Federation and its vicious organ, *The Vigilante*, wholesale Chicago distributor of the anti-Semitic "Protocols of the Elders of Zion," and a prominent figure in "America" movements, was once referred to by McCormick as an "authority on communism."

One example of the kind of use the more violent anti-Roosevelt elements in American life made of *Tribune* editorials is illustrated by an article called "Nothing but the Truth," which first appeared in an obscure publication, *The Constitutionalist,* and was later distributed in quantity by the Women's League for Political Education, in Chicago. This article quoted a *Tribune* editorial: "Mr. Roosevelt has trampled on the constitution deliberately and for his personal advantage. He has violated his oath of office. What he has done is impeachable." The article added: "WHAT HE IS PREPARING TO DO IS UNSPEAKABLE!"

An even more widely quoted *Tribune* editorial appeared in such publications as C. Leon de Aryan's weekly, *The Broom.* This editorial, so like one of Medill's that it might have been written by him, read in part:

## ENEMIES WHOM WE WELCOME

The *Tribune* has its share of critics whom we respect and with whom we disagree. It also has a wide circle of vicious enemies whose attacks we welcome because, in addition to its own reputation, this newspaper is vouched for by these attacks made on it by the enemies of America and Americans.

We are libeled and slandered from time to time by cockroach commentators and the vermin press. We enjoy the hatred of Hatchetman Ickes, the gents' room patriot Winchell, Prevaricating Pearson, the little Cecil Brown, who is trying to prove that he can smell as bad as the big boys. Our abusers include the Adler newspaper chain, whose formula for journalistic success is an editor on each side of the street and a business office in the middle; Mr. Field, who has amalgamated expatriate dollars with British snobbery and Communist theology; and others too disreputable to mention.

Since the *Tribune* isn't a candidate for anything it should be obvious to our readers as it is to ourselves why we are subjected to these attacks. The attackers hope to distract our attention from the patriotic task of ridding this nation of the fatal, un-American curse of Roosevelt's New Deal. They realized the futility of defending the defendant and so have adopted the old dodge of prosecuting the prosecutor. We do not intend to be distracted. We will keep driving toward our objective, but will advise our readers from time to time of any additions to the pack that yaps at our carriage wheels.

Another publication of the same stripe, Court Asher's *X-ray*, which was barred from the mails in 1942 but reappeared later, printed one of the most bitter *Tribune* editorials on August 19, 1944. Even though it was written in the heat of a political campaign, its irresponsibility can scarcely be excused on that score. It read:

## INVITATION TO MURDER

Several years ago, when the Communists were calling Mr. Roosevelt an imperialist war monger, Atty. Gen. Biddle held that the Communist aim in America was to overthrow the government of the United States "by force and violence." At that time Hitler and Stalin were leagued together in looting Poland. Communists were sabotaging the American armament program. Then Hitler invaded Russia and the New Dealers sold out the Democratic party to the Communists.

The sellout was profitable to both parties, but the Communists prospered most because they now control the New Deal party and have Mr. Biddle in their pocket. They are stronger and more active than ever. Moscow ordered them to change their label when the third international allegedly was disbanded, but the Communist party in America was not liquidated. It became fronts and political action groups and its leaders got on the New Deal pay roll. The Communist party platform of 1932 gives the most honest statement of what they intend to do, and that aim hasn't been changed either. They plan to rally the "oppressed masses . . . under Communist leadership in the revolutionary struggle to overthrow capitalism and to establish a government in the United States of workers and farmers."

This is not going to take place without bloodshed. The New Dealers may hold back the revolution for a time by advancing the Communists' plans almost to fruition, but when the New Deal leaders have served their purpose they will get the ax. The Communists intend to overthrow capitalism, which is another way of saying they intend to destroy property rights everywhere. They cannot do this without revolution and murder, and that is what the phrase "revolutionary struggle" means.

The Communists will move as far as they can within the framework of representative government, paying lip service to what they call "democratic principles." If they ever become so strong they know they cannot lose, they will take the "struggle" on from there, by the bloody means they demonstrated so well in soviet Russia. They not only intend to plunder all property, but they intend to murder millions of Americans. They talk now about obtaining the "means of production" for the people. In Russia, the means of production often was a peasant's last cow, and if he did not surrender it to the commissars, he was shot.

The people who support the New Deal ticket this November are supporting the Communists and building them up for the day when they plan to bring the red terror sweeping down upon America. A New Deal vote is an invitation to murder.

This kind of writing was picked up eagerly in Berlin and Tokyo. Often the *Tribune* had the experience of hearing its own editorials quoted approvingly by our country's enemies in propaganda broadcasts beamed to the fighting fronts, and to America itself. Thus it provided ammunition for the enemy, a fact that it cannot dodge.

Sometimes the enemy radio quoted the *Tribune* without needing to add any propaganda devices of its own. On August 8, 1944, Radio Tokyo beamed this Domei broadcast to the general Pacific area, as recorded by FCC monitors: "In a critical editorial 'Blunders in Burma,' the Chicago *Tribune* charged the ineptitude of the Burma campaign and its inability to get going is largely the responsibility of Commander in Chief Lord Mountbatten. . . . The paper said, 'Public opinion in this country is not going to allow the British to cover up their mistakes in Burma indefinitely, and there will be a rising demand either to withdraw American participation from that theater or to turn the command over to somebody like Gen. Stilwell, who has experience in something besides Commando raids.' The paper declared Roosevelt made one of his greatest mistakes in this war when he allowed American armies and fighting units to be merged with those of his Allies under foreign commanders."

At other times these foreign broadcasts were more strictly in the propaganda pattern. Radio Tokyo sent this broadcast in English to western United States and Latin America on April 28, 1943, as monitored by the FCC: "America's designs on Britain have become so apparent of late that the whole world can't fail to see that the United States is only helping her victim. . . . The most candid and outspoken propounder of America's tradition of a [taking?] policy is none other than Robert McCormick, publisher of the Chicago *Tribune*. In the Sunday issue of his paper McCormick went on to say that if Britain, China and Australia can hope for further strengthening of their diplomatic [word missing], trade and currency through the aid of the United States, these countries must expect to be incorporated into the United States as new states. It took the owner of the world's largest newspaper in America to make public America's real motives in this war."

Radio Berlin's exploitation was in the same vein. An example is Hans Hertel's German home service broadcast of August 20, 1944, recorded here by FCC monitors. Hertel discussed American air losses and remarked that it was readily intelligible why such "leading American newspapers as, for example, the Chicago *Tribune*, the New York *Daily News* and the Washington *Times-Herald* have recently stressed again and again that Americans have to bear the brunt of the fighting in Europe and that the British are obviously determined to fight to the last American."

The Chicago *Sun* on April 6, 1945, undertook to prove the paper disloyal by its own definitions. These definitions were set forth in 1917 in answer to a libel suit brought by Mayor Thompson. The *Tribune's* plea, filed in circuit court, charged that Thompson was disloyal because of his public statements and articles printed in the *Republican*, which the paper described as Thompson's mouthpiece. The suit ended in a mistrial, but the *Tribune's* plea stands as at least an embarrassing reminder if nothing more:

The *Tribune* asserted Thompson was disloyal because his "acts and conduct" showed that he was opposed to the entry of the United States into war against the German Empire. A *Tribune* editorial on January 29, 1941, one of many such: "Today we are opposing America's entrance into the war and this time the majority is impressed as we are with the probability that dictatorship and ruin will be America's reward if we go in."

The *Tribune* asserted that after war was declared Thompson "continued to oppose the policies of the President of the United States and of the government in and about the prosecution of the war." Two *Tribune* editorial excerpts among many: "Mr. Roosevelt continually refers to himself as commander in chief in the effort to win public acceptance of rash, ill-considered and disruptive policies of government." (July 7, 1943.) "There is something very wrong with the Washington conduct of the war and evidence points to the self-conscious commander in chief." (February 23, 1943.)

The *Tribune* asserted that the *Republican* on August 18, 1917, made the disloyal statement "in substance that the President of the United States is a monarch, who might as well have the title of king or emperor." One of many *Tribune* editorials on this subject, printed February 2, 1939: "The White House has become an imperial palace and Mr. Roosevelt is acting as if he were the absolute ruler of people who had nothing to say about their own destiny and who could be sold into war as lightly as if they were eighteenth century Hessians."

The *Tribune* asserted that Thompson disloyally said: "Our national officers seem to have their minds set on seeing how much they can spend and how much food they can ship out. It is time they considered their firesides at home." *Tribune* editorial of October 17, 1942: "Everybody [meaning Washington officials] is out to do his stuff in the biggest way possible, spending the greatest amount of funds, and to hell with the country."

In brief, when Thompson said it in 1917 it was disloyalty. When the *Tribune* said it twenty-five years later it was Americanism.

## Chapter 9

# PROFIT AND LOSS

THE FINANCIAL FOUNDATION upon which the world of McCormick rests is difficult to analyze because the *Tribune* is extremely reticent about disclosing the details of its corporate structure or its ledger books, although it often rails at government and labor for precisely the same reticence. Neither of the two standard financial books, Moody's and Poor's, mentions the *Tribune*, daily or Sunday; WGN; the Tribune Syndicate; or any other *Tribune* enterprise. Other Chicago newspapers and radio stations are listed.

The facts that are known, however, only emphasize what a tremendous, far-reaching financial structure the McCormick-Patterson empire encompasses. There has never been any accurate appraisal of its total worth, but a rough estimate would place the figure between seventy-five and one hundred million dollars.

The cornerstone of the empire is the Tribune Company. Colonel McCormick is its president, the late Captain Patterson was first vice-president and chairman of the board, and Eleanor Patterson is a member of the board.

This company has one hundred per cent ownership of eight subsidiaries: the Chicago Tribune Building, net worth about six million dollars; radio station WGN; the Illinois Atlantic Transportation Company; the Ontario Paper Company, Ltd., of Canada, net worth about twenty-three million; the mills of the Quebec North Shore Paper Company; the Quebec & Ontario Transport Company, including seven steamships; the News Syndicate Company, Inc., net worth about ten million dollars, including the New York *Daily News*, circulation 2,036,634, and the *Sunday News*, circulation 3,724,775; and the Chicago *Tribune* itself, daily circulation 964,778, Sunday 1,339,368.

The Tribune Company owns half of the Chicago Tribune-New York News Syndicate, Inc., with the other half owned by the News Syndicate Company. Through Mrs. Patterson, the Tribune Company also includes her Washington *Times-Herald,* circulation daily and Sunday 499,885, as a virtual subsidiary, although Mrs. Patterson controls her own paper.

Behind the hierarchy of company ownership is the famous Medill Trust, by which Joseph Medill left the income from 1050 shares to his daughters Katharine and Elinor, and hence to their sons, McCormick and Patterson. Eleanor Patterson, Elinor's daughter, became an inheritor, and on the other side of the house, Ruth Hanna McCormick Simms enjoyed an inheritance while she was alive. Her husband, Medill McCormick, established a trust for his children with his inheritance when he died, and Mrs. Simms managed it for them. In 1941 *Tribune* shares were estimated as worth between twenty-five and forty thousand dollars apiece. The income from them will be passed on through the creation of trusts.

Next to the 1050 shares embodied in the Medill Trust, the largest slice of Tribune Company ownership is 905 shares owned by three families. Of these, the largest block, 500 shares, belongs to the Lloyd family, which has frequently embarrassed McCormick by its liberal streak. This ownership goes back to Henry Demarest Lloyd, a noted liberal and the first of the muckrakers, who married the daughter of William Bross, one of the *Tribune's* early owners. Four sons came to control the 500 shares, and one of them, William Bross Lloyd, achieved some notoriety as "Chicago's millionaire Communist." He was a pacifist in the first World War, which caused Hearst's delighted *Examiner* to exclaim in headlines: ONE OF OWNERS OF TRIBUNE ATTACKS WAR.

Another block of 305 shares was owned by Alfred Cowles, an early business manager of the *Tribune,* who left it to his three children.

The final 100 shares of this 905-share slice were owned originally by Horace White, an early *Tribune* editor, who left them to his daughters. One of these daughters, Abby, married John Mead Howells, the architect who collaborated with Raymond M. Hood to win the prize competition for the design of Tribune Tower.

Twenty-five other shares were distributed by Medill to employees and they are held today by descendants who have no voice in Tribune Company management.

The last accurate analysis of *Tribune* finances was made by *Fortune Magazine* in 1934, at the bottom of the depression. Although the figures compiled then are now outdated, they furnish a basis at least for estimating the empire's wealth today. In 1933 the *Tribune* grossed $7,000,000 from circulation and $11,900,000 from advertising. This total gross of $18,900,000 was a considerable drop from the boom year of 1929, when it was $43,100,000, and in the boom years of the second World War it is reasonable to assume that the total has considerably surpassed 1929's. The cost of writing, editing, publishing and circulating the *Tribune* in 1933 was about $16,000,000; it may be nearly double that figure today.

Net profits to stockholders in 1933 ran to $2,900,000 from the *Tribune*, $3,300,000 from the New York *Daily News*, and $500,000 from the syndicate—a total of $6,700,000 on which it would be possible to pay, if the company wanted to, an annual dividend of $3350 a share on the company's 2000 shares. Again, net profits today would be much higher—how much higher no one knows except some executives of the company.

The original capital of the Tribune Company was $200,000. This capital structure has not changed since the company got its state corporate charter in February 1861, and in seventy-three years it appreciated more than $38,400,000—an eloquent business argument for single-family control.

One reason for *Tribune* financial success is the kind of advertising salesmanship maintained by the late William Edward ("Big Bill") Donahue, who piled up astounding linage even in the depression. Chesser Campbell replaced Donahue when he died several years ago.

At the annual conventions of *Tribune* ad men in the Drake Hotel, Donahue invoked the kind of inspirational sales enthusiasm which was the dominating factor in his own character. In the depths of the depression he could stir his salesmen to "fight," even in the face of figures showing that the *Tribune* had lost 30,000 lines in retail display. To support his hard-selling methods Donahue could always count on a budget for his department of whatever figure he asked for, depression or no. For years the *Tribune* lost considerable linage by its refusal to take liquor and patent-medicine advertising. It now advertises liquor, and although it still rejects really harmful patent medicines, it came around to advertising such items as reducing tablets and salts.

A second reason for *Tribune* prosperity is the genius of Louis Rose, circulation manager, who calls himself "the Dr. Jekyll and Mr. Hyde of the organization." By this he means that he maintains a suave front-office respectability on the one hand and on the other the roughneck kind of personality that he has needed to fight Chicago's bitter circulation wars.

Rose's day runs from 3:30 P.M. to 3:30 A.M. Until six-thirty he is an executive at a mahogany desk. After his dinner hour at seven-thirty he sweats out the editions among the drivers and mailing-room employees, pushing and cursing them with a splendid impartiality. Like many other good circulation men, he believes that he has a sixth sense which tells him when big news will break that will mean big sales. He claims to have anticipated the attempted assassination of President Roosevelt in February 1933, when Mayor Cermak of Chicago was shot and mortally wounded. He sold 188,602 additional papers that night.

In 1933, with a budget of three million dollars and a staff of 462, Rose sold more papers nightly than any other circulation manager in the country—except his brother-in-law, Max Annenberg, of the New York *Daily News*.

*Tribune* circulation in 1933—and it is in much the same ratio today—concentrated about 450,000 copies daily in the city zone, which is corporate Chicago plus Oak Park. About 150,000 more, daily and Sunday, were sold in the retail trading area, a zone roughly within a forty-mile radius, including such cities as Gary, Indiana, and Aurora, Elgin, Evanston and Joliet, all in Illinois. Finally, about 100,000 daily and 250,000 on Sunday were distributed in the country zone.

*Tribune* circulation methods today are highly organized and businesslike. But old-timers recall the days when gangsters were said to be drivers of *Tribune* and *Examiner* trucks, and rehearsed at their newspaper chores for the later more serious business of assassination and beer running. The exploits of these characters are legendary, and most of the stories have little basis in cold fact. True, however, are the circulation stories of 1907, when Chicago newspapers ganged up on the *Tribune* and tried to force it off the streets, until Medill McCormick brought a charge of conspiracy against them and won a court fight. The same kind of hand-to-hand battle broke out three years later, but customers were so frightened that sales of all papers dropped sharply, which brought about a quick peace.

Probably the greatest circulation idea the *Tribune* ever had was the theory evolved by Max Annenberg, when he was *Tribune* circulation chief, and Managing Editor James Keeley that people would rather read an evening paper than a morning one. Here the talents of all the *Tribune's* chief executives were focused on a single point. Keeley's "personal service" idea contributed much feature material, including fiction, to the paper. He made it look like an evening paper by introducing daily eight-column headlines. Patterson added the final touch with the comic strips he introduced. The result was spectacular proof of the Annenberg-Keeley theory. The morning paper that looked and read like an evening paper established itself firmly in its own field and in time achieved the second largest circulation in the United States.

"Profits," Colonel McCormick once remarked, "are not a true measure of a newspaper's worth."

In the preceding pages there have been estimates of the *Tribune* historically, socially, editorially, ethically, and financially. Against what this composite record shows, consider the *Tribune* as the paper sees itself, what it regards as "a true measure." The following statement was published in 1927 in the Chicago *Tribune* "Book of Facts," but it could be duplicated in substance by any *Tribune* promotional copy today:

". . . Above all else . . . a newspaper must be judged as an agency for gathering and distributing news. Here *The Tribune* shines brightest. Its enormous circulation testifies to the merit of its method of presenting news. Mechanically, *The Tribune* is a model among journalists for the orderly, clean-cut arrangement and printing of news.

". . . On no other paper is a reporter more free to write what he sees as he sees it and to have his story appear uncensored. . . .

"*Tribune* readers take all the above much as a matter of course. They expect 100 per cent—24-carat—AAA1 service from the world's greatest newspaper. They confidently expect to be surprised each morning with a brilliant journalistic triumph, scintillating with wit, throbbing with human interest, replete with great stories of world events, enlivened by news of city and citizens, ballasted by departments of information and service. They expect the unexpected from *The Tribune*—and they get it.

"The sincerity, virility and originality of the Chicago *Tribune* editorial policies have made *The Tribune* loved, hated, admired, feared, quoted, denounced, revered, hissed, defended, attacked —but never ignored. The stand of *The Tribune* is a matter of daily gossip, not only throughout the United States, but in Europe. Notwithstanding this, every reader seems to consider that every editorial is written directly at him. The same identical statement which he passes over in all other papers arouses his bitter resentment in *The Tribune* because he cannot bear to have 'his' paper disagree with him."

A latter-day critic of the *Tribune*, reading this gem of prosody, remarked: "Don't be stingy with that opium pipe, Colonel. Pass it around so we can all have some!"

## Chapter 10

## INSIDE McCORMICK

AT THE HEART of McCormick's world is Tribune Tower. It stretches 36 stories and 456 feet above Michigan Avenue, resting on 60 caissons sunk 125 feet deep. *Tribune* promotion calls it "a symphony in stone."

In November 1945 Colonel McCormick turned the first shovelful of earth for a six-million-dollar addition to the Tower, which adds 2,252,800 cubic feet of space to the group of *Tribune* buildings bounded by Michigan Avenue, Illinois, St. Clair and Hubbard streets. It will rise eight stories from the Illinois street level, and will provide for the expansion of all *Tribune* departments and WGN's facilities, including a three-story studio large enough to accommodate a full symphony orchestra.

The Tower's lobby is known as the Hall of Inscriptions. These inscriptions deal mostly with freedom of the press and with liberty in general. The distinguished names represented include Charles Evans Hughes, the Constitution (First Amendment), John Ruskin, Richard Brinsley Sheridan, Euripides, the Illinois Supreme Court, Patrick Henry, Daniel Webster, Thomas Jefferson, Benjamin Rush, Thomas Erskine, James Madison, John Milton, Louis Brandeis, and the Gospel According to St. John.

For students of McCormick-*Tribune* history the most meaningful inscription of them all is the testament of Joseph Medill, written in the year of his death. Carved into the north wall of Tribune Tower lobby, Medill's words are: "I want the *Tribune* to continue to be after I am gone as it has been under my direction: an advocate of political and moral progress, and in all things to follow the line of common sense."

Medill's line of common sense, in its present manifestations, proceeds in a vertical line from the lobby, passing through the levels where three thousand persons labor every working day (twenty-five hundred of them *Tribune* employees), up to the twenty-fourth floor, where Colonel McCormick sits amid his editorial writers and the *Tribune* library.

In this man is the heartbeat of the empire. It would go on, of course, if he died tomorrow, but it would not and could not be the same. Here is a man about whom hundreds of thousands of words have been written, yet whom few can completely define. Here, at last, is the ultimate riddle of personality from which spring the ideas and actions affecting so many people, even affecting to some extent the course of history.

Theories about the Colonel fall into several broad patterns. There is the school which holds that no matter what the Colonel says or does he is only expressing his honest, sincere beliefs, to which he is entitled by natural and man-made laws. This school believes that no restraints can be placed on the *Tribune* without endangering all other newspapers, and similarly, the Colonel cannot be restricted in any way without placing in jeopardy the individual liberties of all Americans. To this school belong most of McCormick's fellow publishers and nearly the entire body of conservative opinion in the United States. It is also largely the position of the Civil Liberties Union, and so is paradoxically in this case a "liberal" view.

Then there are the people who believe that what the *Tribune* and the Colonel advocate is right. These include not only the lunatic fringe in national politics but those who honestly agree with McCormick, for one reason or another.

At another point are the people who regard McCormick as an arch-conspirator against social progress, both domestic and foreign, who puts his own hates and prejudices ahead of the common welfare—in brief, as a fascist or fascist-minded. A variation on this theme is that the Colonel is an utterly ruthless businessman who, like Medill, uses the editorial and news content of his paper primarily for business ends. An exponent of this theory, a Chicago newspaper veteran who knows the business thoroughly from both the editorial and business sides, maintains that the Colonel built

*Tribune* circulation by pitting one element of the people against another. For instance, he could win Chicago's large Polish population by his anti-Russian policies, and in the same way his Anglophobia could attract readers from the considerable Irish and German elements in the Middle West. This theorist concludes, "McCormick plays it like a pipe organ, and he pulls all the stops." To this general school of thought belong the more ardent liberals, most radicals, and all those people whose hatred of the *Tribune* and what it represents is so intense that they can believe anything about McCormick.

There is a middle-of-the-road school, too, composed mostly of people who don't take McCormick seriously. An old-time Chicago newspaperman who worked for the Colonel six years expressed this theory as follows: "I can't understand what the fuss is all about. That man will be built up to a Colossus! He's not that important. Why, twenty-one years ago [1924] everybody was laughing at Bertie. . . . You know, people enjoy seeing other people excoriated. When the pillory went out of fashion, the newspaper had to take over its duties. And that's what the *Tribune* does."

Only someone with the ego of the Colonel himself would arbitrarily declare that one of these theories is right and the others wrong. An examination of McCormick's life shows quite plainly that there is some truth in most of them.

Robert Rutherford McCormick was born on July 30, 1880. His birthplace, according to trustworthy sources, was a building now numbered 150 East Ontario Street. This building houses the Key Club, an exclusive membership restaurant. The story goes that when Katharine Medill McCormick was pregnant she had an argument with her husband and moved into the building, which was one of the family properties. She had been there only a short time when her son was born in what is now the Green Room, on the second floor. Although Who's Who does not list the affiliation, it is said that the Colonel belongs to the Key Club.

In the infant McCormick's veins flowed Medill and McCormick blood—the aggressive, uncompromising Medill strain; and the eccentric, die-hard, chronically defensive McCormick character so well expressed in Cyrus Hall McCormick, the baby's great-uncle.

The boy grew up among McCormicks and McCormick ideas. Nearly a dozen McCormick families lived in the four-block area around him. His own family in those early years lived in one of the North Side's first apartment houses, the Ontario, and little Robert amused himself by spinning tops on the boardwalks in front of the building and riding his high-wheeled bicycle around Waterworks Circle.

Like other boys, he read avidly of battles, many of them in volumes like *The Boys of '76*, in which British soldiers were villains and Yankees were heroes. Adding to the formation of this pattern, he listened to conversations between his father and Joseph Medill, both of whom were extremely nationalistic and ardent twisters of the British lion's tail.

Apparently the American government did not know or did not care about Robert Sanderson McCormick's anti-British feelings because he was appointed secretary to the United States legation in London when young Robert was nine years old. The family moved to London and there began the long period when he was to see little of his father and mother, as the elder McCormick went on to become ambassador successively to Austro-Hungary, Russia and France.

At first, however, the boy stayed near them while he went to a preparatory school at Lansdown. He was intensely unhappy there. In Chicago he had been a McCormick, with all the privilege and position the name carried with it. In English society, particularly rigid English school society, he was an outsider who did not and could never belong. Young Robert acquired an upper-class English accent, an English attitude toward dress and behavior and a profound distaste for everything English.

His misery was soon relieved. The family sent him back to the United States to finish his education at Groton, where he was one form ahead of Franklin Delano Roosevelt. The popular story is that the enmity between the men began then, but there is little if any real proof. Young Robert spent his summer vacations on Grandfather Medill's farm, or on the old man's ranch near San

Antonio, and was strongly indoctrinated by the patriarch in Medill traditions.

The year 1899 marked another sharp change in Robert's life. His grandfather died, the country went to war, and he himself went to Yale. Before he left for New Haven, however, he made an attempt to enlist in the Army, giving a fictitious age and name. The recruiting sergeant looked him up and down shrewdly and remarked, "Run along now, sonny boy."

At Yale he was only moderately popular because his shyness kept him from mixing freely, but he was well enough liked to make a senior society. He graduated from Yale in 1903, a six-foot-four, awkwardly stiff young man who was alone much of the time and felt that the world belonged to him because he was a McCormick. His favorite sports were riding, polo and hunting to hounds. He was, in brief, a standard Groton product aggravated by loneliness and the traditions peculiar to his family. He wanted to go to Annapolis but defective eyesight barred him from a Navy career. He took a trip to the Arctic on a supply ship and thought of becoming an explorer.

In the end he yielded to family pressure and decided on the law. He wanted to attend Yale Law School, but his father told him that he must study among the people whom he would have to live with later, and so he enrolled at Northwestern University's law school.

He had no affection for the law. Apparently he would like to have been invited into the *Tribune* even then, but his brother Medill McCormick, who was three years older, had the inside track and seemed to be the heir apparent. Young Robert took a bachelor apartment at the Union Club and began to sweat it out between his school classes and a clerkship in a downtown law office. His daily schedule was scarcely inspiring. He was in the office at eight-thirty and he was the last to leave it. All this left him no time for polo, hunting or the other occupations which had formerly filled his days.

McCormick made one friend at Northwestern whose life became entangled with his, and the history of that friendship is one

of the most illuminating episodes in the publisher's life. The friend
was Samuel Emory Thomason. They founded the law firm known
today as Kirkland, Fleming, Green, Martin and Ellis. In their brief
careers as lawyers the two young men came into early contact
with the *Tribune*. McCormick drafted a pension plan for the company; Thomason is said to have been called upon frequently to
settle disputes between the Medill sisters. Five years after Mc-
Cormick moved into the *Tribune's* management in 1913, Thomason became business manager—at the invitation of the sisters, it is
said. He rose in the business to be a vice-president and later general
manager, finally left the *Tribune* in 1927, and started his tabloid
Chicago *Times* in 1929. With that move the liberal Thomason
was transferred in the Colonel's book from old friend to political
enemy.

For a long time the two men were as far apart as the poles in
their policies but they never attacked each other personally in the
columns of their newspapers. The honeymoon lasted until early in
1941, when a *Times* editorial attack on the *Tribune's* opposition to
Lend-Lease, citing Nazi and Italian approval, provoked Mc-
Cormick into an editorial headed: "These Jackals Grow Too
Bold." In the text McCormick or an editorial writer referred con-
temptuously to "fat old men who sit in comfortable offices fanning
hysteria." Thomason took this as a personal affront and wrote an
editorial in reply, titled "The Integrity of Words." In it he wrote
an obituary to the McCormick-Thomason friendship: ". . . The
ownership of rich properties does things to some people—to some
newspapers. . . . Sometimes such owners mistake wealth and its
power for greatness."

The ownership that "did things" to McCormick actually began
at Northwestern, where he turned restlessly from law to cast an
eye on politics. There are various stories of how McCormick got
into the political arena, but the one attributed to the publisher
himself sounds most plausible. The suggestion, he says, came from
Fred A. ("Unser Fritz") Busse, soon to be mayor but then boss of
the 21st Ward. Busse sold coal on the side, and the *Tribune* was
one of his best accounts. In gratitude he told Robert W. Patterson,
McCormick's uncle and *Tribune* editor, that if the Patterson

nephew would run for alderman Busse would guarantee a Republican victory in the uncertain 21st.

As a campaigner McCormick followed the traditional line of politics, which was about as far from his own traditional line as possible. He rang doorbells, set up drinks in tough saloons and concealed his distaste for drinking with the sweaty patrons, and eventually, at the age of twenty-four, got himself elected alderman from the 21st in 1904. Some old-timers say that this victory remains the achievement of which the Colonel is proudest.

As an alderman young McCormick was even more incongruous than he had been as a campaigner. At first the rough-and-ready politicians who made up the City Council were inclined to sneer at the tall young man's fine clothes and his cultured accent. McCormick was oblivious to their open amusement and disdain, and shortly his fellow councilmen detected the quality that other colleagues would discover later on, namely, an unswerving tenacity of purpose and idea.

This quality was quickly rewarded. After a year in the council he was offered an opportunity to run for the presidency of the sanitary district, a sixty-million-dollar sewage-disposal project involving construction of a canal system from Wilmette to Joliet. He won the election and began a five-year period of service.

Again the political prophets predicted failure and again they were wrong. McCormick loved his new job. Dressed in hip boots, he prowled the various construction districts by day and by night. He placated the farmers whose property was threatened by the sewage canals, and he was the relentless foe of wastage and inefficiency. The *Tribune*-like direction he gave the project saved uncounted thousands of dollars and made what might have been a political fiasco a resounding success. By the time he had finished the job the Chicago *Journal* was moved to comment, "Mr. McCormick took office with the prediction of his opponents that he would be a failure, principally on account of his youth and alleged inexperience. Instead of realizing this prediction, the president has proved the American idea that young men of proper character, training and ambition generally make excellent public officials."

While he was engaged in these activities, McCormick found

time to organize his law firm with Thomason (a firm which is the *Tribune's* legal arm today), to serve as a member of the Chicago Charter Convention in 1907 and as a member of the Chicago Planning Commission. He was admitted to the Illinois bar in 1907, a year before he organized his law firm.

Meanwhile, too, McCormick continued acquiring unlikely friends from whom he would find himself alienated later. In 1906, on the North Shore Channel construction of the sanitary district, a young foreman named Edward J. Kelly, a good Democrat, had knocked down a recalcitrant employee, a Republican who happened to be a friend of Fred Busse and the son-in-law of a Republican politician in the bargain. Kelly naturally thought he would be fired, even though his boss, McCormick, had just promoted him to the position of construction foreman. He apologized to McCormick and was flabbergasted when the president told him, "I'm glad someone around here has got some guts. I'll see that you get more money." Next month Kelly got five hundred dollars instead of three hundred in his pay envelope, and McCormick saw to it later that he got a promotion to chief engineer. Kelly went right on rising after that until he became mayor of Chicago.

Some observers are inclined to credit to this incident the otherwise almost inexplicable cordiality between the anti-New Deal *Tribune* and the New Deal regime of Mayor Kelly. It was only with the utmost reluctance that the *Tribune* advocated Kelly's ouster in 1939, and then only because such a move might help unseat Roosevelt in 1940. McCormick and Kelly have never been friends since their sanitary district days, but it seems probable that McCormick, a good engineer himself and a great admirer of gogetters, admires Kelly's ability and his handmade career. It is possible, too, that he feels a certain responsibility for having started that career.

Political adventures came to an end in 1910, when McCormick at last entered into the *Tribune* management scheme. There are a variety of stories about his entry, but the most common one is that McCormick got a tip from a *Tribune* telephone operator that the minority stockholders and the Medill trustees were about to accept a ten-million-dollar bid for the paper from a syndicate headed by

Herman Kohlsaat, of the *Record-Herald*. The story goes that Mc-
Cormick, dressed carefully in morning coat and striped trousers,
broke into the stockholders' meeting and by sheer oratory convinced the *Tribune's* owners that the paper would be more successful if he and his cousin Joe Patterson were allowed to run it.

There are some indications that the story is aprocryphal and
that the entry of McCormick and Patterson into the paper was
probably accomplished on a much less dramatic basis, perhaps a
year earlier; but the legend is so attractive that its perpetuators
insist that McCormick for sentiment's sake wears the morning
clothes he wore that day at his annual New Year's Day reception
for employees.

In any event McCormick and Patterson did join the paper and
began to develop it. McCormick, learning the management of the
business, began to stand out immediately as an astute operator. He
worked hard and he had good teachers. One of these teachers was
William H. Field, who had much to do with breaking in Mc-
Cormick and developing the *Tribune* financially between 1910 and
1919. Field, as business manager, was in control while the cousins
were at war. As he learned the business McCormick also depended
heavily for guidance on James Cleary, called manager of publicity,
actually promotion manager.

During those prewar years McCormick's personality and character began to take form along the lines familiar today. His yearn-
ing toward the military life had led to a major's commission in the
National Guard, and it was not uncommon to see him striding into
the *Tribune* city room in his uniform, with a polo mallet in one
hand and the other holding leashes attached to three German
shepherd dogs. These appearances were made en route to the roof,
where he sat astride a mechanical horse and practiced polo shots.

He found time in 1915 to get married. The bride was Amie de
Houle Irwin Adams. Her first marriage, to McCormick's second
cousin, Edward Shields Adams, had taken place on her twenty-
third birthday. The Adamses had been close friends of McCormick
until they were divorced in 1914, and a year later Mrs. Adams
married McCormick in London. The court records of the Adams
divorce are said to have been destroyed.

Almost immediately after his marriage, so the story goes, McCormick found another reason to hate the British. He made a request to have his wife presented at court but was refused on the grounds that she was a divorcee.

The new Mrs. McCormick apparently was not disturbed. A pleasant woman, diminutive beside her husband, she found much to interest her—social affairs of all kinds and her painting. She produced highly creditable portraits, and pictures of animals. One painting of a McCormick police dog was reproduced as a color page in the *Tribune's* Sunday rotogravure section. McCormick was proud of his wife's talent, but he did not share her love of society. He withdrew almost completely from a mutual social life.

When war came McCormick served first on General Pershing's staff, then as major with the 5th Field Artillery, adjutant with the 57th Artillery Brigade, lieutenant colonel in the 122nd Field Artillery, USNG, and finally as colonel in the 61st Field Artillery, United States Army, before he was assigned to the position of commandant at Fort Sheridan, Illinois. He was awarded the Distinguished Service Medal, and in spite of numerous stories to the contrary, he did fight in the battle of Cantigny, for which his estate is named.

After the war McCormick came into his own. Patterson went to New York to establish the *Daily News* and took Bill Field with him. Cleary left the *Tribune* for the automobile business and McCormick was alone.

At first, until Patterson moved to New York permanently in 1925, McCormick continued his exploration of the paper's mechanical side, for which he had a natural aptitude and interest. He established the paper mills in Ontario. He learned the operation of presses, inside and out, and in fact owns several printing-machinery patents. He put millions of dollars into the *Tribune's* equipment, until it had the best mechanical establishment in the country. To McCormick goes most of the credit for the introduction of newspaper color printing. Only the high cost of color advertising prevented him from realizing his dream of an entire daily newspaper printed in color, rolling from the presses at the rate of fifty thousand copies per hour.

Before long, however, the *Tribune* was a highly successful business venture and the Colonel turned his attention to the more unfamiliar business of political and social evolution. The *Tribune* became more and more his personal political weapon.

Today his domination is complete and magnificent. He runs his part of the McCormick-Patterson empire, most particularly the *Tribune*, strictly according to his own whims and prejudices. Hunched slightly over his red-and-white marble desk, he shoots his ideas by direct wire to Managing Editor Maloney's desk. At noon conferences with editors and cartoonists he produces the thoughts, in monologue form, which come back to him later in the day for approval and polishing in the shape of editorials and cartoons. In the afternoon he gives the same kind of dictation at conferences with advertising, promotion, circulation and mechanical department heads.

The assignments called "policy stories" which are issued by McCormick under his famous RRMc signature are, of course, not peculiar to the Colonel. As types, they are familiar to reporters on most other big dailies, but on the *Tribune* they are inclined to be a little more on the fantastic side.

The kind of policy which governs *Tribune* news columns goes straight back for its inspiration to the kind of personal arrogance that moved Grandfather Medill to tell Abe Lincoln one day, "Take your goddamned feet off my desk, Abe."

In his relations with his employees McCormick is the feudal lord of the manor. He classes them, one supposes, with the people who express majority opinions. "Of course the people want this," McCormick says of such opinion, "but they don't know where it leads them. I do." He insulates himself from the world and gives the people the kind of newspaper he thinks is good for them. Thus it is natural that he is a paternalistic employer. *Tribune* salaries are good and bonuses are high. Employees get free dental cleanings, medical examinations, cheap medical service, life insurance, money from a savings-and-loan fund, and gifts of flat silver when they get married.

McCormick combatted the American Newspaper Guild in an unoriginal but effective way. He heard that the Guild had asked for sixty dollars a week as a minimum wage for experienced men on other Chicago papers, and so he gave all his men that salary immediately. The Guild has never been able to get even a toehold at the *Tribune*.

The result of such paternalism, not forgetting the free coffee which reaches the city room every night, is a loyalty that is intense on the executive levels. Among the working reporters, however, it is more often the kind of loyalty any good reporter gives without question to his paper, no matter what he thinks of the publisher.

The climax of McCormick paternalism is the New Year's Day reception in the *Tribune* lobby, where the Colonel in his cutaway receives his employees and feeds them coffee and sandwiches. It was at one of these affairs that Patterson is supposed to have remarked, "Bertie loves to crack the whip and watch the serfs march by." Attendance at the reception was bad one year and the Colonel declared: "If the employees are not interested in attending the reception, they are not interested in receiving bonuses." There were no bonuses. At the 1945 reception the Colonel and his bride (he had been married a second time only a few days before) greeted the serfs together. McCormick wore his usual cutaway and striped trousers, and across his civilian bosom were spread three rows of military medals and ribbons.

Sometimes, at public events, employees see McCormick with his guard momentarily down. One such occasion came shortly after Pearl Harbor at the annual advertising banquet, where the Colonel gave a fiery, flag-raising speech. After it, he raised his glass, proposed a toast to Colin Kelly and, after it was drunk, shook his head sadly and murmured, "The hardest job in this war is for the stay-at-homes like myself."

Such unguarded moments of sentiment are rare. Most of the time the Colonel's bearing is military and aloof. One *Tribune* employee says that McCormick is most approachable at the luncheons held four days a week in the Overset Club, a private institution for *Tribune* executives in Tribune Tower, and at the meetings held twice a week in the board room on the twenty-fourth floor. On these occasions he regales his executives and editors with dry stories. Sometimes a disparaging remark reported by someone irks him into a response. Personal attacks do not irritate him, but he is disturbed when people dislike the *Tribune* and on that score he once asserted, "There are people who are always willing to argue that the *Tribune* isn't the World's Greatest Newspaper, but those people are the ones who can't nominate a substitute."

To most *Tribune* employees, the Colonel is an awesome, aloof, legendary figure who manipulates their activities with an iron but remote control. His physical manifestations are not calculated to relieve the general feeling that working for McCormick is a little like working for God. As the Colonel walks down the halls of the Tower, he distributes benevolent greetings to his male employees, using their first names if he happens to know them, and occasionally stops to speak to scrubwomen. These exchanges are usually not banal but pleasant and original, though spoken with an effort. During the holidays his constant greeting is "Merry Christmas" or "Happy New Year." He begins these greetings exactly one week before each holiday, never varying from the stereotyped expressions.

His preoccupation with the paper adds to his ordinary reserve. On one of his rare visits to the theater patrons were amused to see the Colonel, sitting in the fourth row center, reading the *Tribune*, spread out like a flag, during intermission. He had beckoned to his chauffeur, who sat at the back of the house, and sent him out to buy a copy. After a quick look McCormick summoned his chauffeur again and instructed him to call up the city desk and make a correction.

Yet, in spite of this preoccupation, his insulation from what is really going on in the city room leads to some amusing tales which have become a part of the McCormick legend. Not long ago an employee originally hired for non-editorial purposes was assigned by McCormick to the job of correspondent. He sent back stories on the way to a distant post, but they were so bad that the cable desk had to take turns rewriting them. When he reached his destination, he sent back a long piece of copy so coherent that the desk was immediately suspicious. A rewrite man checked and found that it had been copied verbatim from the Encyclopaedia

Britannica. When this evidence was placed before an editor, he remarked: "Well, I'm glad to learn that the son of a bitch can read!" The Colonel had no intimation that the man wasn't making good, because the errant one had served the Colonel in a personal capacity and his assignment was an RRMc order. The cable desk decided that the place for this problem child was in Germany. He was no more able to write his own stories there, but he happened upon a sheaf of anti-Nazi stories hoarded by a colleague for a more opportune moment and filed them under his own by-line. The Nazis forthwith fired him out of the country. A *Tribune* reporter recalls that the hapless man's picture ran one day in the paper and a city-room wag cracked, "That's not his picture; it's a composite portrait of the cable desk!"

Another example of the Colonel's aloofness from his employees is the case of Claudia Cassidy, wooed away from the *Sun* to be the *Tribune's* music and drama critic. After a year and a half with the paper, during which she wrote under her by-line nearly every day, she contributed a book review of *Good Night, Sweet Prince*, and that week the book department got this note: "Fine Review. Why haven't we had this woman before? RRMc."

The reporters, as would be the case on nearly any paper, are more remote from the publisher than other editorial employees, yet they feel his hand in numerous and strange ways.

Before the forty-hour week went into effect they were sent out night after night to cover small, insignificant meetings in the hope that something might happen. This system, the Colonel's own, paid off in such stories as the one garnered by an astute reporter the night before a Roosevelt speech in Chicago, when at a meeting attended by only twenty or thirty people he discovered that the WPA was planning a special project to take care of the strikers from the Republic Steel Corporation. The story made page one.

On another occasion the *Tribune* city room whipped itself into an activity unusual for a smooth-running newspaper shop. Outside the Tower, Chicago was enveloped in a drizzly mist, but listeners to WGN heard hourly broadcasts urging them to drive, ride or walk to the airport to await the coming of a special plane. They heard broadcasts from the plane itself. Managers of apartment hotels and residential clubs tacked up notices on their bulletin boards, exhorting their guests to appear at the airport and greet the plane, rain or no.

When it was time for the plane to arrive, a damp crowd of a hundred or so spectators were huddled together, scanning the mists. Suddenly it appeared and the moist throng cheered. The plane landed. Out stepped Colonel McCormick and a family of monkeys which he was delivering in person to the Chicago zoo.

Another city-room yarn concerns a call that came to the city desk.

"Hello," the voice at the other end said, "this is Colonel McCormick."

"Good morning, sir," the desk answered respectfully.

"Can you tell me what kind of weather you're having in Chicago today?" the Colonel queried.

"Yes sir," the desk responded. "It's cool and cloudy, with a strong wind blowing."

"Thank you," the Colonel said, and hung up.

He was calling from London.

Not all of the Colonel's mysterious purposes are disclosed. One day a few years ago the city room got an RRMc assignment that read, "How much would we add to the known area of the world if the ocean bottoms were made into land?" The city editor gave the assignment to a new *Tribune* reporter, who had the reputation of being a geographical expert. The young reporter looked meditative. Obviously there wasn't any known answer, because the ocean bottoms have never been explored. He could arrive at a hypothetical answer, but that would take time, and he was busy at the moment. He tossed the slip of paper into his desk drawer and forgot about it.

Next day the city editor bore down upon him and inquired, "What have you done on that ocean bottom question?"

"Why, nothing yet," the young reporter admitted. "I haven't had time."

"Time!" the city editor roared. "Time! My God, man, that was an assignment by the Colonel!"

"The Colonel? Who in hell is the Colonel?" asked the reporter in innocent wonder.

When the city editor had been revived, he gave the reporter some explicit information and advice. The new man got busy and wired the National Geographic Society, which wired back that it could obtain the answer if the *Tribune* would finance three months' research. Thrown back upon himself, the reporter began to cover sheets of paper with figures. He finally arrived at the conclusion that there were about twenty-million-odd square miles of ocean bottom. Later the American Geographic Society confirmed his figure, stating that it was perhaps the most expert guess yet made. But no one has ever found out why the Colonel wanted the information.

An even more obscure piece of negotiation occurred when the Colonel commanded the presence or telephone number of Chicago's notorious alderman, "Bathhouse John" Coughlin. To its horror, the city desk discovered that it had no address or telephone number for Coughlin, and a reporter was sent out to track him down.

After a long search the reporter found Bathhouse John in a disreputable apartment building in the 1st Ward. Climbing the stairs and knocking at the door, he called for Alderman Coughlin. The alderman sent an intermediary to the door. The reporter, in some embarrassment, gave him the Colonel's message: "The Colonel wants to know if he can breed a couple of his mares to one of the alderman's stallions."

Leaving his post at the half-barred door, the intermediary disappeared and returned a few minutes later to report, "The alderman wants to know what're the blood lines of the Colonel's mares."

"Why, I don't know," the reporter gulped. He went next door to the nearest saloon and called the city desk. Armed with the information and refreshed by a short beer, he climbed the dark flight of stairs again and re-engaged the intermediary. After he had provided the necessary information, the reporter asked why the alderman wanted to know these facts of equine ancestry.

"That's so he'll know what to charge," the intermediary told him. "The fancier the mare the higher the price."

Nothing that happens to the Colonel is alien to his newspaper. A motor terrorist named "Indian Joe" once haunted the western suburbs of Chicago and one day halted McCormick's car. The Colonel had no cash with him and offered the bandit a check. Indian Joe refused it. Highly incensed, the Colonel instructed his automobile editor to start an investigation of traffic holdups.

The personal, vindictive kind of reporting is characteristic of the *Tribune's* Washington news, but here again, say *Tribune* employees, it is McCormick's personality that sets up the vicious circle. The Colonel believes what he reads in the *Tribune*, and the *Tribune's* Washington men, as do his Chicago employees, try to follow the Colonel's own lines of thought. Thus the head of the Washington bureau chooses his own assignment many times and naturally tries to find the one which will please his boss most, and he knows what kind that will be in advance.

The rest of the Washington press corps has never been able to decide whether the *Tribune* men take their boss seriously. Probably the *Tribune* reporters themselves are not always certain. There was, for instance, the Hoover campaign in which McCormick quite naturally supported the Great Engineer. The night before his inauguration the inaugural speech was wired to Chicago for release next day. It evoked a historic telegram from the Colonel in which he disposed of Hoover in five words: "This man will not do."

In Washington, Chicago and wherever else the *Tribune* has employees, they move on the empire's chessboard at the touch of the master's hand, and to the Colonel his employees are no more than chessmen. He once remarked, "It is the duty of the city editor to know the reporters, not mine." McCormick uses telephone, telegram and cablegram to make his moves.

Many observers date his habitual seclusion from the rough days of the twenties, when the *Tribune's* gangster enemies made the threat of physical violence real. Uniformed guards police Tribune Tower and it is said there are machine guns hidden in the building. McCormick's car is bulletproof and his chauffeurs have also functioned as bodyguards. A German shepherd dog, now of advanced years, follows at McCormick's heels wherever he goes in

Tribune Tower and rides to and from work with him. The dog keeps an embarrassingly close watch over visitors in the Colonel's office.

When the Colonel is in his walnut-paneled office, he is securely isolated from everything and everybody because the door appears to be a part of the paneling and opens only by an electric push-button control on the Colonel's desk. This elaborate apparatus may have been installed originally as protection against gangsters, or it may be simply a spark of McCormick's mechanical talent, but in any case it is certainly significant psychologically. Biographers who insist that it is there only to give the publisher an opportunity for amusement as he watches visitors fumble for a non-existent doorknob seem to have missed the point.

For the McCormick personality, when one takes a long, hard look at it, is an absorbing study worth more than the superficial treatment it usually gets. Physically he is a tall, erect man whose military bearing is an index to one of his primary obsessions. His face is a handsome one, in a ruggedly aristocratic way, with heavy arched eyebrows over eyes that often look tired and pouchy. His bristling mustache and thinning hair are a matched gray. He speaks in a deep, gruff, almost explosive voice. The Colonel wears excellent English tweeds and woolens, and he knows how to wear them well. About him is the poised, self-possessed air peculiar to great wealth and great egos, and to aristocracy everywhere.

McCormick's wealth enables him to surround himself with the strenuous entertainments of those who so often have no inner peace. He has a stable of Irish jumpers, a private hunt course, a private plane, and a forty-foot cruiser for deep-sea fishing at Palm Beach. He dislikes public amusements, particularly those which require for appreciation some degree at least of introspection—opera, motion pictures, bridge, backgammon, gambling. McCormick rationalizes his almost complete lack of normal gregariousness by a statement which happens to be true: "The newspaper publisher who hangs around clubs and hotel lobbies, who becomes a crony to sundry businessmen, cannot run a good paper."

Perhaps one index to McCormick is the obvious personality conflict which his actions indicate. Apparently he has the involuntary impulse to withdraw from the world, yet he cannot live with himself and must continually express his overwhelming ego. It is significant that his major overt actions are directed toward trying to preserve those aspects of the world which are familiar to him and to change those that are alien, or constitute a threat to his emotional life. The British have been a threat to his emotional security since his childhood. The Russians represent a political system which terrifies him because it is completely alien. The New Deal represents the same thing. He identifies it readily with Communism, therefore, and it rouses him to a more intense resistance because it is on his doorstep. The only way he can achieve security is to live in a tight little world from which all these elements are excluded and in which he need associate only with people like himself—hence his isolationism, which is violent and extreme in proportion to his psychological need of it. His preoccupation with himself is another facet of his personality which explains an inability to sustain interest.

If this analysis is correct, many of the Colonel's actions become more understandable. For instance, on his deep-sea fishing trips he carries a brief case full of reports and spends little time fishing. The tension generated by his conflict makes him impatient to go ashore after an hour or so. This tension also sends him home from baseball games after three or four innings, and from the theater after the first act. When he drinks, he shows no outward enjoyment and the chronic throat irritation which prevents him from smoking moves him to forbid smoking by others in his presence or in Tribune Tower elevators. Apparently part of his aversion to card games derives from the fact that they bring him into too close social proximity with other people. He operates a party in his home as efficiently as he does his newspaper, but once it is running smoothly, he leaves it.

McCormick cannot bring himself to make close human attachments. The ex-husbands of both his wives were about as near to being cronies as any he ever had, and there is a bachelor neighbor near his Wheaton estate who hikes over the McCormick lands with him, but their conversation is sparse. Away from work, the Colonel will talk to a man who is a technician long enough to pump him dry of ready information, then he will walk away. At the Overset Club luncheons McCormick does not mix with his executives and his guests in any ordinary sense because he monopolizes the conversation almost completely, and sometimes appears to be simply thinking out loud. It is a point of club etiquette that no one touches a course until the Colonel begins.

His tremendous store of mental and physical energy is poured chiefly into the *Tribune*. No other paper in the country gets the concentrated thought from a single brain that McCormick puts into his publication. What energy remains goes into his study of military affairs. He reads history in bed, and he wrote in 1934 a competent study of General Grant. Critics laugh at McCormick's image of himself as an expert military strategist, but Lloyd Lewis, noted author and newspaperman, who is an expert on such matters himself, is said to regard the Colonel as a sound man on many aspects of strategy, particularly Civil War operations, on which Lewis is an authority.

A typical McCormick day would follow this routine: up no later than eight-thirty, out without breakfast to ride or walk around his estate, driven to the office in his bulletproof car with his dog, work all morning, conference at noon, lunch at the Overset Club, conferences in the afternoon, home at night, checking the news with Maloney in the evening over a private wire, reading in the library or in bed.

In his contacts with people at the office who are non-*Tribune* employees his inner tension and essential loneliness express themselves in small ways. An editorial writer from a trade paper who was interviewing the Colonel once asked him a question which veered slightly from the original topic of conversation. McCormick snapped: "Young man, let's not get off the subject. I like my whisky straight!" In several subsequent meetings, the writer said later, McCormick tried to be affable but didn't know how. When he walked to the door of his office with his visitor for the last time, he placed his hand stiffly on the writer's shoulder in a fatherly way, and then quickly withdrew it as though he had told himself, "I shouldn't be doing this."

In politics, where his conflict finds its most explosive expression, he has done such unreasoning things as removing Rhode Island's star from the flag in Tribune Tower lobby in 1935 because the voters had returned a Democratic majority to the Rhode Island bench. In the same pattern, he ordered a daily front-page box, before the 1936 elections, which said, "Only —— days to save your country—what are you going to do about it?" and Tribune telephone operators parroted, "Good afternoon, do you know there are only —— days to save your country?" He could permit such incredible Tribune statements as, "Secretary Perkins urged Governor Davey to kidnap Tom Girdler and Frank Parnell and hold them until they ransomed themselves from the CIO."

Another outlet for McCormick aggressiveness is his fondness for flying his own plane, a Grumman amphibian. The story goes that the Colonel once decided that he could land his plane on the Fox River, near Wheaton. Told it couldn't be done, he did it nonetheless, and climbed out of the wreckage exclaiming, "You see, it *can* be done!" His dream of a private landing field on his Wheaton estate was thwarted by his wife, who raised pure-bred cattle. "It will frighten my cows!" she objected. On another occasion McCormick landed his amphibian at a factory in the East. The plane hit the ground, bounded, and flopped over. Wayne Thomis, a *Tribune* man, wrote the story as it actually happened, telling how the Colonel fell out of the plane and landed on his head. McCormick said he thought it was unnecessary to be so graphic.

It is reported that during the 1945 conferences on postwar air transportation in Chicago McCormick attended one of the sessions and was asked by a Chicago *Times* reporter if the proposed new Chicago airport should not be named in honor of General George Marshall. The Colonel agreed that the honor would be fitting, whereupon the *Times* reporter, with a sly grin, added: "And of course it would be known as Marshall Field." The Colonel said, "Hr-rumph!" and walked away.

One of the most publicized incidents in McCormick's life occurred in 1942. It is used by his critics simply as an example of colossal conceit, but when the whole story is told and interpreted

in the light of McCormick psychology, it is extremely revealing
in a far deeper sense.

The incident was an exchange of letters. On February 19, 1942,
McCormick got a letter from Jacob H. Sawyer, Jr., an employee
of the *Tribune's* national advertising department in the twenties,
now a member of the firm of Sawyer, Ferguson, Walker Co., publishers' representatives. This letter was an unusual document in
itself, completely overshadowed later by the Colonel's reply. Sawyer, in his personal letter to McCormick, unburdened himself of
his own conflict—a dislike of the New Deal and all its works, but
an inability to stomach *Tribune* editorial policy. He pointed out
that, in wartime, *Tribune* philosophy was "destroying within the
minds of millions of people the love and devotion which they
have for their country." Sawyer expressed his respect and regard
for McCormick as editor and man, and he wound up with an
ardent plea "to your conscience and presume to suggest that while
closeted in the sanctity of your prayers you ask to be governed
and guided by God's will and not human will."

This letter struck directly at the core of McCormick's own in-
security and consequently elicited the strongest kind of self-justification, which the Colonel poured into an amazing letter. Reading
it was like looking through a suddenly open window into a secret
room.

DEAR MR. SAWYER:

Thank you for your very temperate letter.

What the most powerful propaganda organization in the
world has misled you into believing was a campaign of hatred,
has really been a constructive campaign without which this
country would be lost.

You do not know it, but the fact is that I introduced the
ROTC into the schools; that I introduced machine guns into
the army; that I introduced mechanization; that I introduced
automatic rifles; that I was the first ground officer to go up in
the air and observe artillery fire. Now I have succeeded in making that the regular practice in the army. I was the first to advocate an alliance with Canada. I forced the acquiring of the bases
in the Atlantic Ocean.

On the other hand, I was unsuccessful in obtaining the fortification of Guam; in preventing the division of the navy into two oceans. I was unable to persuade the navy and the administration that airplanes could destroy battleships. I did get the marines out of Shanghai, but was unsuccessful in trying to get the army out of the Philippines.

Campaigns such as I have carried on inevitably meet resistance, and great persistence is necessary to achieve results. The opposition resorts to such tactics as charging me with hatred and so forth, but in view of the accomplishment, I can bear up under it.

This was the inner McCormick speaking, in the belief that what he wrote would not be seen by other eyes. At other times, making public statements in reply to public attacks, his policy had always been to counterattack and thus cover the driving need for self-justification. Thus, when Archibald MacLeish spoke against him, he would say only, "MacLeish is a Communist." Again, when *Life Magazine* classed him among the "Voices of Defeat," he replied, "It looks like a conspiracy in which the disreputable papers under Mr. Luce's direction have joined themselves to the crypto-communists of Greenwich Village. It is possible to believe that the leadership in this campaign of slander comes from press agents on the Washington payroll. . . . The job of the press agents is to keep the people of this country contented with defeat."

Nor could the McCormick letter be squared with his *Tribune* statements. If he had truly wanted to secure the fortification of Guam, and it is possible he did, he had repressed the thought because Roosevelt wanted it too, and therefore he was compelled to take the opposite view. This is shown by a *Tribune* editorial of March 10, 1939, which asserted:

"No 'impregnable base' can be established at Guam save at a cost for its maintenance which the American people would refuse to pay for the only purpose that could authorize the sacrifice. That purpose is aggressive war in the Far East, the protection of the Philippines, the waging of the war for China, and the British and Dutch possessions in the Pacific. The establishment, or rather the attempt to maintain an 'impregnable base' at Guam is unnecessary in a strategy shaped by the defensive and non-provocative policy demanded by the common sense of the American people. It is inconsistent with such a policy and merely a product of Mr. Roosevelt's megalomania."

In any event the damaging letter to Sawyer fell into the hands of the Chicago *Daily News*, chiefly because its amazed recipient ordered several photostatic copies of it. When the *News* published it under the heading, "Whatta Man," and Carl Sandburg remarked of it sarcastically, "And on the seventh day he rested," the Colonel must have been shocked deeply. It was as though he had been undressed in public. Sawyer was told that when McCormick saw the letter in print he was "fit to be tied . . . furious . . . almost threw a tantrum." A more probable reaction is the one described later by a friend, who said McCormick felt that publication of the letter was "a very dirty trick." He regarded it as a personal letter to a personal friend.

It is possible that this incident, in combination with later events, helped to drive McCormick still further into the seclusion of his private life. As this is written, he is said to be somewhat mellowed by age and a second marriage.

The Colonel has a town house on Astor Street, near Tribune Tower, but he is far more at home on the grounds of his estate, which comprises about a thousand acres in Winfield, west of Wheaton, Illinois. He has several other farms in the vicinity. The story is told that he erected a high paling around his acres so that curious persons couldn't look into the grounds. One side of the paling extended along Roosevelt Road, and county commissioners in charge of the highway found that in winter, when the sun was low and the pavement icy, only the side of the roadway opposite the Colonel's farm would thaw because of the shadow cast by the fence. The commissioners called upon the Colonel and suggested politely that driving hazards might be lessened if he would have the paling cut down about six inches, so the winter sunshine would be able to thaw the roadway sufficiently. Examining the figures presented to him, McCormick acknowledged that they were correct. However, he remarked, according to his calculations they could arrive at the same effect by moving the roadway a couple of feet to the north!

On the estate the Colonel sees his few friends and does his rare entertaining. In the past the place frequently saw the faces of Ed Prendergast, the son of a noted Chicago jurist, who once was a neighbor, and Captain Maxwell Corpening, once of the United States Cavalry, reported in 1945 to be in the Army again. Corpening used to be the Colonel's first assistant at the *Tribune*, played polo with him in his off hours and made himself useful as a sort of general trouble shooter. Once the Colonel asked him to determine why the estate's two black swans, of which he was very proud, did not produce offspring. Corpening called in the experts and made his report to the Colonel: both swans were males.

When Amie McCormick was alive, Wheaton sparkled with her gay parties, which she gave so well. Corpening often took her to the operas, horse shows and other affairs which the Colonel dislikes so intensely, but husband and wife shared other things: they often rode to hounds on the estate. Amie, however, preferred to live in their three-story town house, with its brick and limestone exterior, buried in ivy, and its elegantly quiet interior. Amie once entertained Queen Marie there, but her husband would not come downstairs.

As diverse as their temperaments were, the Colonel nevertheless tried hard to please his wife, often without success. He is, in fact, gallant toward females in his own aloof way, and he likes pretty women. With old-fashioned courtliness he has been known to ask women to leave the room while matters of immorality were under discussion.

Toward his numerous relatives the Colonel maintains an attitude of courteous disinterest, with a few exceptions. One of the exceptions is Chauncey McCormick, who lives near Wheaton. But the McCormick family, nonetheless, is an extremely loyal clan and, including the Colonel, its members stick together when they are attacked collectively.

Probably Amie was a link with his relatives when she was alive, just as she was a connection in many ways between McCormick and the alien world outside his special interests. His enemies say that the two never got on, but it seems more likely that McCormick thought a great deal of Amie and the kind of funeral he gave her is the best evidence of it. When she died in 1939, she was given a military ceremony, with her favorite saddle horse carrying her boots, reversed, in traditional style. A squad from Fort Sheridan fired three volleys and taps were sounded over her grave. Colonel McCormick could give no one a greater tribute.

For five years the aging publisher remained a widower. Then he astonished some Chicagoans by marrying the ex-wife of one of his best friends. The friend was Henry Hooper, president of the Lake Shore Fuel Co. For years Hooper and his wife, the former Maryland Mathison, a Baltimore society belle, had been friends and near neighbors of the McCormicks. Their Naperville farm lay on the acres of the McCormicks' Cantigny Farm, just beyond Wheaton, and the two families often fraternized in these rural surroundings. In town, where the Hoopers had an apartment on Lake Shore Drive, Mrs. Hooper was known as a devoted friend of Chauncey McCormick and his wife, and the Colonel was often seen lunching with Henry Hooper.

But in May 1944 the Hoopers separated after twenty-one years of marriage. They gave up their town apartment and Mrs. Hooper spent the intervening months at the Naperville farm before she got a Mexican divorce in the state of Tlaxcala on November 30. To protect her from divorce-law vagaries, Mrs. Hooper's attorneys got a second decree on December 16 from Superior Court in Chicago; the charge was cruelty.

The Colonel and Mrs. Hooper were married at five o'clock on December 21, 1944, in Chauncey McCormick's apartment at 2450 Lake View Avenue. The bridegroom was sixty-four, the bride forty-seven. There were some similarities between McCormick's two marriages. In both cases the bride was vivacious, popular and a lover of all the social affairs that the bridegroom disliked. In both there was the compensating factor of a mutual taste for horses and hunting. Mrs. Hooper, an accomplished equestrienne, frequently rode with the hunt at Pinehurst, North Carolina, before the war, and in Chicago is a member of the Du Page County Hunt.

The wedding was a major event in Chicago society. Its national significance, evidenced by an elaborate layout in *Life Magazine*, lay in the fact that it brought together more McCormicks in one room than had been seen for many years. Mrs. Hooper's two daughters—Alice, twenty-one, and Ann, nineteen—were almost lost in the gathering of the McCormick and Patterson clans, which included, besides Chauncey, Mr. and Mrs. Brooks McCormick, Captain and Mrs. Joseph Patterson, Mrs. Josephine Patterson Reeve, Mr. and Mrs. William McCormick Blair, Robert H. McCormick, Howard Linn, and Fowler McCormick. The absent members were Katrina McCormick Barnes, family rebel; the ailing Ruth Hanna McCormick Simms; Mrs. Fowler McCormick, described by *Life* as "retired"; Anita McCormick (Mrs. Emmons Blaine), the bridegroom's political enemy; and Eleanor Patterson. Various official reasons were given for Mrs. Patterson's non-attendance, but the most likely excuse was the unofficial one advanced by a friend who explained that "Cissy is still upset over Roosevelt's re-election."

His second wedding obviously overshadowed whatever depression the Colonel may have felt over the outcome of the 1944 campaign. *Life* described him as "excited and misty-eyed as any young swain." Mrs. Hooper, looking extremely smart in her long draped gown of gray crepe trimmed with gray silk fringe, appeared to merit the Chicago *Daily News's* description of her as one who possessed "both beauty and a neat turn of wit." Diminutive beside the Colonel, her purple velvet cap's waving purple plumes did not come far above the bridegroom's shoulders. She carried a gold purse, which the Chicago *Sun* noted had been "loaned for the occasion by Mrs. Howard Ellis."

Captain Patterson was best man, Mrs. Chauncey McCormick was matron of honor and Chauncey gave the bride away. The ceremony was performed by young Rev. Robert B. Stewart, pastor of the Wheaton First Presbyterian Church. Dr. Stewart would make Cyrus McCormick and the earlier McCormick Presbyterians rotate in their graves: he wears shorts in summer and walks with a Russian wolfhound on Wheaton streets.

There were refreshments after the ceremony, and family gossiping over the elegantly set tables. Then the newlyweds were whisked away to Cantigny Farm, the burgeoning ground of their romance, where servants had built a great bonfire to welcome them, tied white satin bows around the necks of the Colonel's pet dogs and shoveled a path in the shape of a heart through the newly fallen snow.

The only untoward incident in the entire affair was an accident. Before the ceremony Chicago newspapers were invited to send "a gentleman photographer" to Chauncey McCormick's apartment, and after an hour of waiting the gentlemen were permitted to photograph the bride and groom, after which they were allowed to drink of the champagne imported to lubricate the festivities. Then, according to the Chicago *Times* columnist, Irv Kupcinet, some of the gentlemen who had partaken too liberally put six champagne glasses in the equipment bag of an innocent photographer, as a gag, and the snapper departed with the glassware. When the hosts began to count their silverware after the wedding, they informed the newspapers that six champagne glasses were missing and that these glasses were distinguished above others by the fact that Napoleon had drunk from them. The glasses were delivered intact a few hours later, wrapped in a brown paper bag.

When the excitement was over, there was some speculation about the McCormick future. The more optimistic echoed *Life's* quotation from a friend of the bride: "This marks the beginning of a new era in the publishing world." Gloomier souls, watching *Tribune* progress after the honeymoon, thought it looked like the same old era. Much of the speculation turned, as it does at births and marriages, to the future of McCormick properties.

A veteran *Tribune* employee recalled privately that, four years before, a block of *Tribune* stock which one of the owners had sold back to the company was to be sold to employees of the paper through the Medill Trust, which gives the employees profits to be derived from the stock, although they may not own the original shares. (It is a Tribune Company rule that every stockholder may sell his stock only to the company, and if he dies the stock may not be inherited but must return to the fold.) There were approximately fifty employees who wished to purchase these substitute shares, and Colonel McCormick invited them all to his office, where he gave them a fatherly talk on the hazards of newspaper publishing in troubled times, particularly for a paper opposed to the New Deal.

"Here we are on the brink of war," the employee said McCormick told them, "and I would never suggest that anyone buy any *Tribune* stock."

He explained further that at his death the *Tribune* would go to the employees, since he had no heirs. The Colonel said he was confident that men would rise out of the *Tribune* organization to carry on.

That was one story. Another, which is a matter of record, concerns the day in October 1941 when McCormick strode into the city room and told his employees, with unaccustomed emotion, of his "heartfelt appreciation" of their loyalty in not deserting to the Chicago *Sun*, which was then recruiting. There had been a few defections, but not many.

The Colonel was quoted: "I want you to know that you won't suffer by such loyalty. I suppose that many of you have wondered what will become of the *Tribune* when I die. I am here to tell you that I made a new will recently and that one fifth of my holdings in the *Tribune* has been set aside for you."

The "I'm-going-to-take-care-of-you-boys" speech, almost a cliché in the business, did not move any *Tribune* reporters to contemplate retirement. If the subsequent report were true that twenty per cent of the publisher's stock would be available on liberal time payments, it meant that an employee who wanted to buy the smallest certificate available, one sixteenth of a share, would have to pay twenty-eight hundred dollars for it, granting that the stock was worth approximately forty-five thousand dollars a share. Even on the paternalistic *Tribune*, few working newspapermen have that kind of investment money.

Life on the McCormick acres these days pursues its tranquil way. The Colonel is fond of showing personal movies in a special room decorated in gold leaf at a cost of ten thousand dollars. The seats are luxuriously upholstered, in case entertainment palls on the guests. Outside the mansion, on the farm, McCormick presumably still charges his employees retail prices for the milk they buy from the farm's depot—plus a deposit on the bottles.

The course of true second love is apparently running smoothly. Mr. Hooper and the children are reported to be living on the estate, and neighbors say that the Hoopers and McCormicks go riding together companionably. There has been only one blot on this scene of domestic felicity. Shortly after his marriage to Mrs. Hooper, it is said, the Colonel ordered the doves around the house killed. Their cooing annoyed him.

## Chapter 11

## CREDO

ALL THAT Colonel McCormick is, and all that his empire represents, is expressed in his writings and speeches, and in the editorial columns of the *Tribune*. The editorials constitute a more formal presentation because they are cast largely in newspaper prose, but in McCormick's speeches and books the man's personality becomes clearer and falls more readily into the pattern already outlined.

The Colonel's first publication was a 306-page treatise on Russian Army tactics and fortifications, titled *With the Russian Army*, drawn up to enlighten the American public on the need for preparedness. It was published by Macmillan in 1915.

In the introduction McCormick complained that he was too young for the war of 1898 and that his parents would not let him witness the Russo-Japanese War. "I had been compelled to devote myself to business affairs for seven years to the exclusion of all wider interests," he wrote. It was his mother, however, who in 1915 used her influence with the Russians so that he could travel with the Russian Army, "not as a war correspondent, but as a distinguished foreigner personally known to the Grand Duke." That gave him "an exceptionally prominent position, which is refused to others. . . ."

Then come these revealing paragraphs: ". . . It came as a distinct shock to me. Ten years had elapsed since I had taken an extended journey. Nearly that much time had passed since I had absented myself so much as a week from business occupation, and I was loath to undertake the discomforts of the one and the idleness of the other. But . . . I wondered whether I retained the physical courage to go upon the battlefield.

"I knew that physical courage was as much dependent upon training and practice as any other form of physical activity. For years I had had none of this training, but, on the other hand, had been steeped as fully as any other in the cult of cowardice which has been such a distinct feature of modern American intellectual thought.

"However, the offer . . . could not be rejected—the only stranger to be invited to the Russian armies. The duty of bringing to America the information which 'was denied to others'; above all, to see from within the military organization of a country geographically so like ours and so eminent in military experience, was a call to patriotism that could not be refused."

The book itself shows that in those days McCormick was far from being an isolationist. He praised Winston Churchill, whom he interviewed, and thought Churchill might have been a great general or admiral if his education had been military instead of academic. The volume, near its close, contains this outburst: "And here I am home again at my desk, where the first thing I see each morning is yesterday's balance sheet, same as it used to be before, and I have written a book, not phrasing it as a wise man should with a single eye to sales, but with no higher aim than to serve my country, and as I look over the daily balance sheets I know that this . . . will not pay.

"But I have tasted of the wine of death, and its flavor will be forever in my throat. The great debauch, which periodically affects mankind, will come to us again, as it has come before, and when it comes I know that a million men must fall, while we are striving to learn in the stress of war, with the best men gone, the lesson that so easily could have been taught in peace. If my book serves to minimize the crime of unpreparedness, what matter a few kopecks more or less?"

Five years later McCormick published his second book. It was titled *The Army of 1918*, published by Harcourt, Brace and Howe. In it the Colonel returned to his favorite theme: "In the early days of my service, while on duty with the General Staff of the A.E.F., I expected to publish my observations upon the development and conduct of that army; but when the war came to a sudden and unexpected end, after a campaign in which I had no part, I abandoned the idea."

Noting that Congress had adopted no postwar policy and that pacifism appeared to be on the rise, he concluded his foreword: "I have, therefore, again changed my mind, and have recorded here my observations and conclusions as a modest contribution to popular comprehension of our effort, its difficulties, its limitations and its achievements, so that another generation as untrained, unorganized and unarmed as we were may not have to face an enemy under the fearful handicaps we suffered."

In Chapter 13, page 253, occur these extraordinary thoughts:

"We have finished another war in which our soldiers suffered unnecessary losses and hardships because of our failure to prepare, while the country at large has suffered almost nothing and the congressmen and the president who failed to prepare for the war have suffered not at all.

"It is, therefore, difficult to establish a military policy based on the lessons of the war. Congress cannot be expected to understand the subject. Our only hope lies in the formation of a sound doctrine which will be accepted by the public and by its representatives.

"We admit . . . the greatest schools of architecture, of art, of acting, and of music are in Europe. Before the war no doctor denied that a medical education was incomplete without a course in Berlin or Vienna. We approached Europe more closely in all these arts than we did in the art of war, and yet we find individual and national difficulty in admitting our obvious military shortcomings. Why is it? It is because fighting is the primeval purpose of the male. In modern times, when fighting becomes necessary only once in a lifetime . . . the urgency is no less great. The fact that it is the male mission is as true as in the stone age.

"Women have entered all forms of industry, of all the arts and the sciences. They play an increasing part in government, so long a masculine monopoly. From war only do they shrink. Here men stand alone, the preservers, the admired of women. Here they glory in their masculinity and resent any suggestion that the males of another race can excel them. . . .

"Of this our lawmakers are ever conscious. They may not think that every man is a soldier but they know that every man is a voter. Hence the blatant oratory, the misleading question: 'How do you account for the fact that our boys after three months are better soldiers than the veterans of Germany?'

"The fact is they were not. 'Our boys' did not fight in this war. Regiments of soldiers of a year or more training fought. Their efficiency varied in direct ratio to the length of· their training. . . . 'Our boys' never fought well. . . . The civilian cannot endure the battle. A complete metamorphosis must take place to turn the civilian into the soldier. Many times must a man overcome the fear of death in his imagination before he can rise triumphant over it on the battlefield. . . .

"There is only one way to have a good army and that is to have every man a soldier.

"Then each one will be exalted in the sense of his manhood."

Those words were written more than a quarter century ago, but the McCormick pattern was already there as it was in his first book: a sense of withdrawal from the ordinary world which included President, Congress, and all other people who did not agree with him; preoccupation with a single theme; suspicion of the motives and actions of others; his own actions based on beliefs held so single-mindedly that they took on the character of delusions; and a certain flatness of emotion, as of one who laughs or cries at the wrong time.

Later, in the decade of the thirties, this pattern was more clearly discernible than ever before. Preparedness had been his preoccupation and the central point of all his thinking in the old days; now it was freedom. In the intervening years the scope of his world had shrunk to a particular freedom—of the press. His suspicions were in a highly developed state, as shown in the *Tribune's* anti-New Deal statements, and this led naturally to the primary delusion that the government and its friends were in a gigantic conspiracy to destroy the *Tribune*. All these things contributed to McCormick's personality withdrawal. The pattern had been seen before in the McCormick family—in old Cyrus and in others.

In 1932, when the *Tribune* was embarking on a period during which its news columns were more indistinguishable from the

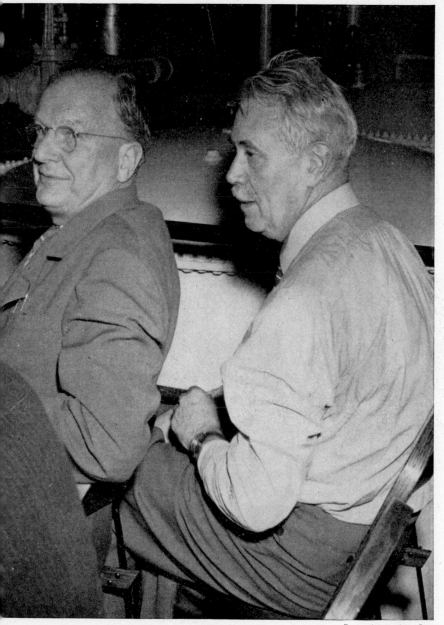

One of the few informal pictures of Colonel McCormick. He is shown with Senator Burton K. Wheeler (left) during a tour of the Ontario Paper Company's industrial alcohol plant, Thorold, Ontario, on June 18, 1943

Mrs. Eleanor Patterson, publisher of the Washington *Times-Herald*, as she looked in 1934

editorial page than at any other time in its history, the Colonel told the twenty-fifth semiannual convention of the *Tribune's* advertising department, "News should be printed in strict accordance with its value as news."

Three years later, on May 20, 1935, when the *Tribune* was conducting one of the most violent hate campaigns in the history of American journalism, McCormick could tell a mass meeting of Sentinels of the Republic, in Faneuil Hall, Boston: ". . . In different sections of the country different appeals to envy and hatred have been made. In some places, the plea has been made to the farmer against industry. . . . Foreign agitators have repaid us for asylum by both insidious and open agitation against our institutions, until today their policies . . . dominate action in Washington.

"Men who have been parasites their entire lives, have never produced anything and never intend to produce anything, who have always lived at the expense of others and plot to live better than the others who support them, have evolved a doctrine that we and our forebears have produced everything and all that remains to do is divide the fruit of our efforts."

Further on in this speech McCormick, whose paper had long been a more savage foe of Henry Ford than any union leader, suggested in ironic vein that the government take over Ford's wealth and distribute it, under the dictation of James Farley. He referred to the "earnings of the Ford factory, which we so savagely begrudge Mr. Ford."

He concluded, ". . . Confronted with this evidence, there can no longer be doubt in the minds of thoughtful men that ambitions are cherished in high places, antagonistic to our constitution, and fatal to freedom. Properly then, we meet in this hall, sacred to Liberty, to take notice of our threatened institutions and our threatened civilization, to send the alarm to our fellow citizens and invite their co-operation in preserving a republican form of government."

It is worth noting that McCormick almost never uses the words "democracy" or "democratic" in referring to the American government. It is nearly always "republic" or "republican."

In his circumscribed world the Colonel visions himself as the primary upholder of freedom of the press in our time. He compiled all his arguments on this subject in 1936 and offered them to the world as a book, titled *The Freedom of the Press*, published by Appleton-Century. The McCormick feelings of suspicion and persecution were at a peak in this volume. He wrote: "Newspapers are frequently under pressure from politicians in power. If it isn't the Building Department, it is likely to be the Tax Assessor. We bring out our papers subject to outside influences and inside inhibitions, and if we are not always fair, let us not be so weak as to favor the men in power over those whom they oppress."

The book went on with a review of recent attacks on freedom of the press, this history being rendered McCormick-style. He recalled the first of these "savage attacks upon our institutions," the city of Chicago's ten-million-dollar libel suit against the *Tribune*, which charged that the paper's criticism of civic fiscal policies had damaged Chicago's credit.

Then, he wrote, "came 1933, and the NRA and NIRA laws, passed without reading, by a thoroughly cowed and corrupted Congress. A panic-stricken public and hardly less panic-stricken press were generally disposed to submit to them without consideration of their effect upon the Constitution and the liberties of the American people."

The *Tribune*, he did *not* add, contributed materially to the failure of early attempts to bring order out of the depression chaos by resisting fanatically any effort made by the government to control any facet of its individual liberty. There was no thought of the good of all, except in rhetorical statements, but only of privilege, unrestrained.

The progressive development of the McCormick credo is an almost frightening thing to contemplate. On February 12, 1936, he was scheduled to give a Lincoln's Birthday address at the Chicago Civic Opera House, but Lincoln lasted for only a few paragraphs, when he was supplanted by this kind of un-Lincolnian talk:

". . . Dictatorship threatens to engulf the liberties of the Amer-

ican people. A band of conspirators, including one Felix Frankfurter, like Adolph Hitler, born in Austria, impregnated with the
historic doctrine of Austrian absolutism, plans to inflict this
Oriental atrocity upon our Republican people.

"The Congress of the United States has been corrupted with
bribes such as history knows no record of. Four billion eight hundred million dollars, or one hundred million dollars for each State
in the Union, has been appropriated to corrupt the electors.

"The unscrupulous organizing mind of Tammany, Jim Farley,
is at work behind the smiling mask of Franklin Roosevelt to bring
the end of self-government in the world. The conspirators write
statutes to violate the rights of our citizens and the rights of our
States, and send these to a thoroughly corrupted Congress with
orders to pass on them in spite of their unconstitutionality. When
their violations of the Constitution have been passed through
Congress by corruption, they tell the Supreme Court it must
not question the constitutionality of an act of Congress. . . .

"By virtue of the Constitution, in due time, all of you will vote
to elect your public servants, for you have no Kings, Fuehrer,
Duces, or Commissars to dominate and oppress you—yet."

Isolationism was a logical part of the development. In a Fourth
of July speech in 1939, McCormick saw an even larger conspiracy,
an even more sinister form of persecution: ". . . we are in the
middle of a conspiracy to throw this country into [another
European] war, and the conspirators are in partnership with a
conspiracy far greater and far more dangerous to our national
welfare—the conspiracy to scrap the Constitution of the United
States and supplant it with the terrorism and communism of
Russia."

On February 15, 1940, McCormick returned to the attack in
a speech given before the Lincoln Club of Jackson, Michigan,
developing the now familiar theme that "the New Deal has been
a persistent effort to overthrow the political and economic systems
and substitute dictatorship and socialism. . . . With our country
stunned by the depression, which he had so ably aggravated, Mr.
Roosevelt struck for a dictatorship."

He went on to tell of his experiences in Europe on a recent

trip, and compared Nazi methods with the Roosevelt Administration. Then he went on to cite Donald Day's dispatch from Riga in August 1936, wherein he quoted Communist leaders as saying, "We are going to work for the election of Roosevelt because we wish to strengthen our influence among America's many radical groups." McCormick related that New Deal newspapers "began a campaign of abuse" against the *Tribune* for printing the story, but that the paper "supported the integrity of its correspondent." Little more than four years from the day McCormick spoke these words, Day was broadcasting for the Germans and the *Tribune* was printing a three-hundred-word statement disavowing the man who had been its correspondent for twenty years.

"Heed well the warning," McCormick concluded his 1940 speech, "for the life of our Republic is at stake!"

The "Republic" became so much a part of the Colonel's preoccupation that he began to have the feeling that many of the things he thought and wrote about it were new and original, although to others they might be the most obvious commonplaces. Thus, in "How We Acquired Our National Territory," published by the *Tribune* in 1942, he wrote solemnly: "About a year ago the idea occurred to me to explain over a radio network the historical circumstances which stamped upon the Middle West its distinctive character. This brought out that all the Middle West did not flow from the Northwest Territory, that some of it was in the Louisiana Purchase." Explaining that he had done research in the history of other annexations, he concluded, "Finally ending at the beginning, I wrote the history of the early settlements which became states, thus producing, I believe, an entirely novel historical volume. . . ."

On September 12, 1942, the Colonel went a little too far in one of his grandiose utterances and brought the wrath of Canada upon himself as the consequence of a paragraph in a speech over WGN, in which he said, "Freedom of the press is simply the right of anyone to print or have printed whatever he wants without interference by the government. It only exists in the United States of America. In Great Britain and the Dominions such freedom of speech and of press as had been achieved were destroyed by legislation a few years ago and these countries have no constitutions to protect the citizens against the oppression of the legislatures and the courts."

British papers did not answer this remarkable accusation, but Canadian papers were indignant. One Ottawa newspaperman remarked later that a high Canadian official, regularly belabored by opposition newspapers, was heard to say that he only wished McCormick were correct.

The kind of freedom which the Colonel advocated was well illustrated in his opposition to wartime censorship. Other newspapers accepted the voluntary censorship code as a necessary evil, and most of them leaned over backward to observe its provisions. The *Tribune* not only opposed the code, but on at least two occasions appeared to have violated it dangerously. Moreover, McCormick's mental pattern made it seem perfectly logical to him to denounce the censorship as "a complete political censorship to control public opinion." He made this charge on November 2, 1943, in a luncheon address to the Chicago Association of Commerce, and concluded, "I take the occasion presented to me today to ask the Associated Press, the United Press, the International News Service, and the New York Times News Service to join with the Chicago Tribune-New York News Service to demand in unison a reform of the dangerous and dishonest censorship under which we are operating."

This appeal was greeted with some dismay by the Associated Press, whose Byron Price was ably directing the Office of Censorship, and whose board of directors included the Colonel himself. Many newspapermen were finding censorship as irritating on occasion as the Colonel found it at all times, and they were further irked by the blunders inevitable in such an operation. But scarcely anyone considered Price's direction "dangerous and dishonest." McCormick's appeal met with profound silence.

All this, however, was consistent with the McCormick pattern. No matter what was suggested by government officials, or by anyone not in agreement with him, he saw only conspiracy and persecution. Speaking at a community festival in suburban Park Ridge on August 7, 1943, he asserted that the purpose of an international army, then being discussed, was "to dominate the United States of America, to take away our Constitution, and our liberties, and put us under a dictatorship." He declared, "In spite of the wishes and the welfare of our people, there exists a diabolical conspiracy among us to destroy the American form of government. . . . At the head of the conspiracy are the power-greedy politicians, who have schemed tirelessly for a decade to overthrow our form of government, to be stopped in the last two years by the vote of the people and an awakened conscience in Congress.

"They tell us smugly that we must give up what they vaguely call some of our independence. They try to conceal the fact that they intend to take from us the right to make war and peace, the right to have our own courts, the right to trial by jury. They intend that our own Army and Navy shall be subordinated and made less strong than an international army and navy directed by a super-government in which the United States will have a small minority vote.

"They conspire to put us under the domination of three foreign countries, the freest of which, Great Britain, has abolished the right to trial before imprisonment and has incarcerated thousands of her citizens under the executive orders of a despot. Next in line, Russia, used Mongolian and Tartar troops to massacre ten millions of its people and has other millions working behind barbed-wire fences. The third country, China, has not now and never has had a government."

This speech elicited only a politely astonished and unofficial denial from the Chinese.

The most complete statement of McCormick's beliefs was made in a speech given twice within a few months. It was delivered first at the Detroit Athletic Club on December 16, 1943. By way of preliminary the Colonel admitted rather frankly that after he had been invited to address the meeting "letters from some of the members protesting my coming were sent to me. A few days later a friend called on me and suggested that I speak on inflation or on labor conditions in war plants. I replied that I am no authority on either subject and that insofar as I am known at all it is for my opinions on Americanism and international affairs." Then he proceeded to enumerate some of these opinions, a sampling of which follows:

*On the Constitution:* "I believe in the American political doctrine as conceived by the great Virginia philosophers, as expressed by Thomas Jefferson in the Declaration of Independence, codified in the Constitution, perfected in the Bill of Rights, interpreted by John Marshall, and expounded by Abraham Lincoln. Since later amendments have extended the Bill of Rights to all citizens, I see the need of but one more amendment—a provision to limit the Presidential term."

*On the Declaration of Independence:* "I believe in the first principle of the Declaration of Independence, 'that all men are created equal,' as strongly as the men who wish to rule others and those who buy into the foreign nobility—and their hangers-on—disbelieve it. Millions of men have come to this country in search of equality. Some thousands have gone abroad to avoid it and to assert arrogant superiority over the many by accepting servile subserviency to the few. Many of them are back here now as refugees and prating, of all things, of patriotism."

*On the government's fight against sedition:* "Attempts by the Department of Justice to imprison political dissentients have been defeated by the courts up to the present. The tyrannies of the unconstitutional alphabet-governments are meeting with increasing resistance and will be swept away."

*On the Presidency:* "I believe in the republican form of government. I believe in an elective senate and house and an elective President, and that the President is President, not 'the chief of state' nor the 'ruler of America.' "

*On freedoms:* "Freedom of speech and of the press include freedom to remain silent. Therefore, if you, or I, or anyone ask candidates or ask publications what is the backing behind them, they have the right to refuse to answer, and the public has the right to put its own interpretation upon this refusal."

*On his critics:* "Do we not perceive that the smears of the Winchells and the Ickeses, the misstatements of the Willkies, and the falsification of history of the Lippmanns have served at great expense to them to furnish audiences for men to refute them which otherwise might not have been obtained?"

*On the postwar world:* "I will say this much of the postwar world: We should insist on retaining such of the islands as we have saved from, retaken, or taken from the Japanese as will secure our future safety from attack; we should retain air bases wherever we have built them; and we should secure now, by treaty, the right to fly directly everywhere we want to go. We should make such other arrangements as will provide for our security. After that is taken care of, we may do what we can for the general welfare of the world. As one means to that end, I think all European governments should be required to liquidate their holdings in this hemisphere."

*On the League of Nations:* "The League of Nations failed because its members would not stand by their agreements. It is utterly false to say that our non-participation had anything to do with the failure."

*On the course of American history:* "Our history appears to me plain. As long as this country was true to itself, it prospered and waxed as no other country ever did; but when it accepted foreign tutelage, when foreign ideologies and foreign systems of government were pressed upon it, it fell into these catastrophes, the end of which is not in sight."

McCormick repeated this speech before the Executives' Club in Chicago on March 3, 1944, but he prefaced it this time with a statement on Communism which needs no comment.

"There are 130,000,000 citizens in the United States of America, of whom not more than 1,000,000 are Communists, and yet this million Communists, less than eight-tenths of one per cent of our population, have dominated our government for eleven years.

"They have done so because there are some 410,000 of them in New York State. Unless they vote with the Democrats, no Democrat can be elected, and unless the Democrats accept their dictation, they will not vote for the Democratic candidates. Bear in mind that New York State has the largest vote in the electoral college.

"These Communists and their abettors not only dominate the Democratic party but are actively trying to control the Republican National Convention as the New Deal did in 1940.

"As long ago as 1936 the Chicago *Tribune* exposed the Communist-Democratic alliance, but the suspicion was vigorously contradicted by all those who profited by the New Deal. . . . The fact is . . . that troops had not been sent to the Pacific in numbers to hold the Philippines and have never been sent in sufficient numbers to recapture them and free American prisoners suffering untold tortures in Japanese prison camps, because the Communists wanted them sent elsewhere.

"It was the Communists who taught the New Deal the tactics of smear and vilification, and the vilest of the vilifiers are Communists. They do the dirtiest work, while near-Communists deal in the less rancid language of the New Deal, and New Deal newspapers and radio chains publish these loathsome diatribes and call attention to them in editorials or more restrained language, in order to pretend they are not partial to the [Communist party].

"These newspapers are without influence with the people, but not without influence with the politicians who do not relish abuse and vilification, and have been largely reduced to silence. Modesty compels me to recognize that your invitation to me is due not to any oratorical skill of mine, but to a distinct lack of competition in standing up against Communist and fellow-traveler abuse."

If observers wondered what the end of the war would mean to the Colonel, they were enlightened by a speech McCormick gave before the Advertising Club in Washington, on October 2, 1945. American victories, he said, meant that "there will never again be a class of groveling snobs who will seek to be better than other Americans by admitting inferiority to foreigners."

In his best chauvinistic manner, the Colonel then went on to say with a straight face that the only serious defeats suffered by American units in the early stages of the war occurred because they were directed by foreign commanders. "All the distinguished admirals and generals of this war are Americans," he said.

Time and history have not changed Colonel McCormick.

Looking back over the history of the McCormick empire, and of its founder, there is a natural tendency to fall into one of two errors. The first of these, overemphasis, would cite the Colonel as the dangerous leader of Chicago and Midwestern isolationism, whose hatreds, prejudices and general personality pattern, coupled with the immense resources of his empire, make him a sinister figure in our national life and a potential threat to the very institutions which he professes to uphold. The second error, one of underemphasis, would argue that McCormick and the *Tribune* empire, wealth and circulation and publicity notwithstanding, are demonstrably incapable of wielding any potent political influence and constitute no more than a gadfly upon the hide of democracy.

There is something to be said for both of these extreme positions. A good many critics have been outspoken in the first view, and the most temperate summary of this position would probably be the conclusion of Robert Lasch, who wrote in the *Atlantic Monthly* for June 1942, in his article "Chicago Patriot": "To the nation's struggle for its life the *Tribune* has contributed suspicion of our allies and also suspicion of our government. It has fought to keep alive the dying embers of isolationism. It has consistently sought to obscure the true nature of this conflict as a worldwide attack upon our freedom and our civilization. It has endeavored to lodge the responsibility for war with ourselves rather than the act of our enemies. Is this the voice of middle-class America?"

To that question the body of opinion representing the other extreme answers an emphatic no. A telling argument on this side points out that the Chicago area—that is, the thirty-five-mile area including the city and its suburbs—has a population of 5,000,000 people. The working population of this area is 2,300,000, according to latest figures from the Chicago Association of Commerce. The daily circulation of the *Tribune* is scarcely a million, and a large percentage of that represents out-of-town subscribers. A reasonable estimate would be that the *Tribune* is read by less than half of the Chicago reading public, and many of these buy it for comics, features, or want ads, either ignoring or disagreeing with the editorial and news pages.

Chicago, like any other large city, attracts crackpots and fanatics. It was only natural that groups like America First and We, the Mothers should spring up. Perhaps the Middle West, because of its natural geographical protection, was a little slower to consider the possibilities and the proximity of war, but there were millions of Midwesterners who recognized the McCormick philosophy for what it was, and disliked him and everything he stood for, long before war was declared.

Chicago is essentially Democratic in its politics; it is downstate Illinois that is preponderantly Republican. In the 1944 election Chicago voted overwhelmingly for Roosevelt and also voted out the isolationist congressmen Stephen Day and Charles S. Dewey, replacing them with liberals sponsored by the Independent Voters of Illinois, and this in spite of bitter *Tribune* opposition.

Surveys also show that in the period 1940–44, when the anti-New Deal campaign of the *Tribune* was at its peak, the shift of voters from the Democratic to the Republican column in Illinois amounted to only 1.4 per cent.

In the rural sections of Illinois, Michigan, Ohio and Indiana, it is true that the *Tribune* is regarded as gospel by a good many farmers, but this is not a traditional isolationism, not the kind of hundred per cent Americanism that the Colonel imagines it is, but rather an expression of the Midwestern farmer's perennial opposition to government, no matter of what dispensation, because no national government has ever solved the perennial "farm problem," and all of them have levied taxes, the farmer's ancient enemy.

Rural America is changing, however slowly, and even though its problems, greatly aggravated by the war, have made it little more sympathetic than ever to Washington or to world planners, there is considerable evidence that the "one world" concept has penetrated to these last strongholds. In the 1944 elections, when the conduct of the war and a satisfactory peace involving our worldwide Allies were the real issues in nearly everyone's mind, an encouragingly large number of Midwestern rural voters rejected the isolationism of extreme right-wing Republicanism, as represented by the *Tribune*, and voted for Mr. Roosevelt's foreign policies, in spite of their distaste for what he did at home.

Thus a convincing argument can be made out for both over- and underemphasis. This writer believes that the answer lies somewhere between the extremes, and an explanation is attempted in the closing chapters of this book.

Part Four


# THE WORLD OF THE PATTERSONS

Chapter 1

# EVOLUTION OF A COLOSSUS

THE PHENOMENON that is the New York *Daily News* represents the peak achievement of the Patterson-McCormick empire in a journalistic sense. Whatever one thinks of its policies or its late owner, the fact remains that its 2,036,634 daily copies and 3,724,775 on Sunday (1945 figures) make it America's largest newspaper. It is a paradox that the influence of the *News* is in inverse ratio to its size.

Captain Patterson borrowed the paper's name when he launched his bold tabloid experiment in 1919. The first *Daily News* in New York was Benjamin Wood's afternoon daily, started in 1867 at 32 Park Row. Frank Munsey bought the sheet in 1901 from the Wood estate and sold it three years later to Thomas Charles Quinn. Under Quinn's ownership it became a Catholic daily, and died within a year. If Patterson had been superstitious, the unfortunate record of his predecessor might have seemed like a premonitory warning in those tense early days of the tabloid's history, when a jeremiad arose from the journalistic prophets who predicted that the *News* would not last six months.

One reason, perhaps, that the *News* got off to such a shaky start was that Patterson intended to beat numerous rivals to the gun, including William Randolph Hearst. Patterson and Hearst were only two among several American newspapermen who had observed the tremendous success of Lord Northcliffe's London *Daily Mirror*. But Patterson had talked to Northcliffe, listened to his advice and burned to establish a newspaper that would be as close to the people as the London tabloid.

At a time when Hearst had a staff going through dry runs of a projected tabloid in a shop on Frankfort Street, Patterson rushed his own plans to completion and the *Illustrated Daily News* appeared. Potential rivals sat back to see what would happen before they invested any of their own money.

The late A. L. Clarke was managing editor of the *News* when it began business in June 1919. On the desk as city editor was Sumner Blossom, a Kansas City *Star* alumnus, now the *American Magazine's* able editor. There were four reporters, but two of them lost their jobs in those early months, so the story goes, because of the paper's desperate circumstances.

They were desperate enough so that Patterson considered writing off the whole project at the end of two months, but it is difficult to understand how the paper could have been as badly off as it is always pictured. It was operated with large slices from the Chicago *Tribune's* swollen income, and the money was certainly not begrudged because it would have gone into taxes otherwise.

On the paper's first anniversary Captain Patterson sent his few hundred employees this message: "The *News* will be a success. I don't think one can say that it is already a success, because it is not yet self-sustaining. When it has become a definite financial success we shall install the Chicago *Tribune's* welfare plan, a substantial bonus at Christmas, sickness and disability pension system. . . . Other liberal plans not yet formulated are in contemplation. We expect to pass from red figures to black on our balance sheets shortly after we get into the new building."

By "new building" Patterson meant a five-story structure at 23–25 Park Place. The *News* moved into this building in April 1921 from its rented quarters in the New York Evening Mail Building, 25 City Hall Place, where the paper was first edited, and printed on the *Mail's* presses.

Patterson had gauged the temperament of his audience accurately when he launched the *News*, and as soon as that audience discovered it, the faltering ended. The restless, overstimulated mass mind of the twenties found horror and scandal in the new tabloid's news columns, escape in its comics and features, sympathy in its editorials, and subway convenience in its handy size.

In the beginning it was a joke in the trade. Other publishers and editors called it "the servant girl's Bible." Newspapermen on regular-sized dailies looked upon the *News* coldly and worked on it only as a last resort. Then, almost overnight, the situation changed. In a year the *News* jumped from eighteenth to eighth place among New York's English-language dailies; in two years it was in second place, behind the *Evening Journal;* within five years it was first. Circulation jumped from its lowest point in August 1919—26,636 copies—to pass the million mark in December 1925. The *Sunday News,* launched on May 1, 1921, achieved fourth place among its competitors during its first full year of existence and averaged 308,318 copies for 1922. Two years later it was in second place, just behind Hearst's New York *American,* and two years after that it overtook the *American* with 1,234,189, thus establishing a new Sunday circulation record in the United States.

When the *News* was four years old and a booming success, Hearst belatedly entered his own tabloid competition, the *Daily Mirror,* but although it survived, the *Mirror* never was more than a dim reflection of the *News.*

In his historic effort to out-*News* the *News,* Bernarr Macfadden then proved conclusively with the *Evening Graphic* that there is a point beyond which tabloidism becomes paranoia. The *Graphic* went insane and was committed to the history books within a few years.

After these attempts the *News* stood alone in its field.

Sex was the keynote of the *News* from its debut issue, when the world's foremost blueblooded heartthrob, the Prince of Wales, occupied the entire front page. The rest of that first issue was an odd mixture of United Press wire copy and *Tribune* features.

The lead editorial asserted: "It will be aggressively for America and for the people of New York. . . . It will have no entangling alliances with any class whatever. . . ." Patterson ran an ad in the New York *Times* to launch his paper, and *Times* readers were startled to find a display that shrieked: "See New York's most beautiful girls every morning in the *Illustrated Daily News.*" There was no local advertising, but some national advertising, including a page ad for Sloan's Liniment. The total 1919 linage, from June 26, was only 61,097. By 1937 it had reached a peak of 20,308,154 lines, the largest display linage in the United States.

The unpromising first issue was good enough to bring the astute Arthur Brisbane into the office with an offer from Hearst of fifty thousand dollars if the *News* would quit the field. Flushed with a first-day sale of 200,000 copies printed and sold, the *News* rejected Hearst's offer peremptorily, although two months later Patterson probably wondered if he hadn't been hasty.

After the quick drop in circulation had reached its lowest point in August 1919 the *News* turned the corner and began to climb for reasons which have never been adequately explained. The theories range from the idea that a popular limerick contest turned the tide to Patterson's own theory that New Yorkers had discovered the paper's convenient size. Probably it was the simple meshing of supply and demand. The *News* had what the postwar public wanted.

There was no lack of material: Fifi Stillman's divorce case, the Daddy Browning amour, the luscious Rhinelander split-up, Fatty Arbuckle's anticlimactic end, and such sex-and-homicide epics as the Hall-Mills and Snyder-Gray cases. These courtroom dramas stood out like pearls among the daily journalistic oysters provided by Waxey Gordon, Al Capone, Legs Diamond, Dutch Schultz and other underworld heroes. Then there were the great news stories of the decade: Queen Marie's visit, Gertrude Ederle and the Channel swim, Rudolph Valentino's enshrinement in the heart of American womanhood, Jimmy Walker and the reign of *laissez-faire* in New York politics, Lindbergh and the *Spirit of St. Louis*.

As Jack Alexander wrote in the *New Yorker* in 1938, "By turns sobby, dirty, bloody, and glamorous, the *News* covered each in the manner that would most effectively appeal to the more elementary emotions of a truck-driver, and to the truck-driver in everyone."

Patterson also invented his own system of reader surveys—a direct process of going into subway and elevated stations with his editors and subeditors and peering through train windows over the shoulders of *News* readers to see what part of the paper they were reading. By the same method he checked buyers at newsstands to see what kind of people were buying his product, and had movies taken of the best-dressed ones to offset any possible objections from suspicious advertisers that *News* readers came from the lower-class, non-buying portion of the public.

It was Patterson, too, who was responsible for the *News's* superior coverage of many of these big stories in the twenties. He anticipated the importance of Lindbergh's flight, for instance, and checked up beforehand to find out whether the *Tribune* had made any provisions for coverage. This "feeling" for the news also made Patterson toss out with no hesitation eight pages of advertising so that the question-and-answer testimony of Jane Gibson, the "pig woman" in the Hall-Mills trial, could be printed, and he did the same thing for a remake on the *Morro Castle* disaster. These actions recall the time that Joseph Medill dumped the *Tribune's* entire classified section to make way for the Johnstown flood story. There was more of the Medill blood in Patterson, apparently, than the family credited him with at first. It is probable, too, that his father had a lot to do with giving him the proper training in the old days on the *Tribune*.

The quarter century of *News* operation is sprinkled with journalistic feats which are tributes to Patterson's news sense and the ability of his editorial executives. One of the greatest news pictures ever published, the *Vestris* disaster picture, was obtained by turning loose the paper's picture staff on the rescue ship when it arrived, in the hope that one of the survivors had made a picture on the scene. Similarly, the *News* put twenty-five photographers on the visit of King George and Queen Elizabeth to New York, keeping them in camera range every minute just in case an attempt might be made on the lives of the visitors.

Months before Ruth Snyder was executed Patterson ordered, "If this woman dies, I want a picture of her." His managing editor, Frank J. Hause, carried out the order and as a consequence the *News* had an unforgettable and exclusive picture on the front page of its final edition for January 13, 1938, and 250,000 extra copies were sold. Against the agonized protests of the business department, which feared that advertisers would revolt against the sensational picture, Hause re-ran the front page in the *Sunday News* to the tune of 350,000 extra copies, and ran it once more in rotogravure on the following Sunday for another extra sale of

400,000. Thus the *News* got 1,000,000 added sales out of one picture.

Patterson bought the Associated Press report for his paper in 1927 by paying the Ridder brothers five hundred thousand dollars for the *Commercial Bulletin*, a financial daily which had an AP franchise. In 1934 he got exclusive New York use of AP wirephotos by guaranteeing seven hundred and fifty thousand dollars over a five-year period, payable at a hundred and fifty thousand dollars annually, a cost considered prohibitive by other New York papers.

In the midst of its growth the *News* changed editorial pace without disturbing its financial status. The change came after the Crash and as the result of a historic, much-quoted speech by Captain Patterson to the editorial department. Patterson announced, "We're off on the wrong foot. The people's major interest is no longer in the playboy, Broadway and divorces, but in how they're going to eat, and from this time forward we'll pay attention to the struggle for existence that's just beginning. All signs point to the prospect of a great economic upheaval and we'll pay attention to the news of things being done to assure the well-being of the average man and his family."

A major result of this decision was the paper's passionate support of the Roosevelt Administration for nearly eight years. Its new policy was consonant with the New Deal's program of social reform and the *News* was as vociferous an advocate of the program as McCormick's *Tribune* was its unswerving enemy. It took the issue of isolationism to make the *Tribune* and the *News* a political as well as a financial axis.

On March 6, 1933, Patterson's news sense had told him that the people were solidly behind Roosevelt in the hour of national crisis and the editorial printed that day, titled "A Pledge to Support Roosevelt," was one more example of the owner's knowledge of his readers. The editorial said in part:

"This newspaper now pledges itself to support the policies of President Franklin D. Roosevelt for a period of at least one year from today; longer, if circumstances warrant. The *News* makes this pledge from conscientious motives, believing that the times call for such a pledge. It is no small sacrifice. . . . One of the editor's chief prerogatives in a free-press nation is his right to tell anyone, from the President down, how to act, and, on occasion, where to head in. This right to volunteer counsel to everybody is a right which most newspaper editors hold sacred. We feel the same way about it, in times anywhere near normal, and certainly expect to snatch up this right again when the times worry around to normality again.

"But these times are anything but normal. . . . Whatever Mr. Roosevelt may urge as methods of attacking these emergencies, we expect to support him, to withhold constructive criticism, to give the new leader a chance. We take the liberty, too, of respectfully asking other newspapers, even if they do not feel they can conscientiously make the same pledge, at least to give Mr. Roosevelt better than an even break—for the good of an embattled nation."

It is ironic now to recall that Captain Patterson gave Mr. Roosevelt far less than an even break when the good of an embattled nation demanded it in much greater degree, and that he snatched up his sacred right "to volunteer counsel" not in a time of normality but at a moment when the times were about as abnormal as they ever were in the history of the country.

But in the thirties the preoccupation of the *News* with the struggle for existence and its shift to a semirespectability did not change its pattern in any radical way. Its many pictures and admirably written stories were slanted, as always, to wage earners who needed romance and adventure in their lives. The news formula was (and is) a deft balance in appeal between men and women. Page two, for example, was usually given a masculine slant, and page three a feminine tone.

The staff was not as gaudy as it had been in the old days, but it shaped itself into a fine newspaper machine. Rewrite men were fired frequently in the search for writing talent, but they got high salaries and joint by-lines with the reporter on occasion, a privilege not accorded on most other dailies. The increasingly heavy flow of national and international news on the wire crowded out more and more local news, as it did on every paper, but Patterson got across much of the flavor of New York life in his paper's superb picture coverage.

Nor did the increasing preoccupation of the *News* with serious issues hamper its liveliness. For example, in less than a year the *News* found itself listening to verdicts handed down in four libel suits. On March 2, 1940, a million-dollar libel suit brought by Walter Wanger, motion picture producer, against the *News* and its columnist Ed Sullivan was dismissed without decision. Wanger had charged that Sullivan intimated his movies weren't as good as Sam Goldwyn's. On October 6 of that year Joseph Gedeon, father of the slain model, Veronica Gedeon, who was the victim in a sensational 1937 murder, was awarded six cents in his five-hundred-thousand-dollar libel suit against the News Syndicate. Only a month before, on September 14, the late Lou Gehrig had brought a million-dollar libel suit against the *News* and its sports columnist, Jimmy Powers, charging that Powers had reported he was suffering from a communicable disease. On January 11, 1941, Mrs. Nikola Cunningham Peabody, who had sued the *News* for ten thousand dollars on the basis of an alleged derogatory line in Sullivan's column, lost judgment in the action and the paper recovered a hundred and twelve dollars in costs.

The liveliness of the *News* is reflected even more in its numerous stunts and promotions, where it emulates the *Tribune* by giving the people circuses as well as bread. It inaugurated a Beautiful Child Contest in the thirties, and until the war it had operated a Golden Gloves boxing tournament since 1927. The Harvest Moon Ball, an amateur dance contest, is one *News* promotion that survived the war and each year fills Madison Square Garden to capacity with happy *News* readers. Other stunts are more extraordinary. In August 1939 the *News* announced results of an experiment on a couple in the paper's employ to study sex predetermination. The result: the sex of human babies cannot be predetermined. During the following month a family undertook, for Patterson's benefit, to go on a week's diet consisting only of wartime food rations decreed by the Nazi government for German civilians. This experiment was designed to determine the effects of the diet on the human system.

On its twenty-first birthday, in 1940, a full-page *News* ad modestly observed the end of the twenty-first year of a "new era in American journalism."

On February 8, 1942, the *News* began broadcasting five-minute radio news programs every hour, twenty-four hours a day, seven days a week, over station WNEW, a popular New York station devoted mostly to recorded dance music. These broadcasts are notable for their melodramatic style of writing and their spoken use of the word "communication" for "communiqué," which Patterson banished from the columns of the *News* because he said it was hard to pronounce and foreign in the bargain. Some listeners find it hard to accept the word audibly, although the eye becomes accustomed to it.

When good local stories are brewing, there is something of the old days remaining in the way the *News* covers them. Probably more than any other New York paper, its reporters and editors are able to go directly to the source of police news. If, for instance, a story breaks in some part of Jersey City, other papers will get their district men on the job and send one of their own reporters later, if the story warrants it. Meanwhile someone on the *News* city desk will be likely to pick up the phone a minute after the first flash and get the Jersey City precinct police station where the story occurred. The desk will probably say, "Hello, Sergeant, this is Joe Doakes over at the *News*. . . . How are you, Sergeant? . . . Fine, and how are the wife and kids? . . . Fine. Say, what do you know about this guy . . . ?" And in a few minutes the *News* has all the immediately available information before the district men from the opposition can get there.

This kind of reporting, common to most newspapers, is highly developed on the *News*. In covering divorces, to cite another example, the tabloid's specialists are able to draw on their acquaintance with all the best divorce lawyers in town, and with the judges who handle these cases. When a divorce scandal breaks, the curious are virtually compelled to buy the *News* if they want the most complete stories. This situation also prevails in murder trials.

In fact the reporting and editing of news stories in the *News* is admirable on the whole; its features are a model of successful publishing; and up to 1940 its editorial policies were highly regarded by everyone except the anti-Roosevelt bloc. When the issue of isolationism was raised, however, the *News* became a target for all except the isolationists, who were in the minority, as it turned out. It was linked with the Chicago *Tribune* and the Washington *Times-Herald* in that cabal which came to be known as "the McCormick-Patterson axis," an epithet used not only in the liberal press but in the many conservative dailies which were interventionist.

While pro-Administration forces were inclined to regard this transformation as betrayal by a newspaper which had been one of Mr. Roosevelt's most ardent supporters, they should have perceived a long time before that the *News*, like the *Tribune*, was fair and objective only to its friends. Some of the paper's attacks on Mr. Roosevelt's enemies were as venomous as those made later on Mr. Roosevelt himself. For example, John O'Donnell, *News* political columnist, in 1940 subjected Wendell Willkie to the kind of attack for which Mr. O'Donnell is justly celebrated, if one may so use the word, and only a year later he was writing in exactly the same vein about Roosevelt.

The pattern that the *Daily News* took is shown by two editorial analyses covering periods from November 1 to December 31, 1944, and January 1–26, 1945. The surveys included editorials, "Voice of the People" (a letters column), and the columns of Danton Walker and O'Donnell. Researchers compiling the material noted that the subject matter of letters to the editor follows closely the subjects discussed editorially. After an editorial denouncing the New Deal, for instance, a large number of anti-Roosevelt letters are printed. This system also works in reverse: a large number of anti-British letters are usually followed by an anti-British editorial.

In the first analysis these major trends appeared:

Anti-Administration: 124 attacks, divided into 43 letters, 41 O'Donnell columns, 31 editorial and 9 Walker columns.

Items tending to destroy confidence in civilian and military leadership: 71, divided into 39 editorials, 21 O'Donnells, 7 letters and 4 Walkers.

Anti-Russian: 42 items, divided into 18 editorials, 16 letters, 5 O'Donnells and 3 Walkers.

Other trends included attacks against the British, labor, the United Nations and the peace. Then there were such "pro" items as editorials, letters and columns which echoed various propaganda lines.

The second analysis confirmed these trends, showing anti-Administration items in the lead, with the others following more or less in order, except that some propaganda echoes were more numerous. As in the similar *Tribune* analysis, all these characteristic *News* themes have been used for propaganda purposes.

The pattern began to take shape in 1939, after Patterson and his wife returned from a trip to Europe. The Captain had been as blind to what he saw as were some other newspaper publishers who had made similar trips. He wrote three signed articles for the *News*, the first of which ran on August 1, 1939, under a three-column head on page three: REICH UNREADY. PERIL OF WAR IN '39 GROWS LESS.

Patterson told of his ten-day motor trip from Berlin to Bayreuth to Nuremberg, Dresden, Eisenach and Cologne to the Dutch border, and predicted that "chances are more than 10 to 1 against a general European war before September and 4 or 5 to 1 against war this year" because of the "condition of the crops and the condition of public roads, particularly the junctions of the big motor roads built since Hitler came to power." He also described the troops and war equipment he saw, but he insisted that war could not be declared until the Germans had completed their new roads.

The second article described Patterson's unsuccessful attempt to interview Hitler, which resulted only in a glimpse of the Fuehrer at the music festival in Bayreuth, where Hitler appeared in a smoking jacket and black tie. Patterson thought the black tie indicated dolor, and he subscribed to one of the current and more conventional bad guesses that Hitler was simply a man who held himself aloof in the role of a mystic or priest.

In the final article Patterson paid tribute to Chamberlain. He predicted that the Prime Minister would hold the confidence of the British people and that the Munich pact gave "his empire ten more months to get ready." The Captain viewed with skepticism the British government's fear of a lightning war and the dire results they predicted if Britain were invaded. He was still not sure there would be a war at all.

A month later, when Hitler marched into Poland, the *News* said on September 2, "Can't we be at least as smart as Mussolini and think of our interests first and last?" Two days later the *News* saw the handwriting on the wall but it still supported Roosevelt: "We must be loyal and obedient to our government to a greater degree than in peacetime. . . . In dealing with the situation Mr. Roosevelt may do things that some of us perhaps would not approve, but he has been chosen by the people, and we must give him support. We cannot have a divided country." Patterson's total inability to understand Hitlerism was expressed in a September 17 editorial, which asked, "Will the British and French masses stand for a long, bloody war for the abstract idea of pulling down Nazism?"

As the war moved through its first year, the *News* correctly surmised that there would be trouble with Japan, but it clung to the thesis that Germany could not be a threat to America, and agreed with Hitler's alibi that Germany's historic role was to keep the menace in the East (i.e., Communism) from overrunning Europe. At that time Patterson still thought of Roosevelt as the man who was keeping us out of "Europe's war," although his cousin, the Colonel, was even then shrieking murder.

But in 1940 the *News* drew completely into its isolationist shell. It not only attacked aid of any kind to the Allies, but it reversed a ten-year stand on the Japanese question and sided with the *Tribune* in advocating coming to terms with Japan, as it did later in regard to the Nazis. The switch, the *News* said, was made because "realistic people and realistic nations have a much better chance of survival than have idealists."

The *News* supported Roosevelt for the last time in 1940, on "the only real issue . . . : Who is the best man we can get for President for the next four years?" But Roosevelt was no sooner inaugurated than the *News* turned on him savagely over the issue of the Lend-Lease Bill, thereafter described as "the Dictator Bill."

The events of early 1941 apparently convinced Patterson that the President was preparing for America's entry into the war. There is a widely accepted story that Patterson's personal bitterness against the President dated from Pearl Harbor, when the Captain offered his services in person at the White House, and Roosevelt is said to have told him that he was too old and reminded him of his paper's isolationist editorials. This rebuff may have occurred, but the editorial record shows that Patterson turned against his friend in the White House on the single issue of isolationism, and that the Lend-Lease Bill was the beginning of the end of his support.

Once he deserted Roosevelt, Patterson showed what the *News* could do in the name of "realism." On October 21, 1941, the *News* said: "Roosevelt's War, we think, is the correct name for the war in which we are engaging more intimately every day. Win or lose, this war should be known to history as Roosevelt's War, because Franklin D. Roosevelt is the man who has got us into it as far as we now are, and is taking us deeper into it. . . ."

By 1942 the Berlin radio was able to cite the *News* and the other McCormick-Patterson papers as typical examples of what the American press faced under Roosevelt's "dictatorship": "These newspapers, being true American papers and representing the majority of American people, are being persecuted by the Roosevelt Administration, even to being accused as saboteurs of the war effort."

The *News* opposed gas rationing. Don't get mad at Hitler, get mad at Roosevelt, was the burden of its message. When some of the more rabid isolationists were indicted for sedition, the *News* rose to their defense. Patterson argued editorially, mostly by inference, that the United States started the war, not Germany or Japan or Italy. He unveiled the logical conclusion to this argument with a series of editorials beginning on July 10, 1942, citing the careers of dictators beginning with Caesar and progressing by easy stages through Cromwell, Napoleon, Hitler and Mussolini, until at the end of July he had made Caesar and Roosevelt synonymous. Next month he was saying forthrightly that Roosevelt had entered into a conspiracy to destroy our form of government and become "first Caesar" of the United States.

The "peace now" theme was boldly exploited, beginning in the darkest hours of the war. These are examples:

October 14, 1942: "The United States could quit fighting Germany now. . . . Germany has not taken an inch of our territory and seems unlikely to do so soon."

August 2, 1944: "If the Germans believed they could save something out of the wreckage a lot more of them would be ready to give up now."

January 17, 1945: "Mr. Churchill in the House of Commons yesterday said he does not think the unconditional surrender demand is prolonging the war and that 'at any rate, the war will be prolonged until unconditional surrender has been obtained.' So it looks as if we're stuck with the Roosevelt-Churchill tactics and diplomacy, for better or for worse . . . unless Stalin by chance should make another deal with Germany."

In 1942 the *News* also advocated a national lottery to bring "real incentive" into the buying of war bonds. It continued to hammer away at its thesis that the military should take over the national wealth after the war, indicating by inference its belief in a bloodless (if possible) coup to displace the Administration. It predicted that the 1942 congressional elections would be called off, refused to take a bet from the New York *Post* on the subject, and alibied later that the elections *would* have been called off "if we, or somebody, hadn't squawked loudly."

In 1943 Patterson's editorials dwelt on the "Red menace," defended Father Coughlin and those indicted for sedition, and forecast the possible formation of a third party dedicated to the interests of isolationism.

The election year of 1944 was devoted primarily to fighting the President and opposing his re-election. One quotation, from an editorial of October 26, will indicate the character of the entire campaign. "Mr. Roosevelt has come around again with the same old arguments. He and his New Deal-Communist-PAC backers argue that the world crisis is still upon us, and that only Franklin D. Roosevelt, among 135,000,000 Americans has the wisdom and the experience to see the nation through this crisis. If the American people buy this bale of goods, they will buy themselves a monarch along with it, and sell out democracy. That is what Mr. Roosevelt is asking us to do; that is what he is running for. The fourth term is the issue." This final sentence appeared at the end of almost every editorial column in the *News* for a month before election.

Only once during this campaign was the *News* caught off base. That break came with the resumption of the "Presidential Battle Page," in which the Democratic and Republican parties were offered equal campaign space in columns running side by side. This had been a popular feature in 1936 and 1940, when the *News* was considerably less sensitive about what was said, and asked only that combatants provide an indemnity bond with libelous material.

The page ran for seventeen days in 1944. Then the Democrats printed a cartoon which showed Governor Dewey speaking from a platform, and in the cellar beneath it a gang including Hamilton Fish, Gerald L. K. Smith, and a figure identified by the label "Bertie." The caption read: "Look in the cellar, Mr. Dewey."

Next day the *News* announced discontinuance of the Battle Page with these words: "Tempers are rising on both sides. Some below-the-belt blows have already been registered, and the probability is that more and more will be. . . . We have been furnishing the Battle Page free of charge to thirty-five other newspapers. If the Battle Page should involve us in libel troubles, we don't see how other papers carrying the Battle Page could escape being involved, too. If we should undertake to censor the Battle Page copy, we would promptly be accused of doing it in a partisan manner, and its value and probably its interest would sag off. We are sorry to call it off, but it seems the wisest thing to do."

Robert E. Hannegan, Democratic national chairman, remarked, "Patterson can dish it out, but he can't take it." Newspapermen, however, discounted that as much as they did the *News's* editorial reasons. They pooh-poohed the fear-of-libel excuse, not only on the basis of the tabloid's aggressive record but because eighteen other newspapers immediately offered to print the Battle Page. They did not believe, either, that the *News* really wanted to spare its readers from old-fashioned political slugging. They did not even believe that Patterson minded the sneer at his cousin. Their guess was that Patterson did not want any contrary ideas put in the heads of *News* readers; he wanted them to concentrate on *News* philosophy without distractions.

The election of Roosevelt, in spite of the paper's opposition, did not upset Patterson, notwithstanding the fact that New York City, where he had boasted of his paper's editorial influence, voted for Roosevelt as always. He returned to the same old pattern of attack and maintained it until the day of the President's death.

The *News* did not carry an obituary editorial on Mr. Roosevelt in its first edition after his death; it was probably the only daily newspaper in the country not to do so. It ran, instead, a column of outstanding Roosevelt quotations—an added feature in the coverage of most other papers—and it enjoyed the distinction of being the only newspaper, at least among the major dailies, to include the "again and again and again" quote, which had been a bitter Republican barb in the 1944 campaign.

Next day Danton Walker's column shared with a Boston newspaper the bad taste of making a mystery out of the artist who was with the President before he died. "What everybody wants to know is, why did the couple make such a hasty departure from Warm Springs, instead of remaining there for questioning?" Walker wrote.

In the same issue the *News* got around to its Roosevelt editorial, an editorial radically different from every other paper's contribution, and unmatched anywhere for sheer arrogance. It ran, in part:

## ROOSEVELT IN HISTORY

It is too soon to try to make a complete evaluation of Roosevelt's place in U.S. and world history.

Some of the domestic reforms introduced in the early years of his New Deal looked and still look good. There were Social Security, with its old age pension and unemployment insurance features; stock market supervision by the SEC; federal bank deposit insurance; the Wagner Labor Relations Act; the TVA, a notable success as a project for flood control, soil conservation

and power production, and a forerunner in all likelihood of related projects in the Missouri and Ohio River systems.

About one of Roosevelt's achievements there is no dispute.
It is historic fact that he was the first U.S. President to win and
serve a third term, and to be elected to a fourth. . . .

It is the matter of Roosevelt's foreign policies which make a
final assessment of his rank in history impossible at this time.
Such an assessment will not be possible, we'd guess, for 20 or
more years.

There were grave misgivings in this country over Roosevelt's
open sympathy with the Allies from the outbreak of the European war in 1939. Furious differences of opinion were aroused
by his One World ideas after we got into the war. . . .

The war is still going on. No one can now say with authority
whether the U.S. could have stayed out of it to its own ultimate
benefit, whether it will eventually add up on the plus or the
minus side as regards human welfare and progress, and so on.
The decision on those questions must be left to history. . . .

As to the new President, we think the common sense thing to
do is to—GIVE TRUMAN A BREAK—and not to begin dif-
fering with him from the word go. That can come later. . . .

We cannot see how any of us can hurt ourselves, our country
or our war effort by rallying around and giving President Truman a hand and a buildup as he takes over the burdens of the
toughest political job in the world today.

When President Roosevelt was first inaugurated, back in 1933,
we promised to withhold adverse editorial criticism of him for
one year, for what looked like practical as well as patriotic
reasons. . . .

. . . We do say now that we'll be editorially respectful,
friendly, and helpful according to our lights, toward President
Truman for at least the next three months, and probably for the
next six months.

That was the generous *News*, giving Truman a break and permitting history to judge the dead President, although it had been
eager to anticipate history when he was alive.

The arrogance of this editorial was more than matched by the
bad taste of another which appeared on May 5, 1945. It was a

familiar excursion into *News* "realism," titled "Three of the Big Ones Dead in a Month." After opening with a listing of American war casualties, it went on to a discussion of "three departed headmen—Roosevelt, Mussolini, Hitler. . . . Then it said:

"These day-to-day deaths of numerous young men do not get the public interest or the newspaper space devoted to the recent departures of three prominent older men.

"President Roosevelt died April 12, 1945. Benito Mussolini was executed (polite term for it; lynched is the correct word) April 28. Adolf Hitler is believed dead, death being dated April 29 by most reports, though his cadaver has not been dug up at this writing.

"These occurrences, we imagine, have stimulated some long thoughts in the brains of Winston Churchill, now 70, and Josef Stalin, now 65. Stalin seems to be the toughest baby of the lot.

"The chief thought which these deaths have stirred in us concerns the holes that have been blown by these deaths in the 'indispensable man' theory."

The New York *Post's* shocked rejoinder was fitting; "Captain Patterson, at 66, is well within the age bracket which his editorial said should give Stalin and Churchill reason for 'some long thoughts.' We offer Patterson one long thought. Roosevelt's grave, guarded in spirit by all freedom-loving people, is safe from dishonor by him. He dishonored only himself, and the grave in which he will eventually lie."

Patterson died almost exactly a year later.

But the editorial columns of the *News* are not the only purveyors of its party line, and it would be unfair to minimize the efforts of other *News* experts.

One of these is C. D. Batchelor, who came to the *News* in October 1931. Like John T. McCutcheon, of the *Tribune*, Batchelor is a Pulitzer prize winner. He won an award in 1937 for a pacifist cartoon showing the deathlike prostitute figure of another World War beckoning to a young man, the caption reading: "Come on in, I'll treat you right. I used to know your daddy."

In theme Batchelor's cartoons are remarkable, like McCutch-

A study of the late Captain Joseph Patterson

*Wide W*

Alicia Patterson as she looked in 1942, going over a copy of her tabloid *Newsday* in its Hempstead, Long Island, plant

eon's. Both have reflected their respective papers' bitterness against Roosevelt in much the same way.

The most violent expressions of *News* opinion are found in the letters column, "Voice of the People." A good many people believe that the department would be more aptly titled "Voice of the *News*," for the letters are certainly hand-picked to fit the paper's purpose. Critical letters are published under slanted heads. Here are a few samples of the kind of thing purveyed by these letters:

"This war with Japan is needless and insane. That Japan made the first overt move is not as important as that our government labored for years to provoke it. There are those of us who believe we will be rendering our country the greatest service by never ceasing to cry out for peace against the monstrous injustice of this war."

"I think the poisonous New Deal is mainly to blame for the defeat at Pearl Harbor. Many people are uneasily afraid that our President is constantly being misled by the strange people with whom he surrounds himself."

"Several suggestions for F.D.R. about naming the war: the Pyrrhic Victory; the Raw Deal; the Slaughter Pen; the Revenge of the Refugees."

"If we keep on copying the British rationing system, I am going to ask Mahatma Gandhi to will me his sheet when he kicks the bucket."

"You Voice squawkers about food rationing are yourselves to blame for it. You have invested heavily in War Bonds, without insisting that the money be used by the Government to buy war materials. So the Government turns around and buys large stocks of foodstuffs to give to foreign peoples. So, dear fellow saps, if you want to eat heartily in the future, you'd better make haste to secure passports for Malta, England or Russia."

"I predict that the casualties we shall suffer in this war will make it impossible for the indispensable man, after the present term, to be elected dog-catcher."

Another able Patterson ally was John O'Donnell, who writes the Washington column, "Capitol Stuff." O'Donnell's style is decep-

tively simple. He is an excellent writer who makes his propaganda
points in such a way that it is difficult for opponents to quote him
effectively or to put a finger on anything precise of which he may
be accused. O'Donnell's "Stuff" runs well up in the *News* format,
on pages where it will get attention.

Here is a typical example of the O'Donnell method, which he
uses with little alteration day after day: " 'Are you kicking in with
your 100 bucks for the Washington Birthday dinner?' One of
New York's office-holding Democrats was asked by a brother who
also had been tapped for the fund-raising meal sponsored by the
Democratic National Committee.

"We liked his reply.

" 'No. I just wrote back and suggested that the National Committee tell the White House that the dinner should be held on
Texas Guinan's birthday—not the birthday of the founder of the
country. I think I'd come if they only wrote on the invitation:
"Hello, sucker." ' "

There have been one or two serious attempts to analyze O'Donnell, trying to determine why he is what he is, and why he turned
against Roosevelt, with whom he was so friendly earlier in his
career on the *News*. These students point to his Irish-American
background in New England as an explanation for his isolationist,
ultraconservative attitudes, which emerged at a time when some
Irish-Americans were fighting for neutrality and most of New
England was a hotbed of Roosevelt-hating.

In the column on October 3, 1945, however, there appeared a
piece unbelievable even for O'Donnell and his paper. It was a story
by which he intimated that the late General Patton was ousted as
commander of the eastern half of the American occupation zone in
Germany because of a plot. The column began with this paragraph:

"Behind the successful drive to disgrace and remove Gen.
George S. Patton from his army command in occupied Germany
is the secret and astoundingly effective might of this Republic's
foreign-born political leaders—such as Justice of the Supreme
Court Felix Frankfurter of Vienna, White House administrative

assistant Dave (Devious Dave) Niles alias Neyhus and the Latvian ex-rabbinical student now known as Sidney Hillman."

In an early edition of the Washington *Times-Herald*, this paragraph was followed by another, reading: "An honest birth record, spelling out the names of the paternal grandfathers of this triumvirate would be interesting, even if the educated Christian American couldn't read it." Apparently this was too much, however, even for O'Donnell's bosses. The paragraph was dropped in later editions of the *Times-Herald*, and it did not appear at all in the *Daily News*.

The column then went on to reveal, for the first time, according to its author, that the soldier slapped by Patton in Sicily "was of Jewish descent and that the general, hot and fatigued and fresh from the fighting front, used the words 'yellow-bellied' or 'yellow-streaked' linking them up with a direct reference to the patient's racial background." O'Donnell further implied that the face-slapping incident was fed to Drew Pearson, the radio commentator, by Robert S. Allen, formerly Pearson's partner, who he intimated was attached to Patton's staff. When Pearson brought the incident to light, O'Donnell wrote, Morgenthau and Frankfurter "bellowed in the White House that the important issue was that Patton used the word 'Jew' in reprimanding" the slapped soldier.

Some estimate of O'Donnell's accuracy may be made from what happened after this column's publication. The slapped soldier came forward to prove that he was not Jewish. Allen disclosed that at the time of the incident he was on maneuvers in Louisiana. Morgenthau branded the reference to him as "an absolute untruth."

In the end the *News* was forced to apologize for the column to an interfaith delegation which visited its offices. The apology was tendered through the managing editor, Richard Clarke. But the damage had been done. It was a long time before various public forms of anti-*News* agitation subsided.

When the case of John O'Donnell is boiled down, it may be the truth about him is simply that he is another example of what happens to a man when he is given a printed outlet for his prejudices and opinions. There are thousands of unpublished O'Donnells and Peglers in America, but writing talent and circumstance have placed such columnists in a position to transmit their thoughts to millions of people. The sense of power this position gives them has a tremendous elevating effect on their egos, which makes these men attach an importance to what they say out of all proportion to the ideas they express.

Critics of the *News* disparage it by saying that nobody reads O'Donnell or the editorial page anyhow, that people only buy the paper for the sex stories, the comics, the columns and the racing entries. It is undoubtedly bought primarily for these features, but the poison is taken too. Reader surveys show that *News* editorials have a higher readership than most of its extremely popular comics, and O'Donnell also has a far higher rating than the political columnists of most dailies.

A primary reason for the editorial page's popularity is the language it uses. It is the language of the people. Writing men admire the way *News* editorials are written; their simple wording and direct expression of complex opinions and ideas are in shining contrast to the omniscient tone and dull rhetoric of most editorial pages.

Reuben Maury, who wrote the editorials in close collaboration with Captain Patterson, came to the *News* in 1926, the year after Patterson moved to New York permanently. Maury was twenty-six years old at that time, a lawyer who had never had any newspaper experience, but his *American Mercury* pieces about his native Butte, Montana, attracted the Captain's notice. Within three months the two were working together as an editorial-writing team. In less than a year a *News* editorial was quoted for the first time in the *Literary Digest*.

Maury's editorials are not as grammatical as the *Tribune*'s, nor as polished in execution, but they are more effective because they do not hesitate to use colloquialisms or common usages and, like the rest of the *News* editorial page, do not hesitate to use profanity, vulgarity or profound overstatement to make a point.

A sample of colloquialism in the *News* is the letter in "Voice of the People" which appeared on Washington's Birthday, 1943: "To the lousy filthy skunk, sneak and rat that made me get off the bus the other day with my two small kids because he thought I had offered him a lead half dollar—you must have been cockeyed drunk, skunk, not to see that it was a perfectly good half dollar, and may the devil haunt you the rest of your days, you old crab."

The *News* has never since reached the peak of distinction it attained in 1934 when it became the first newspaper in America, perhaps in the world, to use the words "son of a bitch." This violation of newspaper standards brought only a mild slap on the wrist from the business's trade journal, *Editor & Publisher*.

The whole theory of *News* editorial presentation is that the people will read and believe if ideas are given to them in words they can understand. Captain Patterson believed that the kind of "realism" the *News* purveys editorially represents mass thinking. Priding himself as a student of human nature, who had observed it at first hand on its lowest levels, he designed his paper to satisfy its demands. It is true that Patterson did understand people well enough to establish an enormously successful paper, but there is plenty of evidence to indicate that his success is not based on his editorial policies.

Patterson himself was sure that his policies were the reason for *News* success, and for the success of McCormick's and Mrs. Patterson's papers. "Why this popularity?" the *News* asked itself editorially when it attained its circulation peak at a time when it was under heaviest attack. Patterson pointed out in this editorial that the *News*, the *Times-Herald* and the *Tribune* were all leaders in their respective areas. He concluded: "We think the answer must be that a lot of people . . . like these papers' editorial policies and approve of them. Anyway, that's our story, and we're going to stick to it until and unless it's disproved."

Yet the *News* has no more concrete political influence than the *Tribune*, despite the high readership of its editorials and columns. Its own circulation figures prove it. New York voters go Democratic no matter on which side of the fence the *News* finds itself. The candidates it backed in 1944 were defeated, as were the *Tribune's*, and there is not the slightest evidence that Patterson's attacks on Roosevelt had any more practical political effect than his support, and his isolationist views actually had a contrary effect on New York voters in 1944.

To make the point even more specific, in 1944 the *News* had 48.1 per cent family coverage on the lower East Side and this figure has remained relatively constant since Patterson's pro-Roosevelt days, although the paper's constant baiting of foreign-born citizens would scarcely make it popular in that section of the city at any time. During the war there was only a 5 per cent increase in Yorkville, the Manhattan district where Bundism flourished and where *News* isolation would be highly popular, if anywhere. Similarly, family coverage is 80 per cent in Greenwich Village, the city's most liberal district and the one in which the *News* is probably most cordially hated. Nor is economic status any measure of *News* circulation. It shares such impoverished districts as Hell's Kitchen almost exclusively with Hearst's *Daily Mirror*, but along the better residential parts of Fifth Avenue it runs ahead of the conservative *Times* by about 2000 copies daily.

Thus it appears that Captain Patterson was not the voice of the masses, that he was instead a victim of the disease which has attacked other publishers of magazines and newspapers who find themselves reaching millions of readers and begin to play God. This God complex was the subject of a Patterson editorial in 1936, before the Captain was stricken with the disease himself. The editorial appeared after an election in which most of the nation's major dailies had opposed Roosevelt and taken the first of three sound beatings.

Patterson was in a jovial mood that day. He not only poked sarcastic barbs at the anti-Roosevelt publishers, but he dismissed any pro-Roosevelt influence the *News* might have had and asserted that people read newspapers for facts. The Captain urged his fellow publishers to examine their souls, and he concluded, "The smugness of some newspaper editors passeth all understanding."

Years later his fellow publishers were able to return these sentiments in kind. Even the Republican *Herald Tribune* accused him of promoting wartime disunity.

In the end, Joseph Medill Patterson arrived at the same point as his cousin, Colonel McCormick, although by a far different route. They started out as individuals apparently completely different; later, as publishers, they seemed even further apart in their conception of journalism. At last, however, they proved that blood will inevitably tell, and they were sharing the same unhappy throne when Joseph Patterson proved that even he was not indispensable.

## Chapter 2

## POOR LITTLE RICH MAN

PATTERSON surveyed his world from Room 906 in the thirty-six-story Daily News Building, 220 East Forty-second Street, a $10,-700,000 structure opened in February 1930. His office was unpretentious. It had a globe in it, which he consulted frequently, and a venerable mahogany desk carried over from the paper's Park Place era. The cork walls were background for thumbtacked pictures of plant operations. A green carpet covered the floor; Patterson insisted on it in preference to a more lush type which decorates the offices of other executives.

Just as the Tribune Building reflects some of McCormick's personality, so does the *News* illuminate its late owner. The difference between the two buildings is a case in point. Whereas the inscriptions in the *Tribune's* lobby deal mostly with lofty principles, the News Building has a quotation from Lincoln over its entrance: "The Lord must have loved the common people, He made so many of them."

The lobby floor is in the pattern of a great compass, and its focal point is a twelve-foot revolving globe, tilted to the earth's own inclination and illuminated from below. The seventeen panels on the lobby walls are occupied by meteorological charts, maps and indicators. The atmosphere of the *News* is educational, not rhetorical.

The master of this realm in the McCormick-Patterson empire was a proud man, six feet tall, with gray, bristling hair, a square face heavily seamed, lips straight and thin, eyes deep-set, his hands heavy and thick. He walked with a heavy, decisive step. In sharp contrast to the Colonel's sartorial elegance, the Captain was often dressed in a way that would shame his reporters, and at his best he was no more than baggily orthodox.

Much has been made of Patterson's kinship with the proletariat as opposed to McCormick's essential aristocracy, but a closer study of the two men shows that they had a great deal in common psychologically. From that standpoint Patterson was nearly as unusual a personality as his cousin.

Like McCormick, he got off to the wrong kind of start. Born into a rich family, living on Chicago's fashionable North Side, he seemed at first to be destined inevitably for the kind of conventional rich man's life that his socially conscious mother had mapped out for him. He was sent to private schools in Chicago and France, and in 1890 found himself at Groton.

McCormick began his rebellion against the world at private school in England. Patterson opened his at Groton, where he underwent the same kind of cruel teasing. McCormick was teased because he came to Groton with the accent he had acquired in England; Patterson suffered because he came to the school with a typical Midwestern accent, rendered incongruous by his English blazer. All in all, Patterson had a rough time at Groton and came to have a healthy loathing for most of the young snobs who went there.

Still following his cousin's footsteps, Patterson moved on to Yale, but his college years were distinguished chiefly by the vacation between his junior and senior years, when he went to China for Hearst's New York *American*, as aide to the reporter covering the Boxer Rebellion. He left Yale in 1901 and went to work immediately for the *Tribune* at fifteen dollars per week, actually a gesture on the part of the management because the young man currently got a ten-thousand-dollar yearly allowance. The gesture did not make him happy, however.

A year after he went on the paper he married Alice Higinbotham, the daughter of Harlow Niles Higinbotham, one of Marshall Field's partners and president of the Columbian Exposition. Marriage did not cure his restlessness. He thought the *Tribune* was disgustingly dull and found no interest in his own work. He looked with admiration upon William Randolph Hearst and the meaty Hearst papers.

The rebellion within him against the pattern of living which had

brought him nothing but unhappiness had to find expression somehow, and young Patterson found that he could voice his protest
in politics. In 1903 he made speeches for the municipal reform
movement then agitating Chicago, and although he was only
twenty-four, his performances so impressed the reform group that
they made him their nominee for the state Legislature. Patterson
ran on an anti-boss ticket and won. This victory was probably the
first real satisfaction Patterson had ever obtained from life. It was a
recognition of him as a person, as contrasted with his former
position as a conventional figure in a conventional kind of living.
He played his new role for all it was worth. In the Legislature
he won public notice by starting a riot during the hot debates
over Chicago's traction problems. However, he suffered another
severe psychological setback when his father told him that his
election to the Legislature was the result of a backstage bargain
between the *Tribune* and Republican bosses. Hurt and humiliated,
he left the *Tribune* temporarily and never ran for an elective office
again.

The incident only sharpened his zeal for reform, and he plunged
into the cause with new fervor. In 1905 he put his public-speaking
talents at the disposal of Judge Edward J. Dunne, the Democratic
candidate for mayor, who was running on a platform which was
pro-municipal ownership and anti-Big Business. As editor in chief
of the *Tribune*, the elder Patterson found himself in the somewhat
embarrassing position of opposing editorially a candidate who was
backed publicly and ardently by his son.

This time the son was on the winning side without help from
the father. Moreover, young Patterson was appointed commissioner of public works by the victorious candidate, and he began
fulfilling his party's campaign promises by waging war against
the big department stores which were making female sweatshops
out of their bargain basements. Turning in another direction, he
took a decisive step to end a bloody circulation war between the
*Daily News* and the *American* by sending wagons from the Department of Public Works to haul newsstands away to the city
dump. The warring newspapers took the hint and desisted.

These activities were satisfying to Patterson's ego, but before long he began to encounter the same kind of frustrations he had suffered in his former pattern of living. Practical politics, he discovered, was a long way from the moral Utopia he advocated, even when it was a reform party safely in power. His zeal for reform, a passion born of his revolt, was left unsatisfied by the practical limitations imposed on his every move.

Consequently it was not actually surprising, though it astounded a good many people, when young Patterson announced his conversion to Socialism in 1906. The announcement was dramatic, made in the form of a letter to Mayor Dunne written from the Pattersons' Washington, D.C., residence at 15 DuPont Circle, on February 28, 1906. Patterson wrote in part:

"The whole body of our laws as at present framed is ridiculous and obsolete. They are designed always to uphold capital at the expense of the community. I realized soon after I took the office that to fight privilege under the present laws would be a jest.

". . . Money is power and dominion. It is wine and women and song. It is art and poetry and music. It is idleness and activity. It is warmth in winter and coolness in summer. It is clothing and food. It is travel and sport. It is horses and automobiles, and silks and diamonds. It is books. It is education. It is self-respect and the respect of all others. No one possesses it but it possesses everybody.

"In other words," he concluded, "as I understand it, I am a Socialist. I have hardly read a book on Socialism, but that which I have enunciated I believe in general to be their theory. If it is their theory, I am a Socialist."

This pronouncement was received in the widest variety of ways. At one extreme was the New York *Times*, which took "Mr. Patterson's Socialism" seriously in an editorial of that title. The *Times* commented on Patterson's youth, noted his work with the Socialist leader J. G. Phelps Stokes, and concluded, "While other men have been money-grubbing, Mr. Stokes and Mr. Patterson have been observing and thinking. When some men have reached the age of 27 they throw away 'the poor squeezed orange of the world.' Mr. Stokes and Mr. Patterson are going to reconstruct the orange."

At the other extreme stood the Chicago *Inter-Ocean*, which accused Patterson of resigning as commissioner not as a result of political conviction but in consequence of a marital scandal. Most people paid little attention to either extreme; they divided themselves over the simpler question of whether Patterson was a misguided young rich man who might get sense in his head later on, or whether he was a dangerous betrayer of his own class who dealt in radical plots to destroy the hands which had fed him.

A week after he had announced himself as a Socialist Patterson met his father in New York, where the son was attending a Socialist convention. Both men gave interviews to the newspapers on the subject of the moment. The son reiterated his belief that all sources of production should be vested in the people, and that there should be no monopoly of the natural sources of wealth, nor of wealth-producing agencies. Wealth, he said, should not be inherited.

The elder Patterson was far less rhetorical. He remarked bluntly that Socialism was fanatic, and he warned his son that the *Tribune* would not support him if he decided to run for mayor of Chicago. This was not a particularly potent threat, in view of the *Tribune's* record as an opponent of young Patterson's political interests.

As though in answer to this interview, Joe went to Chicago a few weeks later and made his first Socialist speech, received sourly by the *Tribune* but widely acclaimed by numerous sympathizers. However, the new turn in Patterson's career had not yet taken definite direction by mid-year, a fact underlined by a story in the Philadelphia *Ledger* on July 21, in which Patterson was quoted as having decided to become a farmer, to take a course in agriculture at the University of Wisconsin and work on an Illinois farm, to write a book on Socialism, and to study German.

Patterson was sincere about his conversion, and with the compulsion to justify himself he wrote an article titled "Confessions of a Drone," which appeared in the August 30, 1906, issue of the *Independent*. This extraordinary confession was reprinted in amended versions for the next ten years; tens of thousands of copies were distributed. In it, Patterson wrote:

"I am talking about myself, the type of the idle, rich young man, not myself the individual. . . . I have an income of between ten and twenty thousand dollars a year. I spend all of it. I produce nothing—am doing no work. I (the type) can keep on doing this all my life unless the present social system is changed. . . . My income doesn't descend upon me like manna from heaven. It can be traced. Some of it comes from the profits of a daily newspaper; some of it comes from Chicago real estate; some from the profits made by the Pennsylvania and other railroads; some from the profits of the United States Steel Corporation; some from the profits of the American Tobacco Company. . . .

". . . It takes to support me just about twenty times as much as it takes to support an average workingman or farmer. And the funny thing about it is that these workingmen and farmers work hard all year round, while I don't work at all.

"I have better food, better clothes, and better houses than the workers who supply me with money to spend. I can travel oftener . . . I have horses to ride and drive, domestic servants . . . the best physicians. . . . My children will never go to work in a cotton mill or a sweatshop. In short, I lead a far more highly civilized life than the working people. I have offered me the choice of all the best things that man in his stay upon this earth has discovered, evolved or created. The working people do not have this choice offered them. There are left for them the shoddy things of life—hard work and small reward. I have little or no work and the earth's best for reward.

"The work of the working people, and nothing else, produces the wealth, which by some hocus-pocus arrangement, is transferred to me, leaving them bare. While they support me in splendid style, what do I do for them? Let the candid upholder of the present order answer, for I am not aware of doing anything for them.

"It is said that I supply a wage fund out of which their wages are paid. Nonsense. If every bond and stock certificate and every real estate abstract were burned today in a huge bonfire, the vacated titles of ownership falling naturally to the community, trains would pull out on schedule time tomorrow. . . .

"That my life is so much completer than the lives of the workers who support me has been excused on the ground that they are less 'cultivated,' and, therefore, less fitted to enjoy things which please me. But that seems a little like begging the question. I don't think it was entirely natural aptitude that marked me out for a university education, since I remember that frequently I had to pay money to tutors to drill into my head information of a remarkably simple character. I was fond of a good time—and that I had. Of course, it took money, which was obligingly supplied, via my family, by the pressmen, the switchmen, the cigarette girls, the rolling-mill men, etc.

"I started at the bottom. . . . But I knew it was play-acting all the time. . . . I was not living on a $15-a-week basis. . . . I wasn't afraid of losing my job. . . . I got an 'allowance' in addition to the fifteen, and the allowance was by considerable the more substantial figure. . . . It was just this 'allowance' that makes all the difference.

"If a man produces $2,000 worth of wealth a year, and consumes $10,000 worth a year, he is overpaid. If he is overpaid, some must be underpaid. Socialism urges the underpaid to unite and insist on receiving the full amount of the wealth they produce."

If some shocked readers thought these statements radical, Patterson himself apparently felt they didn't go far enough because he amended the above conclusion to make it stronger, in one of four reprints of the "Confessions." George Seldes, in his *Lords of the Press*, notes the progress of these reprints and cites Patterson's more emphatic conclusion, which was appended to a reprint for the Pocket Library of Socialism, No. 45. Patterson added: "So it is with all capitalists. Insofar as they receive interest, profit and rent, they are economic idlers, taking toll of the labor of others and returning nothing; insofar as they actively further business, by superintendence or otherwise, they are laborers, worthy in many cases of their hire. The wealth appropriated by capital through the agencies of rent, profit and interest is obviously appropriated from the working people, the creators of all wealth. Therefore it is to the working people that Socialism addresses itself, urging them to veto their own further exploitation."

His confession was attacked almost universally in the newspapers, and Patterson answered these press critics in the fourth reprint of his pamphlet: "Since the foregoing appeared in the *Independent,* many criticisms of it have appeared in the capitalist press. The burden of practically every criticism has been, 'If young Patterson feels that way why doesn't he give his money to the poor?'

"From which it is fair to surmise that the capitalist press cannot explain what useful economic functions young Patterson and the rest of his class perform. The article was written about the whole capitalist class, as explicitly mentioned in the first paragraph. The reason the whole capitalist class doesn't give away its money and go to work is because it doesn't want to. It is quite satisfied with its present arrangement of luxury, dominion and idleness. As long as the working class is satisfied with its present arrangement of poverty, obedience and laboriousness, the present arrangement will continue. But whenever the working class wants to discontinue the present arrangement it can do so. It has the great majority."

"Confessions of a Drone" made Patterson such a success with the Socialists that they put him on their national executive committee, in the company of Clarence Darrow and Big Bill Haywood. However, he had found a new satisfaction and a new outlet in the business of writing. He bought a farm near Libertyville, Illinois, next to Samuel Insull's estate, and for the next four years devoted himself largely to that occupation. He went up to Chicago in 1907 long enough to oppose Mayor Dunne for re-election, with words which showed how far he had carried his psychological revolt. "Dunne," he told the voters, "is against the laborer and always will be. He is a lawyer, and one who is accustomed to receiving big fees from corporations and employers. Every lawyer generally sees only the side of the employer. And Dunne is no different from the rest. . . ."

Back in Libertyville, Patterson turned out a playlet titled *Dope,* attempting to prove that drug addiction was the result of slum conditions, and implying that Socialism was the antidote for this unfortunate condition. The capsule drama was a hugely successful vaudeville skit for years, played for its melodramatic values rather than for its moral message.

Gaining skill and speed in his writing, Patterson next turned out a novel called *A Little Brother of the Rich*, published in 1908. It was a variation on a theme of Upton Sinclair's, and its message was that rich men lived empty lives and had nothing in the end to show for their lifelong devotion to the making of money. The book's characters were economically divided into heroes and villains, the poor as heroic as the rich were villainous.

The reception of the book was curious. The Chicago Public Library would not circulate it. The literary critics sneered at it, especially the young novelists and playwrights whom Patterson upheld in the book as compared with their soulless elders. These people, whose approval he mistakenly sought, amazed him by applying the same kind of snobbery to his novel that Patterson so deplored in the rich. Nonetheless, the book was a huge success because the public at large appeared to feel that they had a champion in Patterson and they bought his book in satisfying quantities.

Reading the reviews of *A Little Brother of the Rich*, Patterson must have felt the first sharp pains of disillusionment. The New York *Post's* reviewer wrote loftily that the material from which the book was taken was hardly worth touching by the "artist." The New York *Press* rested its case on a high moral plane. It predicted that the book would cause Patterson to be ostracized socially, and asserted, "The book presents a picture of society which if it were true is too vile and revolting for words." With consummate bad taste, the *Press* article ended with the statement that Patterson was rather unpleasantly mixed up in the divorce suit of Mrs. Preston Gibson, one of the smart set of Chicago.

Patterson wrote another proletarian novel, this one unsuccessful, and turned out three plays which were produced on Broadway, *The Fourth Estate* (with James Keeley and Harriet Ford), *By-Products* and *Rebellion*. The latter was reworked into a novel, published under the same title.

In those four years of writing, however, Patterson's Socialist clock ran down and stopped. Again frustration was a prime factor in this new turn of his life. He found that the party was increasingly split by factional disputes, and he observed that there was no real, continuing zeal for reform in the large body of his fellow travelers, except in words. Patterson became convinced that the Socialist party was not a practical means to the end of social reform.

Coincidentally with his disillusionment came the death of his father and the circumstances by which he was precipitated into the *Tribune* management. In 1911 he was quoted by the New York *Sun* in what was almost an obituary to his writing career, and at the same time was an unwittingly accurate forecast of his future career as publisher of the *News*. "Most of what I have written," the *Sun* reported Patterson as saying, "is possibly Socialistic or radical on some lines, for if you see things at an angle it more or less tinges your view of what is right."

Patterson saw the first World War at an obtuse ideological angle. In the *Tribune's* isolationist stand before American entry the thinking of both Patterson and McCormick on this point was clearly established, and their minds never changed thereafter. This isolationism was first voiced in August 1914, when the *Tribune* printed an article by its circulation manager, Max Annenberg, who had just returned from a trip to Europe. Travel, apparently, had qualified Mr. Annenberg as an expert on foreign affairs. He wrote these astonishing words: "Germany will win, is winning now, by both might and right. . . . Here and now I forecast that a week from Sunday will find France and Belgium conquered by Germany, England suing for peace, and Russia not even in the fight."

Meanwhile Patterson had made his junket in 1914 as *Tribune* correspondent to the scene of the Mexican troubles at Vera Cruz. Returning in 1915, he turned his thoughts to the war in Europe and came to the conclusion that we should enter the conflict, not for moral reasons but because neutrality might cost us the friendship of both Germany and the Allies, so that if the Germans and Japanese attacked us later on we might not be able to get the protection of the British Navy. Only one thing disturbed Patterson about his own logic. He remembered the *Lusitania* and he asked himself whether the reality of fear could be identical with the reality of safety.

Just as McCormick declared that he exposed himself to enemy fire as a correspondent in order to test his courage, Patterson risked being torpedoed to find out how he would react to the imminence of death. In September 1915 he sailed from Europe, where he had gone to cover the German occupation of Belgium, on the British ammunition carrier *Cymric*, a lumbering craft which would have been a sitting duck for enemy torpedoes. Before he left Paris to embark Patterson thoughtfully left a note with a friend requesting that the embattled governments not make him an international incident if the *Cymric* were sunk.

The ship made New York intact and confirmed its neutral passenger in his cynical opinions. He cabled the *Tribune* from New York: "So let us choose England on our side and, in the holy name of the Monroe Doctrine, after the war sit tight on our own hemisphere and make money."

While the *Cymric* wallowed through the Atlantic, Patterson had time when he wasn't watching for submarines to write six articles which were published collectively in 1915 as the *Notebook of a Neutral*.

In this collection Patterson displayed the hard face of his isolationism in words which might have been written a quarter century later: "No American has a right to consider any interest save the interest of America. Any American in a position of power or influence who allows any consideration but the selfish interests of America to guide him is a traitor—unconsciously, perhaps, and without a sense of guilt, but still a traitor. . . .

"Any American who suggests or even hopes that America should go into the war on the side of the Allies because he loves France, or because he sorrows for Belgium, or because of the *Lusitania*, or because he thinks it would be unfortunate for humanity in general to have Germany triumph, is a traitor to America. . . ."

He also made one accurate prophecy, rising from his obsessive fear of Japan, although he called the Japanese "remarkable little people." He wrote, "When (or if) the Japanese attack us we shall immediately present the same alibi for our defeats [lack of preparedness] but with even less excuse. The other nations at least tried to prepare for the probable onslaught of the great military empire of Germany. We are not even trying to prepare for the probable onslaught of the great military empire of Japan. . . . One thing is certain. If the Japanese decide to fight us they will try to surprise us and obtain for themselves that initial advantage."

In 1916 came the period of service in Mexico already described, during which he rose from private to sergeant while chasing Villa with the Illinois Field Artillery, a National Guard unit.

When America entered the war, Patterson presumably had not changed his mind about the ideology of the conflict but he went overseas as a second lieutenant of artillery and fought with distinction. He saw action in the Lorraine sector for three months, participated in the defense of Champagne under Gouraud, and fought at St.-Mihiel, the Argonne, and in the second battle of the Marne. He wound up as captain and commanding officer of Battery B, 149th Field Artillery, of the famed 42d, the Rainbow Division. His men called him by the affectionate nickname of "Aunty Joe," or sometimes "Sloppy Joe," the one because of his solicitude for his men, the other for the carelessness in dress already characteristic of him.

The war was only an interlude in Patterson's intellectual progress. After it was over, and he had gone to New York following a brief, unhappy straddle in Chicago between *Tribune* and *News,* he went on thinking and writing in much the same way as he had before the war. More and more, as the years went on, his personality showed itself as like his Chicago cousin's in many respects.

Like McCormick, Patterson presented a dictatorial, stubborn, ruthless and unstable side to the world—a personality characteristic of Cyrus McCormick, Joseph Medill and other strong men of the dynasty. Like McCormick and the others, he had a charming side to his personality which only a few intimates ever saw.

He had eccentricities, such as his spells of hero worship for unlikely people. Clyde Beatty, the lion tamer, was a conspicuous example, but there were many others, most of them female stage or screen stars. His restlessness was expressed, like his cousin's, in a love of flying. He had McCormick's unpredictability of mood, and his deep suspicion of things alien, some of his compulsion to withdraw from the world at times, and some of his flatness of emotion.

Patterson's day began about 6 A.M. on his Ossining estate, when he awakened after six or eight hours of sleep. Lying in bed, he worked his way meticulously through the morning newspapers, including the *Daily Worker, Wall Street Journal* and the *Journal of Commerce*. Breakfast at seven did not interrupt his reading.

Next on the schedule was exercise. The Captain did it with ball throwing, or with roller skating on his private rink in summer and ice skating in winter—his favorite sport. Then he and his wife drove to take the commuters' train down to the office, arriving between 10 and 11 A.M. Before his second marriage in 1938 to Mary King, Patterson drove to work frequently so that he could study traffic problems.

At the office—and again like his cousin—he began to translate the ideas he had accumulated. He made a round of the editorial department to take an informal look at whatever was going on. He usually stopped first at the Sunday department and originated several stories in a few minutes of conversation with the Sunday editor. He often drew the picture editor or a reporter into the discussion, so that he might communicate his ideas directly.

On his rounds Patterson was likely to stop at the paper's color studio, one of his particular prides, where celebrities hand-picked by the publisher himself were photographed. Patterson liked motion pictures, too, and before the war sometimes saw movies several afternoons in a week, as well as on Sunday in Peekskill with his wife. He believed that movies were another index to what people were thinking.

Patterson made an early stop at the city desk as he circulated through the plant, talked over the day's news and gave his instructions about treatment. The desk was tense during those brief sessions, as it is on some other newspapers, because the publisher had been absorbing the details of the news since six o'clock and believed that his editors should have the same background, no matter how different and more complicated their personal living problems might be. Patterson sometimes went over his own

"JMP" assignments (reminiscent of "Must, JM" and "RRMc") with the reporter who was handling the story, and he did not hesitate to tell the underling how to write his lead.

Another occasional stop was at the picture desk, where again Patterson gave instructions about special coverage and learned what the desk had scheduled for the day's work.

When he got back up to his own office the most important part of the day began for Patterson, as he sat down with Maury and Batchelor to plot the next day's editorial pronouncements. Although he worked with these men for years, they called him "Mr. Patterson" or "Chief" or "Captain." Like McCormick, Patterson could not bring himself to be chummy with people. Only Burns Mantle, whose friendship with Patterson dated back to *Tribune* days, called him "Joe."

The conference with Maury and Batchelor usually ran between 11 A.M. and noon, although it was sometimes as short as five minutes. Patterson and Maury talked while Batchelor sat quietly and sketched. The Captain rarely wrote an editorial himself, but he scarcely needed to because Maury's cameralike mind, sensitive from long practice to his boss's every meaning, recorded exactly what Patterson wanted to say. Sometimes, if an editorial tied in with a policy story running in the news columns, the reporter assigned to it was called in to provide facts.

Patterson had Monday luncheon conferences with the five administrative heads of the *News*. He did most of the talking and the others spoke when they were addressed. Lunch was served them, for which they were billed individually at the end of the month. Aside from these meetings, the executives did not see their boss unless he came to their offices with something on his mind.

Monday was "cleanup day." On Monday afternoons at four-thirty Patterson had another conference with the heads and assistants of all the paper's departments, and someone representing the syndicate. These sessions were intended to air complaints and eliminate friction between departments, and although they were designed to preclude alibis, the meetings were called the Alibi Club by other employees. Earlier on Monday afternoons Patterson usually went over comic strips and other syndicate products.

The publisher spent other afternoons dealing with various facets of his business. In the evening he usually took a brief walk after dinner and then spent a considerable amount of time in reading, mostly history, biography and military books.

In all his operations at the office there was the constant reminder, as there is at the *Tribune*, that the *News* was a one-man newspaper and the imprint of its owner was everywhere. One potent reminder, rare in other newspaper offices, was the installation of time clocks in 1932. Patterson broke several of these clocks by punching them too hard and finally exempted himself from the duty, but he refused to excuse anyone else and the clocks remained as an ironic commentary on the mind of the man who later had so many bitter things to say about regimentation.

The most famous of Patterson eccentricities was his penchant for mixing incognito with the masses to find out what they were thinking. Sometimes the mixing was commonplace, like eating in cafeterias and eavesdropping on conversations at nearby tables; at other times it took the form of dressing like a bum and mingling with the down-and-outers in such places as Chicago's old and disreputable 1st Ward and the Bowery in New York. He was known to take the subway out to Coney Island for a happy afternoon of mass enjoyment. In all these excursions Patterson's purposes seem to have been sincere and his enjoyment of them genuine. They undoubtedly paid off in many ways, but the Captain's celebrated understanding of human nature appears to have been greatly exaggerated.

For all his publicized love of the masses, Patterson was psychologically withdrawn from other people. He disliked to shake hands and avoided it when he could. His various suspicions included the rich man's fear that others were preying upon his money. He had a quick, destructive temper and he did not hesitate to use his newspaper to attack for personal reasons which had nothing to do with the making of a newspaper, even when the act involved obviously prejudicial handling of the news. When his anger was directed against an employee, the man might as well have begun to look for another job because Patterson forced him into resigning if he did not fire him outright. Burton Rascoe and Percy Hammond were among the more noted victims of Patterson's vengefulness. They were writers, and Patterson had a strange contempt for writers.

Another Patterson personality trait was claustrophobia, somewhat exaggerated beyond the normal streak most people have. He is said to have had a hatchet hung on the wall of his private bathroom in the Tribune Tower days, so that he could hack his way out if he happened to get locked in. As a further safeguard he ordered a telephone installed.

With a stubbornness reminiscent of old Cyrus McCormick, Patterson fought his great fear of flying by learning to fly when he was past fifty. It was hard going. He lacked co-ordination and the proper judgment of distance, and his first attempt at a solo, stolen against his instructor's orders, ended in a ground loop. But he tried again the same afternoon and made a successful flight, after which he swore off flying entirely for a while. Two years later, however, he was back at it and got his private pilot's license. At one time he owned both a Laird biplane and the world's largest amphibian, a five-ton Sikorsky that cost him fifty-five thousand dollars, named *Liberty* for his ill-fated magazine venture. He wrecked the amphibian in a take-off at Roosevelt Field, escaped death by a miracle, then immediately took off again in his Laird. When the reaction hit him, and he thought about the good fortune that had prevented the Sikorsky's three hundred gallons of gasoline from igniting, he took the pledge not to pilot again himself, and kept it.

When Patterson left Chicago for good, he left behind him his first wife, who won an uncontested divorce in 1938 on grounds of desertion. A substantial settlement was arranged. A month later the Captain married his old *Tribune* friend, Mary King, who had come to New York to be woman's editor of the *News* and fiction editor of the syndicate. They were married by a New York Supreme Court justice in the Bronx County Court House, and sailed the same day on the *Queen Mary* for a honeymoon tour of Ireland, Scotland and Wales.

They returned to live in the house at Ossining, which Raymond Hood, the Tribune Tower's architect, had built to order for the

Captain on a wooded estate overlooking the Hudson. Patterson ordered the house built ugly so that it wouldn't be a show place, had it painted a neutral gray, and demanded metal doors in the place to soothe his claustrophobic fear that wooden ones might swell with the heat and trap him.

At the time the house was built one of his daughters, Alicia, was living with him. She was a seventy-five-dollar-a-week book reviewer for the *News* until 1940, when she became a newspaper publisher in her own right with a tabloid, liberal daily called *Newsday*, published in Hempstead, Long Island. It was typical of Patterson enterprise that Alicia should launch her journalistically experimental paper in a circulation field already dominated by the conservative, well-established *Nassau Daily Review-Star*, a paper which faithfully reflects the county's ardent Republicanism. But *Newsday*, excellently edited and brought along imaginatively, has succeeded in a field which experts had regarded as virtually impossible to crack. Alicia inherits her father's ability. She was in sharp disagreement with him politically—*Newsday* in general supports New Deal principles—but there was a strong affection between them, and she is more like her father than any of the other children. Alicia, once divorced, married an insurance man and ex-Colgate All-American tackle named Joseph Brooks. She married again, this time Harry J. Guggenheim, former United States ambassador to Cuba.

Elinor, the Captain's oldest daughter, also once divorced, later married a banker, Griffith Mark, and went to live in Greenwich, Connecticut. A strikingly beautiful girl, she was an actress when she was eighteen and once played the nun in a Salzburg production of *The Miracle*.

Josephine, the youngest daughter, was a Chicago *Daily News* reporter before she married a Chicago lawyer. When they were growing up, Alicia and Josephine were much together. They learned to fly, earned transport pilots' licenses, and once hunted big game in India and Africa. Besides the three daughters, there is an adopted son, James.

As McCormick sometimes entertains lavishly at Wheaton, Captain Patterson occasionally put aside his seclusion and entertained on his seventy-acre estate. One of the place's beauty spots, aside from its rambling drives and trees of every description, is its large, beautifully kept garden. This garden has a massive greenhouse in its midst and it was there that a ritual took place on the Captain's social occasions. On summer evenings he walked his guests toward it after dinner so that he might display his botanical triumphs. As he approached the greenhouse door, he was likely to pause and turn to his guests and ask them to guess the temperature. He noted their responses, then walked alone to the greenhouse door, near which a thermometer was fastened. He read the temperature, returned to the group and asked, for example, who guessed 78 degrees. The lucky guesser found himself walking with the Captain, who regaled him with further intimate facts about the fauna and flora on the estate. He imparted to one guest the strange news that some of the dells and ravines on his property had the largest fireflies in the county.

Captain Patterson was an accomplished swimmer and diver. It was the custom of women guests, dressed in their picture hats and summer finery, to sit near the pool on his estate. They were unsuspecting victims of the unheralded approach, dive and drenching splash caused when the Captain flung himself off the fifteen-foot board. Patterson himself was oblivious to these disturbances. He swam the length of the pool and back before climbing out. A few minutes later he would be dressed and mingling pleasantly with his guests. By that time the ladies would have moved back to the pool's edge, damper but not wiser, for suddenly they would behold the Captain, once again attired in swimming trunks, poised on the edge of the diving board. They would grit their teeth and wait for the splash which drenched them again.

In attempting to size up Patterson's state of mind in his latter days, some observers insist that it was his divorce from the New Deal which left him out on a mental limb, where he sometimes appeared to be sawing himself off.

When the New Deal was young and going in Patterson's direction, he stayed overnight at the White House many times, was consulted by the President, sent up trial balloons for him, and in general mixed with the Administration far more than his principles allowed, for, like McCormick and Joseph Pulitzer, he felt that publishers should not mix with people they might have to criticize.

In those days of the thirties he was the Peck's Bad Boy among the publishers. His characteristic pattern of revolt took the form of standing for all the things that his fellow publishers hated; he was the newspaper business's severest critic. When his isolationism swung him away from Roosevelt, and the public's support of Roosevelt cost him also the sure feeling that the *News* was interpreting the thinking of the masses, the revolt simply shifted to defense of rich publishers and their interests, both of which he had once scorned, and to holding out for the political ideas which the American people consistently rejected at the polls.

This was in line with what is probably the best single estimate of Patterson ever written, an appreciation penned by his ex-employee, Burton Rascoe, in Rascoe's autobiography, *Before I Forget*. Rascoe wrote of the Captain: "He has always had a social conscience; he is by nature, by action and by conviction democratic and equalitarian. . . . He is impulsive, erratic and impatient, unpredictable, a man who acts and works on hunches. He is devoid of all except the most elementary reasoning powers, and his mistakes have been made through the initial errors of assuming that he was thinking when he was merely feeling, and of attempting to apply a logical process to matters of pure instinct and emotion. His most charming quality is that of trying to live up to his principles. And half the time he does not know what his real feelings are, so numerous are they, . . . so checked and leashed by obligations to his conscience, to his employees, to the handful of heirs of the Chicago *Tribune* properties, to his belief in his mission in the world and to his innate, half-repressed, half-satisfied quest for a full, free life of admirable action and true noblesse oblige."

These words were published in 1937, when Rascoe and Patterson were on opposite sides of the political fence, and may therefore be taken with some reserve. If Rascoe ever revises his memoirs, it will be instructive to see whether the common bond of Roosevelt-hating brought the two men closer together.

Patterson's own estimate of himself, his dynasty and their position in the world was contained in a two-part editorial, "Family Portrait," which appeared in the *News* on October 7 and 8, 1941. It was inspired by Patterson's irritation over *Time Magazine's* continued reference to the "three furies of isolationism"—meaning the Captain, his sister Eleanor and the Colonel.

The editorial is remarkable for its extremely short perspective and lack of understanding of family history. In the first part Patterson argued without particular point that Henry R. Luce had neglected a "fourth Fury," Senator Medill McCormick. The Captain pointed with pardonable pride to the fact that Senator McCormick had, indeed, been of considerable help in wrecking the League of Nations. He recalled, too, that both he and the Colonel had done what they could to keep the United States out of the first World War, but he did not recall that the cousins' thinking on the subject had been static for twenty-five years, an almost classic example of the closed mind.

While this argument could still legitimately come under the head of opinion, there was much less substance to Patterson's next point, an excursion into family history designed to prove that the original Medills and Pattersons and McCormicks were not like the original Cabots and Roosevelts and Byrds. The latter, he said, wanted to "set up a new England here, with lords of the manor and a servant class and all the rest of it." The progenitors of his own dynasty, however, were "another breed of cats," being Scotch and Irish, anxious to get as far away as possible from England and "English aristocratic ideas."

They were Scotch and Irish, true enough, and they probably hated the English, but Patterson's subsequent statement that "they did not stop on the anglicized Atlantic seaboard," but "moved west to the fringes of civilization," gives an entirely erroneous impression. The facts show very clearly that the immigrants in all three families stopped on the anglicized seaboard long enough to acquire land, marry well and become well-to-do in their time and place before the rolling tide of colonization sent them into the interior.

As for the Pattersons in particular, the evidence indicates that they came to America not out of distaste for English aristocracy but to escape English religious intolerance. They came relatively poor, but there is nothing to show that they did not live well before they were long in America. The Medills came to this country as the result of a family dispute over religion. Joseph Medill started life a poor boy, but he made money rapidly. By the time the three families were joined by marriage on "the fringes of civilization," they were all comparatively wealthy. It was the acquisition of wealth that took them there, not a desire to get as far away from the English as possible.

In the second part of his editorial Patterson repeated the myth that the dynasty's ancestors came to America "because they wanted to get shut of Europe's eternal wars, intrigues, oppressions and snobberies." He went on to assert that "when they could see some point in a war, they were for it," and cited the *Tribune's* backing of the Civil War—overlooking those other members of the McCormick clan who opposed that war as bitterly as their cousins opposed the world conflicts that were to come.

Patterson reviewed the already familiar history of his own and the Colonel's isolationism before he advanced the novel thesis that Henry Luce was an interventionist because he spent his youth in China, "surrounded by servants who at that time could be hired" for very low wages. "It is therefore natural for Mr. Luce to feel that the United States ought to rescue China from the Japanese and the French, Dutch, Belgians, Russians, etc., etc., from the Germans." The Captain shortsightedly overlooked millions of Americans who had never been out of their own country, never had a servant, and had no knowledge of English ancestry, if they had any—millions who felt that the issue was the survival of democracy.

"Family Portrait" concluded smugly, "But it also is natural for us, with our Midwestern background, to think first of America in times like these, and to hate to see Americans kidded and cajoled into impossible crusades to remake the whole world."

On a historical basis, of course, the McCormicks, Pattersons and Medills were Johnny-come-latelys to the Middle West, and almost from the first they were separated from real Midwestern life by the wealth and position they enjoyed. Judged against the ordinary Midwesterner of the last century and of today, the three families' individual members were about as untypical of the region as one could imagine. Moreover, although they were Anglophobes, they set themselves up as an aristocracy in Chicago and exhibited the snobbery and other obnoxious characteristics of social position of which they were forever accusing the English.

Coming down to Patterson himself, there is little in his life to show that he was anything more than a rich man born into wealth and the ownership of newspaper properties, who at first tried to evade the responsibilities inherent in both because of his strong guilt feelings. When he created wealth by his own efforts, he lost his guiltiness and slipped gradually into the traditional ways of money and power.

Joseph Medill Patterson died on May 26, 1946, in Doctors Hospital, New York, of a liver ailment complicated at the end by pneumonia. It was a Sunday, and every hour on the hour stay-at-home New Yorkers heard the dead publisher extolled on the news broadcasts over WNEW. These *News*-written eulogies celebrated him as editor, soldier, statesman, novelist and playwright, and reiterated again and again the remark General Douglas MacArthur is said to have made to Lowell Limpus, *News* military analyst, that Patterson was "one of the greatest natural-born soldiers who ever came under my command."

Patterson had been ill since November, and at the time of his death the *News* already seemed like a different plant, according to some of its staff members, although the Captain was more or less in touch with the paper as long as he was able. It was reported that there was even a telephone in his oxygen tent, but if true, this may have been a final expression of claustrophobia. His wife, his daughter Alicia and his son James were with him when he died.

The reaction to the passing of so controversial a figure was more subdued than might have been expected, probably because it came in a period of postwar anesthesia to strong emotion. The editorial column of the *News* carried only this notice, centered: "Joseph Medill Patterson, publisher of this newspaper and the man who directed this page from the day the *News* began, June 26, 1919, is no longer with us. The story of his death will be found in the news columns. Those who are left behind will do their best to keep this page and the paper what we believe he would want them to be."

That was all. As A. J. Liebling remarked in the *New Yorker*, "There was nobody left to tell the highly paid editorial writer what to think." However, Mr. Maury was only momentarily stunned, apparently, because the *News* editorial page has continued in its customary way. Its responses are automatic by this time; it does not need to be told.

Carl Warren wrote the paper's official obituary, which ran for five columns. It began, "Joseph Medill Patterson once wrote the obituary of his best friend. It was a three-line memo to Max Annenberg which said in part: 'Good-by. I am going to miss you a lot. . . . Hope to be seeing you some day. J. M. Patterson.' Perhaps he would have liked some such unpretentious farewell written to him now. It was typical of the man who, to himself, was an humble person. To others he was a genius who possessed and used the magic gift of human understanding."

Warren did not mention Patterson's affair with Socialism.

The obituary was printed in full and without changes, inside black borders, by the Washington *Times-Herald*, but the *Tribune* made several alterations in keeping with the World's Greatest Newspaper. It added, "Patterson was the eldest of a family trio of publishers whose exploits, leadership, and genius for success made history in 20th century journalism. . . . Surviving members of the famous trio are his sister, Eleanor M. Patterson, publisher of the Washington *Times-Herald*, and Col. Robert R. McCormick."

The *Tribune* moved the story of Patterson's career as a novelist down to the end of the obituary, and substituted in the chronology the vague statement that he "worked on the *Tribune* intermittently during this period." Another drastic change in emphasis was the burying of an anecdote Warren had placed near his lead, in which he recited the publisher's love for the people, a love that had caused him to have the quotation from Abraham Lincoln inscribed on the front of the Daily News Building. ("Like Abraham Lincoln, who was his idol," the paper's newscasts reiterated that Sunday, "he belongs to the ages.")

In place of this anecdote the *Tribune* inserted another which told of Patterson's insistence on being boss. Further down it deleted entirely General MacArthur's citation of Patterson as the greatest natural-born soldier who had ever served under him, because as Liebling observed in his *New Yorker* summary of these affairs, "Everybody on the *Tribune* knows that Colonel McCormick is the most brilliant, natural-born soldier that ever served under anyone."

The *Tribune's* editorial on Patterson was meditative, and in all respects true to form. It ran in part: "You can't wholly explain genius. A very few men—and Capt. Patterson was one of them—have it and the great majority don't. Somebody, some day, may find out why this is so. The best we can do now is to say that he was born of the right parents, in the right place, and at the right time. He inherited the blood of the founder of this newspaper, the grandfather for whom he was named, and he inherited also an interest in the ownership of the *Tribune*. . . . These circumstances, surely, are not the whole explanation of the man and his career, but they are a most important part of it.

"In early manhood he was a Socialist," the *Tribune* went on, having found a way to explain the sins of the deceased, "because, as he once said, he couldn't find answers to the arguments of his Socialist friends. When he did find the answers he quit the movement. He had joined because he saw Socialism as the hope of the common man. Years later, in much the same spirit, he supported Mr. Roosevelt thru two terms. He broke with him dramatically over foreign policy. Capt. Patterson, who knew war and history better than Mr. Roosevelt did, couldn't believe that the common man's lot in America was going to be improved on European battlefields."

As for the theory that Patterson had "the right formula" in making the *News* successful, the *Tribune* was disdainful. "All such talk is likely to be pretty silly because he didn't have a formula in the sense in which the word is commonly used. People who talk learnedly about formulas have in mind the size of headline type, an arbitrary length to which stories are limited, the quantity of space devoted to the various categories of news, the number of comic strips, and all such measurable things. If great newspapers could be made by formula, we would have not a half-dozen of them in the world but hundreds and maybe thousands, because any publisher possessed of a bankroll and an agate rule could be as successful as any other. It is just because such publishers operate by formula that most of our newspapers today are the colorless things they are.

"In this sense Patterson had no formula. What he had was something infinitely more precious, and that was a sure sense of what the masses of the people, rich and poor, smart and dumb, were interested in and how to tell it to them. The *Tribune-News* comic strips disclose this understanding, but it should not be forgotten that what he did in developing these cartoons here in Chicago and later in New York offers merely one evidence of his ability to penetrate the minds and hearts of people. His whole paper and the feature pages of the *Tribune* as well, tell the same story. It was that quality in him which made his editorial page sing.

"That, and a boyish gayety and a playful wit that provided a nice balance for his earnestness and candor. If the editorial pages of this country's newspapers are ever freed of ponderosity and cant, Patterson will deserve most of the credit for the achievement. His editorials have shown the way. Nothing can be more certain than that he would have quit the newspaper business if it had not been fun for him, or if he had thought for a moment that any other occupation could give him the same lusty pleasure and the same solid satisfactions."

Numerous anecdotes about the Captain were related after his death. One of the most revealing, although intended to be complimentary, was narrated by Lowell Limpus to *Editor & Publisher*. Limpus said that he was making up the paper one day in its early period when an unassuming middle-aged man offered him some ideas for an editorial. Limpus glanced through the opening sentences and threw the whole thing into the wastebasket. "The thing was that bad," he said. "It looked like it would get us into a lot of trouble. I didn't know the gent who gave me the copy was Patterson, so I gave it the heave-ho. Shand [Robert G. Shand, now city editor] dashed up as I was dropping the last few sheets into the basket and hurriedly retrieved them. 'That's Mr. Patterson,' he said. 'Anything he writes goes into the paper.'

"I told Shand I didn't know who the man was; I thought he was one of the printers and the only reason I even looked at it was because I thought it would be amusing to see what a printer thought would be an editorial idea. I told Shand that even if the owner had written the editorial, it looked like it needed checking, but he brushed that aside, repeating that what Mr. Patterson wrote would appear as he wrote it. I still remember that editorial, which later became famous. It was one of Patterson's frequent attacks on what he termed the 'idle rich,' and had to do with an important family of the time living in New York. It led off like this: 'What a filthy tribe of vultures they are.' Well, the editorial appeared as he wrote it, and that little incident was my introduction to Captain Patterson."

*Editor & Publisher* also recorded that Patterson was so anxious to be on the spot where news was made that he would often turn up unexpectedly and tell the reporter who was on the assignment, "Here I am. What's to be done? Understand now, you're the boss and I'm working for you. What angle do you want me to take?" No record exists of how many good reporters were stricken dumb for life by these tactics.

For a day or two there was considerable speculation as to who would control the *News* now that its strong man was no more. Few people knew that Patterson had anticipated this situation fifteen years before and had created a five-man board of *News* executives to operate the paper in the event of his death. There had never, as a matter of fact, been an official publisher or editor of the paper. Patterson, as president of the News Syndicate Company, was called publisher for the sake of convenience.

At the time of Patterson's death the board of control consisted of Roy C. Holliss, general manager; F. M. Flynn, business manager; H. B. Sherwood, advertising director; Richard W. Clarke, managing editor; and Ivan Annenberg, circulation manager. This board was responsible to the board of directors of the News Syndicate Company, composed of Colonel McCormick, Mrs. Patterson, Mrs. Ruth Miller, daughter of the late Ruth Hanna McCormick

Simms; Dr. Henry D. Lloyd; Alfred Cowles; E. M. Antrim, business manager of the *Tribune;* Flynn and Holliss.

Speaking for the board of control, Clarke told *Editor & Publisher* that there was "no change contemplated in the operation of the paper in the forseeable future." He added that the board would resolve all of its publishing problems as far as possible, but would refer "more important situations" to the directors.

There was little prospect that Patterson's son James would succeed to the throne. Although he had once been a copy boy on the *News,* he still had two more years to go at West Point and after that, according to the Point's unwritten law, would have to serve at least four years in the Army, a career for which he already showed aptitude and interest.

Patterson's will, filed for probate at White Plains, left the bulk of his fortune to his wife and children, and his Ossining estate to Fordham University. Much of his money, it appeared, was in a trust fund which he had created in 1932 with McCormick.

On May 29, 1946, a caisson drawn by six white horses carried Captain Patterson's body into Arlington Cemetery, where it was laid to rest near the tomb of the Unknown Soldier, at the Fort Myer gate. It was the kind of funeral which would have pleased him, for he preferred to think of himself as a soldier instead of a publisher. Those he left behind, however, could not help remembering him as a publisher, the kind of strange and wonderful publisher he was. Friends and enemies alike knew that the New York *Daily News* might survive indefinitely, but its heart had stopped beating.

Patterson had scarcely been in his grave three months before disaster struck the *News* again. Roy Holliss, who had been directing the paper as acting president, died in a Connecticut auto accident. Superstitious folk shuddered at the coincidences surrounding Holliss's death. He was the second *News* executive to die in a wrecked car: Harvey Deuell, called by many the greatest managing editor of all time, whose six-figure salary was certainly the highest ever paid for that job, had suffered a heart attack on a Sunday afternoon in 1939 while he was driving to work and had also died in a ditch.

Even more striking was the manner in which the *News* itself had forecast, if one were superstitious, the deaths of both Patterson and Holliss, in each case through editorial matter aimed primarily at the hated Roosevelts. There had been the May 1945 editorial, "Three of the Big Ones Dead in a Month," in which Roosevelt was linked with Mussolini and Hitler—a piece followed by Patterson's death a year later. Holliss's passing was an ironic commentary on the *News's* traffic safety campaign, conducted mostly through the cartoons Batchelor had drawn for nine years, titled "Inviting the Undertaker." These grim art works pointed out driving errors. The two hundred and sixty-fourth cartoon in the series depicted a tombstone and, in the paper's own peculiar way, was intended to slap at Eleanor Roosevelt for her recent accident, although no one had been injured seriously in it. The final edition carrying this latest sample of *News* taste had been closed only an hour and a half when Roy Holliss was killed.

Three days later the News Syndicate Company's board of directors was reshuffled. Cissy Patterson was made chairman of the board; Richard Clarke, managing editor since 1939, was elected secretary; and Business Manager Flynn took on added responsibility as treasurer. Fifty-year-old Clarke, son of the paper's first managing editor, was given the new title of executive editor, and it was understood that he would run the paper and be responsible to Cissy, inasmuch as McCormick had said in Chicago a short time before that he didn't think the *News* needed him. The new board told reporters from other papers that no statement on future policy would be made. It was not hard to guess, however, what *News* policy would be as long as Cissy was chairman of the board.

## Chapter 3

# THE FEMALE OF THE SPECIES

ELEANOR MEDILL PATTERSON, publisher of the Washington *Times-Herald*, was once termed by Stanley Walker "an everlasting problem child." This is a kinder way of saying that she is a rich woman who has always had her own will about virtually everything. Her newspaper is successful and it is published with even more of the spirit typical of the *Tribune* and the *Daily News* because Mrs. Patterson adds feminine temperament to the other characteristics of the family.

This redheaded member of the clan was born (November 7, 1884) into the newspaper business but, like Captain Patterson, she came into the actual practice of it reluctantly and after trying to make a different kind of life for herself. As a child she had the example of her father, who became the respected editor of the Chicago *Tribune* in spite of the fact that he married the boss's daughter. Eleanor adored her father and idolized her brother Joe, who gave her the nickname "Cissy" by which she is known familiarly today. In the family manner, however, she permits only intimates to use the nickname; she is Mrs. Patterson or The Lady to everyone else.

The early fixation on the male members of her family led to a protest against the well-ordered feminine social world represented by her mother, who had planned a career in society for her. Cissy was critical of her mother until the elder Mrs. Patterson died in her Drake Hotel apartment in Chicago in 1933.

According to Cissy, the family was not wealthy, measured by the fact that the Patterson home had only one bathtub. They were anything but poor measured by Chicago standards, however, and the girl grew up in an atmosphere of turn-of-the-century elegance. Her revolt against this way of living did not have the deep psychological roots implicit in her brother's soul struggles. It was far simpler, and at first took the shape of trying to be like the family's male members. In brief, Cissy was a tomboy. A former neighbor recalls the day that Cissy climbed the steeple of St. James' Church, an Episcopal church on the near North Side. This feat brought a gratifyingly shocked response at home. In general, the family accepted her tomboyishness resignedly.

Meanwhile her mother worked assiduously to guide Cissy's wayward steps into their preordained path, and at the proper time the girl went off to Miss Hersey's School in Boston, with the hope that she would be "finished" in the correct mold. By the time she was graduated, a lovely child of seventeen, Cissy was ready to be launched, both in Chicago and at the Pattersons' big, formal house on DuPont Circle in Washington, which was architect Stanford White's monument to Mrs. Patterson's social ambitions.

Once launched, Cissy plunged into the accepted social life of fashionable Washington, interspersed with junkets abroad. It was on one of these trips, in 1902 in Paris, that she met Count Josef Gizycki. The count was an amiable, handsome young Polish cavalry officer, a bit low in his bank account, who felt that fate had brought him this charming and wealthy young American girl. He pursued Cissy about Europe in his ardent continental way until the hypnotized maiden brushed aside the objections of her family and friends and married the dashing Gizycki in a large and fashionable wedding at the DuPont Circle mansion.

That was on April 4, 1904. Cissy spent the next four years regretting her romantic hastiness. Her life with the count was like a Lubitsch movie, star-crossed with a bad novel. It was a marriage that made no one happy except newspaper editors and columnists. The count took her to his castle in the Russian Ukraine, as he had promised, but it turned out to be a gloomy pile full of bad plumbing and completely surrounded by mortgages. Moreover, Gizycki took the traditional European attitude that there was to be no more nonsense permitted from a woman after the ceremony, that she was henceforth a chattel.

Intolerable though it must have been to anyone of Cissy's background, she refrained from murdering the count in his sleep and endured the situation until her daughter Felicia was born in 1907. Then she took the baby and went to England without saying good-by, thereby precipitating an international incident. The count followed her to London, kidnaped Felicia and hid the child in an Austrian convent.

That action was the impulsive Gizycki's major mistake. He brought the full weight of the McCormicks and Pattersons down on his head. A battalion of private detectives ferreted out the abducted child; President Taft made representations to the Czar of Russia; the ambassadorial McCormicks went about Moscow pulling wires; and the count got an appallingly bad press in America, where he was relegated to the class of "foreign fortune hunters."

Cissy made a triumphal re-entry into America on August 18, 1909. Like a first-act entrance in a Pinero drama, she walked down the gangplank of the *Kaiser Wilhelm der Grosse*, a small-waisted, fashionably dressed woman, the picture of femininity triumphant over man's inhumanity. Little Felicia clutched her hand tightly. The New York *World* reported, "The countess is tall and still girlish, with a look of sadness about her eyes."

But the count was not ready to give up his income so easily. He fought Cissy through the courts for eight years while she tried to divorce him, and it took the fall of czarism to defeat him. Cissy got her divorce in 1917; the count was allegedly a half million dollars richer and promptly disappeared from public view.

Back in good old familiar America again, the ex-Countess Gizycka returned to the traditional American life she had exchanged for a life of foreign frippery. She frequented the flossy haunts of New York, Washington and Chicago society. She rode and hunted on her ranch near Jackson Hole, Wyoming. Cissy drifted.

It was love that changed her life again. First it was the love of her rebellious daughter Felicia, who was willing to trade her debut for the privilege of running a San Francisco eatery but decided instead in 1925 to marry Drew Pearson, then a struggling Washington newspaperman.

Left alone, the countess surprised her friends by getting married herself a month later to Elmer Schlesinger, a New York lawyer who had won a name for himself as counsel for the United States Shipping Board. Schlesinger had one unsuccessful marriage behind him and came out of it with two children and a temperament which apparently made it difficult for him to get along with the mercurial Cissy. In any event this second marriage was not satisfactory to either party. It ended in 1929 when Schlesinger died suddenly of heart failure at the Palmetto Golf Club in Aiken, South Carolina. After some legal squabbling over the estate Cissy was able to add a third of her husband's two-million-dollar fortune to her capital resources. The courts also obliged the widow by changing her name legally to Mrs. Eleanor Patterson.

At forty-six Cissy had done virtually everything the other members of her family had done except run a newspaper. She had dabbled in literature with two novels, *Glass Houses* (1926) and *Fall Flight* (1928). The first was received in an innocuous way by the critics and in grim silence by the author's Washington friends, who got in it their first taste of what Cissy could and would do to them in print. The literary quality of the book may be estimated roughly by a remark made by her heroine: "Don't let's ask too much. But we can be happy, most of the time, I suppose, when we have learned to compromise."

In *Fall Flight* Mrs. Patterson paid her belated respects to the count and became so engrossed with assassinating him fictionally that she let her plot fall apart. With this book Cissy established herself as a newspaperwoman.

Entering the parlous thirties, she was at loose ends. Her daughter had divorced Pearson and was destined to follow her mother's footsteps in 1934 by marrying again, a marriage that also broke up, after which she became a novelist.

At this critical point in Cissy's life she got into the newspaper business through the back door, by virtue of her friendship with William Randolph Hearst. Cissy and Hearst were old friends. In 1920 she had contributed some Idaho hunting articles to the Chicago *Herald and Examiner*. They had dined together, ridden together, and partied from coast to coast, and they saw eye to eye on the subject of journalism.

Consequently Hearst had every reason to trust his judgment when in 1930 Cissy talked him into letting her be editor of his Washington *Herald*. He paid her a ten-thousand-dollar annual salary, moreover, a figure which was scarcely reflected by the *Herald's* fluttery circulation. It was one of Hearst's better speculations, because Cissy promptly brought personal journalism to Washington in the old familiar family manner. Her initial blast was inspired by a Washington rumor that Cissy's worst enemy, Alice Roosevelt Longworth, might be adviser to Ruth Hanna McCormick, then about to run for the Senate. Cissy dignified the rumor by replying to it in a signed front-page box, a personal insult running in the news columns. This much-quoted piece read:

## INTERESTING, BUT NOT TRUE

The news is that Alice Longworth will not only be the confidential adviser to Mrs. Ruth Hanna McCormick but that she will campaign publicly for her lifelong friend. Interesting, but not true.

Mrs. McCormick takes no advice, political or otherwise, from Mrs. Longworth.

Mrs. Longworth gives no interviews to the press.

Mrs. Longworth cannot utter in public.

Her assistance, therefore, will resolve itself, as usual, into posing for photographs.

The resulting circulation jump indicated primarily what everyone knows: that Washington likes to read about itself. In the national capital, where intrigue has always been the major industry, Cissy's personal approach was just what the doctor ordered. As the paper went along under her direction, Cissy supplemented the diet with features, an element previously inclined to undernourishment in Washington newspapers. The combination nearly doubled the *Herald's* 60,000 circulation from 1930 to 1936. By that time Cissy was in the saddle and already had the publisher complex. She differed in some respects with Hearst's anti-Administration policies, and in 1937 she leased the *Herald* so that she could express her own views. Later in the same year she leased the evening *Times*, published from the same plant, and in

1939 bought the properties to publish them as the Washington *Times-Herald*, in morning, evening and Sunday editions.

These papers compete against the conservative and advertising-rich *Star*, afternoons and Sundays; the afternoon Scripps-Howard tabloid *News*, which has never been a financial success but is often first with the news; and Eugene Meyer's liberal, superbly edited morning *Post*.

The *Times-Herald* has never approached its competitors in the primary matter of news coverage. Like the other family properties, it is edited with a fine disregard for objective reporting. Nor is it the equal of the other Washington papers in news presentation (the Sunday edition is a particular disgrace), but when the figures are added up, the *Times-Herald* outsells its competitors. Its total circulation, daily and Sunday, is 499,885. There are minor factors in this success, but the principal reason for it is feature coverage. Brother Joe was a profitable tutor for Cissy, and she often sought his advice, which he gave her freely.

In the course of her career as a publisher Cissy has followed the family's methods faithfully. She went even further in the early days of her newspapering by doing actual reporting. In 1931 she looked into Washington's unemployment situation by utilizing a typical Hearst technique and disguising herself as an out-of-work maid so that she could study at first hand what the city was doing about one of its major problems. Similarly she investigated reports that school children were not being properly fed, and as the result of her crusading series on the subject Washington school children got hot lunches. On still another occasion she talked her way into Al Capone's Florida mansion and got an exclusive story from the ex-underworld czar.

Cissy's position in society turned out to be helpful in her newspaper career. Well knowing the predilections of Washington newspaper readers, she provided the most complete coverage of society news in the city—pages as compared to her competitors' columns—and, working this snob appeal in another direction, she wined and dined potential advertisers to attract them into the *Times-Herald* fold.

The similarities between Cissy and the other publishers in her family are many. Like the Colonel, whom she is supposed to have once called "that old Bourbon, my cousin Bertie," she is stubborn, willful, moody, domineering, contradictory and utterly convinced of her own rightness. Like him, she loves riding and the good things that money buys.

Cissy even has that shy, human side which the world does not see. She confided to a friend that she gets moody sometimes when she wakes up in the morning, looks in the mirror, sees that she is getting on, and concludes that she will never know love again. "Then," the friend reported, "she goes down to the office and gives the Administration hell."

She has used the name-calling technique with *Tribune*-like fervor. In the course of a long feud with her rival publisher, Eugene Meyer, her paper normally refers to his paper as "our venerable lady friend, the *Post*" and "our narsty-nice morning contemporary."

Her operation of the *Times-Herald* differs in one important respect from that of both the *Tribune* and the *Daily News*. Both McCormick and Patterson have made efforts to keep their employees happy, even though their papers were strictly one-man shows, and the turnover in manpower is small. But Cissy is a woman, as well as a member of the dynasty, and the combination has proved overpowering to many a good newspaperman in her employ. In the first ten years of her editorship seven news editors came, heard and departed.

The principal difficulty in getting along with Cissy, according to one veteran who resigned, is that she runs the paper strictly according to her own whims and ideas, no matter what sound newspaper practice dictates. She will not listen to men who have spent their lives making newspapers, even though events prove her to be completely wrong. What is even harder for some employees to stomach is her disposition to let prejudice dictate. For example a photo editor going over a picture layout with her was ordered to use a bad shot in place of the acceptable one he had selected because the bad one showed off a society friend of Cissy's to better advantage.

A much worse example of how far blind prejudice goes in the

making of Cissy's papers occurred in the first days of 1945, when with unpardonable bad taste the *Times-Herald* carried a picture page of American war victims, captioned with President Roosevelt's 1940 "again and again and again" quotation. That layout cost Cissy her able managing editor, George DeWitt, who is said to have told his boss, "Either that layout goes, or I go."

Cissy's theory of newspaper publishing was enunciated in November 1939, in a New York *Herald Tribune* interview written by Emma Bugbee. She was quoted: "What I am trying to do is to put out a paper which depends first on its news value. Features must come second in my opinion. . . . And I want my paper to give its news honest and unbiased. We all say that—all newspaper proprietors—but I really mean it."

Perhaps Cissy really meant it, but the record of her newspapers even at that time indicated that her conception of honest and unbiased news was a long way from the higher standards of journalism. The *Times-Herald* was violently isolationist, in its news columns as well as on the editorial page, in line with the publisher's belief that the United States must be kept out of war "at any cost." In April 1938 she had published on the front page an open letter to the President, asserting, "This fear is fear of you," and urging him to cease his reform measures and to keep silent. There spoke true McCormick omniscience.

Like Patterson, Cissy had supported Roosevelt in 1932 and published a signed editorial assailing the "whisper" about him, although her own voice after 1938 scarcely fell below the level of a shout. She took little part in the 1936 campaign, and thereafter she departed even faster than the *Daily News* from Administration support. The real split was on the issue of intervention. And though Cissy had once called Mrs. Roosevelt editorially "the noblest woman I have ever known" and asserted that she adored her "above all women," the *Times-Herald* did not hesitate to repeat all the worst canards of the Roosevelt-hating press after 1940, and invented some of its own.

Mrs. Patterson's political attacks follow the familiar pattern of those in the *Tribune* and *Daily News*. In general her paper is closer in tone and treatment to the *Tribune* in its use of slanted headlines and news stories, studied emphasis in display of news, and generally exclamatory method of attack. The *Times-Herald's* equivalent of John O'Donnell has been Frank C. Waldrop, who is the paper's nominal editor and writes a column even more direct than O'Donnell's. This is supplemented by Helen Essary's column, which says the same things in other ways.

For example the *Times-Herald* was against unconditional surrender from the first for reasons obvious to all observers of McCormick-Patterson policy. A column on this subject was written by Waldrop on July 24, 1944, in which he rang the changes on the bells of piety:

"On the one side, politicians who want the war to go on to 'unconditional surrender' for reasons of their own will have powerful weapons in the natural human lust for revenge.

"On the other, American Protestantism and Roman Catholicism join to sound 'the voice of moral authority' as a brake to violence.

"A real jolt has been handed the 'unconditional surrender' warriors by highly influential Protestant American churchmen who quote Pope Pius' call for 'wisdom and moderation' as the way to peace.

"The *Christian Century* asked, 'Is the United States to be the principal agent in this hour of world crisis in padlocking the lips of the Pope as he attempts to speak with the voice of moral authority?'

"Washington can only guess at what was said about 'unconditional surrender' at recent conferences between the Pontiff and Secretary of War Stimson and Myron C. Taylor, but the old-time crack about the Pope being 'the prisoner of the Vatican' is going around here again, as official policy calls for strangling all sentiments opposed to the Roosevelt-Churchill 'unconditional surrender' line.

"In America there will be name-calling again, reminiscent of the foreign policy debates of 1940–41, as the peace' pressure grows."

A prime example of the *Times-Herald's* treatment of news is its February 1945 headline on the Yalta Conference. The eight-column front-page banner proclaimed: CRIMEA PACT A

CRIME—BERLIN. This had been the spoken verdict of Dr. Goebbels. A one-column head at the bottom of page one read: CONGRESS HAILS CRIMEAN PACT.

These headlines appeared in the first afternoon edition. The second edition showed the banner only slightly altered, with the emphasis remaining: CRIMEA PACT A CRIME, BERLIN CHARGES. To underline its stand the paper's final edition had a new banner, EXILE POLES REJECT BIG 3 PACT, and underneath it a three-column head reading, BERLIN CALLS YALTA DECISIONS "GREATEST POLITICAL CRIME." The story on the favorable reaction of Congress still ran below the fold.

It is all very well to argue that such play of a story is a matter for individual editorial opinion, but it is quite another thing for the publisher of such a paper to pretend that the news in it is "honest and unbiased."

As in the case of the other McCormick-Patterson newspapers, the *Times-Herald's* words were quoted with approval by the enemy radio and were cited by the rabid isolationist publications, including those which were subsequently barred from the mails. Such stories, for example, as the one originating in the *Tribune,* in which McCormick charged that top United States jobs were held by Rhodes scholars who were undoubtedly British propagandists, found ready space for reprinting in these Anglophobic sheets which parroted the German propaganda line. They were equally avid to get McCormick-Patterson stories like the editorial which asserted that the OWI was creating an army of spies resembling the Gestapo, and another which sniped in a snide fashion at the alleged influx of refugees on government pay rolls.

Again it may be argued that a paper cannot be held responsible if the wrong people agree with its views. Liberal papers are often embarrassed by the support of American Communists when the Kremlin's party line happens to coincide with liberal thinking.

But the sins of the *Times-Herald,* like those of the *Tribune* and *Daily News,* are not simply those of ideology. They are those resulting from the presentation of news by strongly prejudiced, willful people who apparently feel no responsibility to the people who read their newspapers. Possibly they are sincerely convinced that they reflect a certain body of public opinion which, although it is obviously in the minority, is right and the rest of the world wrong. No one but they themselves should presume to answer for the sincerity of their motives.

The inescapable fact, however, is that the people are entitled to unbiased reporting and presentation of the news, and from this study it seems self-evident that the McCormick-Patterson papers do not fulfill that primary, fundamental responsibility.

Part Five

# McCORMICK, THE PATTERSONS AND FREEDOM OF THE PRESS

# Chapter 1
## THE DEFENSE RESTS

FREEDOM OF THE PRESS is a subject big enough to accommodate all the tongues and pens that burn to argue about it. The range of opinion runs from Colonel McCormick and other publishers to whom freedom of the press means a freedom without limits except those which the individual chooses to impose upon himself, all the way to the Communists, who argue that complete government control of the press in the Soviet Union is the only free press because the government is the people.

As an arbitrary starting point for this particular discussion, let us accept the truism that the American press is the freest in the world, however much it may abuse its freedom. Unfortunately the abuses are seldom the subject of argument because the owners of newspapers customarily restrict discussion of press freedom to the maintenance of the status quo against real or imaginary attempts at control by government. There are few critics of the newspaper business within the business itself, and those outside are habitually scorned by the publishers as lacking knowledge and actual experience. Consequently the public is given the impression that freedom of the press is the exclusive property of newspaper proprietors, who must constantly defend it against both government regulation and the criticism of outsiders who are not convinced that the status quo is the best of all possible states.

An example of the kind of lullaby that publishers sing to each other when they foregather is contained in a speech by John S. Knight, whose Knight Newspapers include the Miami *Herald*, Akron *Beacon-Journal*, Detroit *Free Press* and Chicago *Daily News*. Speaking to the New York State Publishers' Association in Syracuse, on September 11, 1944, Mr. Knight assured his willing listeners, "The President himself has delighted in throwing barbs at the newspapers, even though, with a few notable exceptions, he has had the fairest press in the history of American government."

He followed this scholarly piece of historical analysis with a familiar jab at those non-newspaper owners who presume to examine the press critically. "Then," he remarked, "we have the professional critics of the press like Morris Ernst and George Seldes, the columnists who delight in spearing the profession that brought them into being, and the bright, young radio salesmen who tell the advertiser that the press has 'no influence.' "

The little band of persecuted publishers presumably went home greatly consoled by the assurance that they were the stout defenders of freedom against villainy.

At times Colonel McCormick gives the impression that he and his paper are the only barriers between a free press and total bondage. He has spoken and written hundreds of thousands of words on the subject; he was first chairman of the ANPA's general committee on freedom of the press; he has even caused the publication (in 1944) of a book called *Liberty and the Press,* by the *Tribune's* biographer, Philip Kinsley, which is blandly subtitled, "A History of the Chicago *Tribune's* Fight to Preserve a Free Press for the American People."

The history of the *Tribune's* fight for the *Tribune's* conception of press freedom, however, began long before Mr. Kinsley's book says it did, and the consequences are somewhat different from those imagined by the Colonel.

Joseph Medill's theory of press freedom was first enunciated in a *Tribune* editorial of January 22, 1864. It expresses clearly the idea of a free press subject only to the control of the individual publisher, who of course never publishes anything except from the highest motives. The editorial declared:

### THE INDEPENDENCE OF THE PRESS

Within the last quarter of a century the metropolitan press— that portion at least devoted to freedom—has become thoroughly independent. The people have fostered and approved the change and now even demand that their paper shall be the organ of no mere clique or faction but that it shall earnestly advocate the right and combat the wrong, come from whatever source it may.

So thoroughly zealous are Americans on this point that nothing can be more injurious to a paper than for it to swerve from these principles and become the party organ of any man or set of men, no matter how towering his or their ability may be.

For the last few years *The Tribune* has been ruined scores of times in the estimation of party hacks and even well meaning friends when it would not lend itself to their schemes of personal aggrandizement, or because it denounced incompetency in generals and demanded more vigorous measures to put down the rebellion. But every leading measure so advocated has become from necessity the policy of the government and from "the grave digger" of Chickahominy all through the list, the do-nothings have been laid on the shelf, just as we predicted they would be.

In brief, therefore, the independent press wants no friends—it must have none—except only as they represent truth, progress, and patriotism and in the ratio that men have the will, the energy, and the ability to promote these in that ratio will the press labor with them to secure and to advance the intellectual, the social, and the moral welfare of the whole people.

To it, social and personal relations, wealth, high position and even past service, are nothing. The questions to be decided are, Are the measures proposed intrinsically right and adapted to promote the welfare of society?

An early example of this philosophy in practice, not to be found in the *Tribune's* book on the subject, was the libel case brought by Mrs. Frances M. Wilkinson against the *Tribune* in 1868. George Buckley, a reporter, published the speeches of counsel for the plaintiff (Rounds & James, Chicago, 1869) because, as he put it, "The *Tribune's* side of the case, in all its fullness, has found all the publicity of that paper's circulation, in its so-called report of the trial, in its columns. The plaintiff's case can be only so slightly and imperfectly gathered from the *Tribune's* professed report—the only one published—that there would seem to be propriety and justice in a fairer and fuller presentation of her side of it to the public. . . ."

The case originated with a *Tribune* story of October 1867, carried under the headline, SCANDAL AND TURMOIL. A WIFE BREAKING IN ON HER HUSBAND'S DEVOTIONS. THE AFFRAY CARRIED INTO THE POLICE COURT. It was the kind of story quite common in newspapers of that time, a highly editorialized narration of what happened when the wife of a real estate agent allegedly surprised him in the midst of amours with one of his tenants. The "other woman" sued for libel, however, and the *Tribune* published a retraction, asserting that the story had gotten into the paper by mistake in spite of such precautions to prevent its publication as writing "out" on the margins. The retraction was followed by a plea of justification in which, as plaintiff's counsel argued, the victims were accused all over again.

The jury heard the testimony, held a short consultation, and returned a verdict of guilty; damages were assessed at seventy-five hundred dollars. This verdict brought an outraged cry from the *Tribune* on January 1, 1869, in part as follows:

### A MALICIOUS VERDICT

The public have had an opportunity of reading in all the papers of the city, during the week, the trial of the libel suit in which a Mrs. Wilkinson claimed damages of the *Tribune* for the accidental publication of a report of a Police Court case in which she, Mr. A. C. Ellithorpe, and his wife, were parties under arrest. The facts of the publication are known to the public, and were known to the jury. In the face of the facts of the case, the jury, as if in defiance of common sense, law, justice and public decency, have rendered a verdict for the plaintiff, awarding her $7,500 damages. Had the jury been co-plaintiffs, and each man entitled to a pro rata share of the damages, their own self-interest, overriding all other considerations, would not have permitted them to have given a great sum damages [sic]. We question whether there is on record a verdict which bears upon its face such incontestable evidence of ignorance and malice as this one. . . . There is no person who will question the overbearing malice which marks this verdict. The effort to justify it on the ground that the Tribune Company is wealthy, is but an additional proof that the verdict proceeded from the lowest of all springs of human action—malicious ignorance.

The verdict will not arrest the publication of the *Tribune*. . . . It is in behalf of the freedom of the press—in behalf of the freedom of every other paper published in this city, and in the country, and in behalf of the liberty of the people themselves—that we arraign this verdict as an embodiment of an ignorance whose stolidity is only equalled by its personal malignity. There is not a man who sat on that jury who does not owe the liberty he enjoys, and the peace and security of his family and of his business, to the protecting power of the public press. Men of such intellects and instincts would be serfs in any country, where there was not a free press to shield them from the tyranny of the powerful and unscrupulous. . . . Such verdicts prevent a newspaper publishing any facts or news unless it has the power to prove their truth, and in addition, the faculty of overcoming the low-born malevolence of a besotted jury.

. . . If such a verdict is to stand, to mark the narrow boundary in which the press may be free, there must be an appeal to that higher tribunal—the people—for that sweeping remedy that will teach treacherous jurors that the liberties of the people are so bound up with and so intimately blended with that of the press, that the one cannot be assailed and outraged without doing violence to the other.

An indignant letter in response was written by the jury's foreman, John M. Cyrus, and cosigned by other jurors. Medill refused to publish it, but the Chicago *Republican*, the *Tribune's* rival, was only too glad to give it space. Cyrus wrote in part: "Gentlemen, you have had your own reporter in the court room during the progress of the trial. Have you not *distorted* the evidence to suit your side of the case? Have you not *tinged* and *colored* every incident that seemed to disparage the plaintiff? Can you say, under the sanctions and solemnities of an oath (for bear in mind the jury were under oath), that *your* report of the evidence and the arguments of counsel were fair and honest? . . . Why all these epithets upon the jury; why all this particularity of names, occupations and private residences, unless to injure us in our business, and to scare any future jury which might be called to try a case in which the Tribune Company was one of the parties to the suit?"

The courts later established that a newspaper could indeed not publish "facts or news unless it has the power to prove their truth," except in the case of such privileged matter as editorials and signed columns, under limitations prescribed by the law of libel. News stories of the kind the *Tribune* ran in 1867 disappeared from all newspapers, whether they were true or not. Or rather, they were written from a more objective, less editorialized standpoint, within the limits outlined by practice and court decisions.

The instructive moral to be derived from the case of Wilkinson vs. the *Tribune* is that the paper, as early as this in its history, set a pattern from which it has scarcely deviated: the publication of anything it chooses, and an attack on those who dare to oppose it as enemies of freedom of the press. This freedom, even in 1868, if one may believe the testimony of the jury foreman and other parties not involved in the suit, included the right to publish one-sided news stories about the paper's enemies.

In its long fight for its own kind of freedom the *Tribune* has concentrated almost exclusively on infringements by government, resting its cases on the belief, as Mr. Kinsley puts it, that "The power of the press must stem from the power of the people; its restrictions must emanate from the people, not from any governmental authority."

While no sane student of the problem would argue in behalf of any form or variety of governmental control, it is equally clear that the press cannot evade responsibility by shifting it to the people. The *Tribune* argument, followed to its logical conclusion, would result in exactly the kind of irresponsible press for which McCormick has always argued.

The *Tribune* has spent about three million dollars in its court fights involving the free-press issue. The briefs prepared by its able lawyers, while they have been fashioned naturally to further the interests of the client, have also contributed in a large measure to the legal framework upon which our present press freedom rests.

Reviewing these cases in his book, Mr. Kinsley begins with the Henry Ford trial. As has been shown, this is one case where it can be argued legitimately that a six-cent verdict for the plaintiff is not a moral victory for the defendant, yet the *Tribune* regards it today as a further establishment of the right of fair comment, even though the jury in the case ruled that this right had been violated.

In the next case, the city of Chicago's libel suit against the *Tribune* in 1920, the paper was on firm ground in defending the principle that a newspaper has the right to comment on the conduct of a government, and the Supreme Court of Illinois so ruled. But here again there was no limit set to the privilege, and when the *Tribune* abused its right during the Roosevelt Administration, nothing could be done about it.

The old question of whether a newspaper should be treated as a public utility or as a private business was tested in 1922 by the Chicago *Journal of Commerce* in an injunction suit brought against the *Tribune* during the course of a circulation fight. Judge K. M. Landis upheld the *Tribune's* position that newspaper publishing was a private business—legally correct, but the ruling added another support to the *Tribune's* argument of privilege. Other private businesses had to be regulated in later years to conform to the public interest, but the *Tribune* argued then that newspapers were different from all other private businesses and were not subject to regulation of any kind.

In 1928 the *Tribune* was again in a solid position when it entered the controversy centering around the suppression of the Minneapolis weekly, the *Saturday Press*, which had been closed by the Fourth District Court of Minnesota after it had accused county officials of underworld collaboration. The basic question of whether a state had the constitutional right to censor newspapers was decided in the only reasonable way—by a United States Supreme Court ruling in 1931 that such a state statute was a violation of the Constitution.

This decision was effected largely by McCormick, who brought the case to the attention of the American Newspaper Publishers' Association and led the move to appeal the decision of the Minnesota Supreme Court. The victory was a personal one for the Colonel, and he was widely acclaimed by newspaper publishers everywhere, who felt that their collective interests had been successfully defended. Once again the principle of freedom from governmental control had been vindicated. Yet the question remained unanswered: Should the press be responsible to no one? Only to the people, McCormick had said, but there had never been any indication that the people were in a position to accept responsibility.

This question, always in the background before, moved to a more prominent position in 1933 with enactment of the National Recovery Act, and the formulation of a Newspaper Code under it. The crux of this argument was whether a specific Bill of Rights provision should be inserted in the code which, in effect, would have put publishers in a privileged position over all other businesses and would have made the code virtually unenforceable in their case. McCormick's counsel argued that newspapers could "contract away the right of free publication" by signing the code. The government denied that there was any intent to use NRA's licensing powers against the press in violation of its constitutional rights. The publishers won their point and got their emasculated code, whereupon some of the most influential of them contributed to the assault upon NRA which eventually killed it.

Once more it had been firmly established that newspapers could not be held responsible by government, and in this case, where it might be argued that they had acted selfishly against the common interest in a time of national emergency, there remained unanswered the question of who had the right and power to hold them responsible. The people, in 1933, were helpless to do so.

The Associated Press case, initiated in 1943, is the latest issue involving freedom of the press in general and the Chicago *Tribune* specifically. The question of whether the AP is a monopoly operating in violation of the anti-trust laws is a legal one which has been decided in the affirmative by the United States Supreme Court, and any comment on it here would be meaningless, except to note that some publishers, including the McCormicks, could not bring themselves to accept the decision. Some of the circumstances surrounding the case, however, and particularly the part the *Tribune* has played in it, are legitimately open to criticism, especially because the whole question of responsibility is involved.

The immediate preliminary to filing of the government's suit was the historic annual meeting of the Associated Press membership in April 1942, one of the stormiest in AP history, at which Marshall Field's application for membership on behalf of his Chicago *Sun* was refused.

There was an atmosphere of high tension as the editors and publishers representing AP members met in the Waldorf-Astoria in New York. Rumors of impending government action against the press association had been freely circulated and many, but not all, of the members were apprehensive that the franchise character of the organization was threatened, that it might be compelled to sell its service on the open market, like the United Press, instead of existing as an exclusive kind of club—exclusive in the sense that prospective members could be blackballed for reasons having nothing to do with their eligibility as newspapers.

Marshall Field had filed application for membership on the preceding February 9. Silliman Evans, using his Nashville *Tennessean* membership, spoke for Field at the convention; he was then the *Sun's* editor. Evans said Field had tried to buy a membership from "a member of the Hearst organization" for two hundred and fifty thousand dollars. This Hearst member was the *Herald-American*, whose publisher, Thomas J. White, explained that the offer was inadequate and that the *Herald-American* could not sell its indivisible seven-day morning rights without losing the Sunday franchise, which it was using. White and Cissy Patterson are old friends.

McCormick himself did not speak against Field, but his sports editor, Arch Ward, took the floor with the proxy of the Norwich (Connecticut) *Record* to make a fifteen-minute prepared speech. It was a homey kind of speech, couched at first in baseball talk. Ward spoke of the "imported slugger" who convinced the Chicago Cubs after a few weeks that he "couldn't hit major league pitching," and he proclaimed that he had spent his life "among men who play the game according to rules and who do not expect to have the rules changed in the middle of the game." Ward went on to attack Field as a rich man, whose acquisition of an AP franchise would hurt the *Tribune* and thus hurt *Tribune* employees because he could afford to sell advertising space at giveaway rates and hire away reporters at three times their *Tribune* salaries. "To my knowledge," he said, "no one on the *Tribune* fears competition. All we ask is that our competition be clean, wholesome and fair."

This kind of attack was more than some of the other editors present could take. John D. Ewing, of the Shreveport (Louisiana) *Times*, rose to reply. Ewing said he had never been a sports editor, but he surmised that an education at V.M.I. and infantry service in the first World War had taught him "a little bit about sportsmanship," and "I never heard a more unsportsmanlike thing in my life." If he were McCormick, Ewing added, he would "rather have another paper come into Chicago than to see a 50,000-watt radio station come in."

Joining Ewing in the reply to Ward was Charles D. Osborne, of the Auburn (New York) *Citizen-Advertiser*, who declared, "I'm not a sports writer and I have no sob stuff, but I want to bring before you the fact that the country has changed." He reminded the publishers of Archibald MacLeish's admonition at another session to "police" their ranks against defeatists. "We all know through the vermin press that we have traitors in our ranks. An important part of the duty of the AP is to give unprejudiced news. To do that there must be some other Chicago AP paper in the morning field, and the way to do that is to vote this membership to Marshall Field."

The unpopularity of that kind of plain speaking was apparent in the quick murmur that ran through the room, and there were calls for a vote. The debate had gone on for forty-five minutes and it was obvious that the courageous opposition was in the minority. The old fear of government interference had already been effectively revived by such statements as McCormick's: "The heat was put on. The FBI men were sent to talk with the members. There were threats of indictment and court action. . . ." The proponents of this point of view had done some skillful preliminary spadework. Another important aspect of the voting, according to some expert observers of the process, was the coalition of small-town editors who thought to themselves, "If we allow another morning paper in Chicago to have an AP franchise, what's to prevent someone from starting a rival paper in our own town and securing a franchise in the same way?"

Apparently it was a merging of fears that governed the vote on Field's application. There were 971 ballots cast, divided 684 against and 287 in favor. Even under newly adopted rules requiring a majority vote for admission instead of the old four-fifths rule, this vote was enough to insure defeat.

There were still two applications for membership before the meeting: Cissy Patterson's, for the morning and afternoon report; and McCormick's, for an afternoon paper that he alleged he was going to start.

Although she was not an AP member, Mrs. Patterson was present at the meeting and got permission to speak. She said in part: "Thurman Arnold sent for me two years ago and said, 'If you want an AP membership I can get it for you. I won't start it myself, but if you will send a member of your staff around the country and get some complaints from newspapers in your situation—that is, without an AP membership—I'll guarantee to break that monopoly and get you that membership.'

"I come from four generations of newspaper people and I didn't like it—I didn't like the smell of it. I went home and thought it over and I refused to act."

Having shut out Field, however, the membership could scarcely give Cissy a franchise and her application was turned down by a vote of 514 to 242. It is instructive to note that there were some members who saw no inconsistency in refusing it to Field and granting it to Mrs. Patterson, who had asserted correctly that her papers dominated Washington anyway, without AP membership, thus raising some doubt about the good faith of her application.

To the surprise of no one, Colonel McCormick withdrew his own application after the balloting, with this curious speech: "It doesn't seem to have occurred to anybody in this room that the Chicago *Tribune* is not publishing an afternoon newspaper, and therefore it is not in order to ask for a membership. So that you won't think I played a joke on you, I will say that when the pressure was very severe upon the Chicago *Tribune* not to maintain its protest right it occurred to me it would be a good thing to have other members in Chicago which would not waive this right. Hence this application. The other members didn't waive their protest rights, so if any action was to have been taken against me it would have to be taken against all and I didn't think that was likely. I withdraw the application."

Thus ended this exercise in newspaper self-government. The day after these events Colonel McCormick released a statement through the AP which left no doubt about the kind of thinking he brought to the entire operation.

"I hope the overwhelming vote of yesterday," he said, "means that the Gestapo is out of American newspaper offices forever. Some of the members were so apprehensive they asked the ballots be burned so they could not fall into the hands of the FBI. It is to the eternal honor of American publishers that they will not stand for that coercion. It is not at all a question between Mr. Field and myself, but one between a free press and government coercion."

Although it was difficult for some observers to conceive how a free press might be endangered by wider circulation of the AP's morning report in Chicago, it was evident that such doubts were not entertained by a majority of AP members, nor by publishers at large. *Editor & Publisher*, the business's foremost trade publication, which exists by virtue of newspaper advertising and support and naturally reflects the thinking of publishers, attacked Thurman Arnold editorially the following week, and at the same time criticized the Chicago *Sun* in its "Shop Talk" column for the *Sun's* views on government advertising. A week later it was repeating the familiar McCormick-Patterson canard that *PM*, Field's New York paper, was in league with the Communists—because *PM* had attacked McCormick, Patterson and Hearst.

Nothing was said in *Editor & Publisher*, or by any single publisher, about the kind of slanting and editorializing which the *Tribune* regularly puts into its news columns, including AP stories

—a fact which seems a far more fundamental danger to journalism than any issue involved in the AP fight. An example of this editorializing was contained in the *Tribune* news story covering its answer to the suit against the AP. The second paragraph asserted, without any qualification: "The suit was launched by the national administration after the AP's members voted last April to deny membership to Marshall Field's Chicago *Sun* and Eleanor Medill Patterson's Washington *Times-Herald*. It proposes to reduce the AP to the level of a public utility, subject to government regulation and control."

The fourth paragraph of this story stated, without the qualification that it was a paraphrase of the *Tribune's* answer: "It marks the first determined attempt in an English-speaking nation since the days of the Stuarts and the Tudors to monopolize, stifle, and control the press."

These statements were opinions, pure and simple, yet they appeared in the news columns, where real freedom of the press demands they should never appear. This utter lack of responsibility evoked no comment from McCormick's fellow publishers, whose interests were threatened by it.

In October 1942 occurred another incident which displayed McCormick's inflamed state of mind. Marshall Field had made a speech in Petersborough, Ontario, where he had told the Ontario-Quebec Circulation Managers' convention, according to the United Press, that "a government victory in its anti-trust suit against the Associated Press would be one of the most important moves ever made toward real freedom of the press in American journalism."

Next day, in New York, McCormick issued a statement carried by press services and printed widely in many American newspapers. It was a statement unsurpassed for arrogance, even by the *Tribune's* publisher. "Marshall Field," he said, "is an authority on horse racing, yacht racing and grouse shooting but he knows little about newspapers and nothing about the great constitutional subject of freedom of the press. It is an evil thing, therefore, that some weasel-minded lawyer should have written a disingenuous speech for him to declaim on a spot where freedom of the press does not exist, for the purpose of prejudicing a lawsuit which the government has started for his financial benefit."

The implied slur against the Canadian press brought a storm of protest from that country's newspapers, ranging from Premier Hepburn's query: "Has the man gone wrong in his head, or something?" to the Petersborough *Examiner's* outraged comment: "We are pleased to tell this clamorous colonel that he is talking through his brass hat and that everybody knows it except himself and a few poor thousands of deluded morons who believe the editorials in the Chicago *Tribune*."

Other editorials were more temperate but just as scornful. One in the Montreal *Gazette*, signed by Paul Bilkey, its vice-president and editor in chief, expressed the opinion of many American newspaper readers. "We think Col. McCormick is mistaken. . . . His own conception of newspaper freedom is newspaper license, freedom from fact and freedom to sling mud. Naturally, he has misunderstood a self-imposed restraint on the part of Canadian newspapers, the drawing of a rigid line between freedom and the abuse of freedom."

As though to confirm this opinion, the *Tribune* began a series of articles a few months later, in January 1943, under the initial headline, TRACE ATTITUDE OF NEW DEALERS TOWARD PRESS. AP SUIT CLIMAX TO LONG HARASSMENT. These articles were actually editorials running in the news columns, and privileged because they were signed by a writer named William Fulton. If Marshall Field's speech was given "for the purpose of prejudicing a lawsuit," as McCormick had asserted, it would be difficult to find an accurate name for the kind of prejudicial utterances about the case which the Colonel allowed to be published in his newspaper. The tone for the whole series was set by the lead in the first story:

"This is a story about the cloak and dagger work behind the administration's treatment of the press from the days of the NRA Blue Eagle to the anti-trust suit against the Associated Press. . . .

"This article will be followed by a series of stories telling of the sordid activities of a motley crew which entered into a cabal with the objective of 'getting *The Chicago Tribune*.'

"Washington officialdom figures largely in the picture, but the conspirators also include communist agitators, pink fellow travelers, and the internationalist snob social set on the eastern seaboard.

"*The Tribune* has weathered a number of below-the-belt blows from this crew in recent months, blows aimed at this newspaper because of its forthright demand for an all-out war program pointing to victory and the removal of proven incompetents among Washington politicians.

"Reprisals have been attempted for months, especially just before the last election. Swarms of federal bureau of investigation agents, secret service operatives, and naval intelligence officers have been sent out with orders to 'get *The Tribune*.'

"Their forays have proven fruitless. Time, money, and energy that could have been spent in tracking down those responsible for the Pearl Harbor debacle, and the saboteurs and spies at home, have been wasted.

"Against the mosaic of harassment, and political persecution, the administration suit against the Associated Press should be viewed."

The second article rehearsed McCormick's argument that the New Deal had harassed the *Tribune* ever since the Colonel led the fight on NRA, and that the suit against the AP was the latest result of this "bitter animosity," a phrase aptly descriptive of the *Tribune's* harassment of the New Deal.

The fourth article was an elaborate alibi for Stanley Johnston's Battle of Midway story, an alibi which went out of its way to smear Attorney General Biddle on the ground that he served only a little more than a month in the Army in the first World War, as compared with Johnston's record in both wars, specifically his bravery as a civilian correspondent in the battle of the Coral Sea. No one questions Johnston's personal bravery, nor the fact that his reporting of the Coral Sea battle in newspaper and book form brought him a deserved recognition, but anyone who has ever talked to Johnston knows that he often sounds like McCormick himself when he speaks, that he appears to be wholeheartedly committed to his boss's philosophy, and that he presumably would not hesitate to handle news as McCormick would order it handled.

The facts in the Midway story, as recited before, speak for themselves.

The seventh article was more scurrilous than the others. Headed REVEAL "ANGELS" FINANCING PLOTS AGAINST TRIBUNE, it was full of melodramatic and erroneous statements about Fight for Freedom and the Friends of Democracy, the two principal groups which the paper charged figured largely in the "conspiracy" to get the *Tribune*. This article asserted, "Both organizations have been financed principally by eastern millionaire interventionists and Long Island cookie-pushing society friends of Wendell L. Willkie, ex-Republican nominee for President."

The *Tribune*'s Mr. Fulton, if he had been interested in getting the facts, could never have written such a statement nor topped it with his next sentence: "While the two groups loudly beat the drums and cried for war when the United States was at peace, few of their leaders stepped into uniform after Pearl Harbor. Some of the younger ones got public relations and press agents' commissions." This slur, so typical of *Tribune* attack, does not stand up against the facts in this case, which are well known to anyone acquainted with the personnel of both organizations.

In this article the *Tribune* also made personal attacks against its ex-correspondent, Edmond Taylor; Herbert Agar, brilliant editor of the Louisville *Courier-Journal* and first president of Freedom House, successor of Fight for Freedom; the Rev. Leon Birkhead, president of Friends of Democracy; and Rex Stout, head of the Writers' War Board. In identifying these people the *Tribune* indulged in such smear tactics as calling Agar "a non-fighting lieutenant commander in the United States Navy," and making sarcastic references to his "arduous" duties.

Still another article in the series was devoted to an attack on the "international set," including Wendell Willkie, "high priest of the international cult"; Henry Luce, Willkie's "good friend and apologist"; Clare Luce; the New York *Herald Tribune*, "now the leading Anglophile organ of the country"; Thomas Lamont, another "leading Anglophile"; his son, Corliss Lamont; Dorothy Thompson; Bundles for Britain; the British War Relief Society;

and Winthrop W. Aldrich, Chase National Bank chairman and "bellwether of New York society."

These were the articles in which the *Tribune* attempted to establish the existence of a conspiracy against the paper and against freedom of the press. They are well designed to show the kind of press freedom in which Colonel McCormick believes.

# Chapter 2

## THE PROSECUTION RESTS

RALPH MCGILL, distinguished editor of the Atlanta *Constitution* and one of the few critics of newspapers within the business, put his finger on the core of the free-press problem when he pointed out that freedom of the press means different things to an editor in actual newspaper practice and to the man who reads a newspaper. The editor, McGill said, believes it means the right to say what he pleases and to hold back at will, while to the man on the street it means that he can depend on the paper to tell him the whole story.

That the man on the street has become increasingly aware of this discrepancy was shown by the results of a *Fortune Magazine* poll in 1939. To those skeptics who sneer at the validity of public-opinion polling, it may be pointed out that *Fortune* polls have shown consistently a nearly hundred per cent accuracy. This basic survey of 1939 disclosed some figures which many publishers found so unpalatable that they put their heads in the sand and refused to believe them. These were some of the results:

*How do you get your news?* Newspapers, 60 per cent; don't need newspapers to get news, 40 per cent; radio, 25 per cent—and there were twice as many poor people as well-to-do people in this last percentage.

*Which does the better job of supplying news?* Radio, 39 per cent; newspapers, 38.3 per cent.

*Which is the most free from prejudice?* Radio, 49 per cent; newspapers, 17 per cent. In a breakdown of these figures, it was shown that the higher the economic class the more regard for the press.

*Which do you prefer for interpreting the news?* Radio, 39.3

per cent; newspaper editorials, 25.9 per cent; columnists, 10.7 per cent.

*Which would you believe on conflicting versions?* Radio, 40.3 per cent; newspapers, 26.9 per cent. This in spite of the fact that newspapers are demonstrably much more accurate.

Breaking these figures down further, only 45.1 per cent believed that news stories were usually accurate, and about 30 per cent thought that headlines were usually misleading.

A total of 63.4 per cent believed the press was free, and of the minority who didn't, 22.9 per cent put the blame on newspaper owners.

Edward L. Bernays, the public relations counsel, recalled these figures in the course of an address in 1944 before the National Newspaper Promotion Association. He pointed out that "there is a great gap between the platforms of the newspapers and public acceptance of them. Particularly is this the case in the field of news dissemination, freedom and independence." He went on to advocate that newspapers use public relations techniques to convince the public that they were truthful and accurate, particularly in the spheres where the public doubted their fairness, namely, politics, labor, business, foreign affairs, religion and race.

This speech was printed in the *Journalism Quarterly*, and Mr. Bernays sent reprints of it to a large mailing list of editors and publishers for comment. The response was overwhelming, and the tone of the many hundreds of letters received indicated that the owners of newspapers generally were concerned about the encroachment of radio and about the increasing lack of confidence in their product. They regarded it rightly as a dangerous tendency.

But there were some who scoffed at the whole business, and unfortunately these few constituted the most powerful elements in the newspaper business, measuring power in terms of circulation and influence among other publishers. McCormick's *Tribune* denounced Bernays and his speech editorially.

This brings us around to another important aspect of the problem that has a direct bearing here, and that is the steady shrinking of the daily press through chain journalism, consolidations and plain failures. The more smug defenders of the status quo say that the papers which disappear would never be missed, thereby evading the point that it is diversity of utterance that is being strangled. It is this diversity, this wide range of editorial thought and clash of opinion, that produces the truth.

Yet, in terms of circulation, what kind of newspapers provide Americans with the bulk of their journalistic thinking? The three McCormick-Patterson papers account for a considerable slice of total circulation, and it is concentrated in the most strategic areas. The Hearst newspapers add up to an imposing percentage. The Scripps-Howard chain reaches another large segment of population, and the Gannett chain still another. On a remarkable number of important issues in the past few years all these newspapers have thought substantially alike; they have differed on only a few public questions. All of them have, at one time or another, used their news columns freely to promulgate editorial policies; none of them has hesitated to distort and slant the news when it suited its political purposes. Further, they represent a class of publishers who think more or less alike and who dominate their field.

Morris L. Ernst, one of the hardest-hitting newspaper critics and one who has made a particular study of the shrinking "market place of thought," points out that fourteen owners (eighteen papers) control 23.7 per cent of the total daily circulations; these papers, less than 1 per cent of all the daily papers, have roughly a quarter of the circulation pie. In the Sunday field this disproportionate control is even more apparent; nineteen papers (3 per cent of all Sunday editions) own 47.2 per cent of the total Sunday circulations.

Looking at it from another angle, Ernst shows that "the total number of one-paper or singleton towns, as opposed to those with a diversity of papers, have doubled in number in the period from 1910 to 1939. While population increased by 43 per cent in these years, the number of singleton towns also grew by 43 per cent. We are traveling fast in the wrong direction."

Mr. Ernst cites a good many other statistics and approaches to the problem, all of which add up to the inescapable conclusion that there has been an increasing standardization of journalistic thought, both through the shrinkage of newspapers and in the spreading of the same ideas to millions of people through syndication and chain journalism. The reason that there are not more newspapers, and a consequent greater diversity of opinion, perhaps was best expressed by Mark Ethridge, publisher of the Louisville (Kentucky) *Courier-Journal* and *Times,* who remarked, "The newspaper business has gone beyond the stage where a man with ideas or even brains can start a newspaper. He must have money."

In Mr. Ernst's view it does not matter what the newspapers say as long as there are more of them and a diversity of thought so that the truth can be served by the conflict of ideas. Almost any observer will agree that the diversity is essential, but to this writer it seems that the present comparative standardization is even more harmful in that the newspapers which reach the greatest proportion of newspaper readers are guilty of editorializing the news. The result has been a loss of reader confidence, a growing cynicism, a lack of trust in newspapers by the people who read them at a time when that trust is most needed.

The papers which have contributed most to that state of mind, and thus to the detriment of the entire American press, are the McCormick-Patterson papers. These papers have also demonstrated, in their editorial formulas, that people turn to newspapers more and more for entertainment rather than for the accurate, unbiased presentation of news and responsible leadership on the editorial pages.

It is a truism that cannot be too often repeated that the press in general has come to regard freedom of the press as a privilege, instead of the responsibility it is intended to be in a democracy.

There are all too few great dailies in America practicing this concept of responsibility—the St. Louis *Post-Dispatch,* the Louisville *Courier-Journal,* the Richmond *Times-Dispatch,* and the *News-Leader,* the *Atlanta Constitution,* the Chicago *Sun* and perhaps a half-dozen others, certainly not more. Even the New York *Times,* which keeps telling itself that it is the world's most distinguished newspaper, is not above running an Arthur Krock editorial disguised as news in its front-page news columns. The

*Times* may honestly believe these expositions are news stories, but in at least one case the piece was a cruel and unfair political attack.

Robert Lasch, in a July 1944 *Atlantic Monthly* article, defined the ideal: "the kind of newspaper owner who can make the press free." Granting that it is an ideal beyond most mortals, at the same time it is one toward which the mortals in question might well strive. This owner, said Lasch, would be "a man who can divorce himself from the associations and outlook that normally go with wealth; a man who can sacrifice even his own short-range interest as a business entrepreneur in favor of his long-run interest as the champion of a greater cause; a man whose passion for the general welfare overcomes his desire to impose his own ideas on the community; a man of wisdom and humility, character and devotion, courage and modesty. . . ."

A month later, in another *Atlantic* article, Ralph McGill outlined the changes he believed must be made to save freedom of the press. He advocated three major changes:

1. Publishers and editors will have to regain, "if they have lost it," the vision of serving the people of their state and community. They should keep out of other enterprises which affect their newspaper interest.

2. Editors and publishers must realize that freedom of the press means not merely the right to publish but the giving of a complete and unbiased picture of the news. The man in the street may keep reading a paper for its comics or features and his attitude won't show up in the circulation figures, but that doesn't mean he has a free press.

3. Newspapers must interpret America to the people, a task at which they have "failed miserably" in the past. Because of the newspapers' failure, such phrases as "free enterprise" and the "American way of life" are no more than undefinable phrases today, mocked in some quarters, misused in others.

The greatest obstacle to the achievement of these ideals is the attitude of the press itself. The Associated Press, built upon the highest standards of accuracy, elects to its directorship Colonel McCormick, who has shown repeatedly in his newspaper that he has an entirely different conception of accuracy. Influential publishers, with a few praiseworthy exceptions, not only are silent about the violations of professional ethics in the Tribune Company's newspapers but actually defend them in a large sense, though not specifically, as the general body of newspaper ownership tends to resent and defend any criticism at all, no matter how justified. Edwin L. James, managing editor of the New York *Times*, reflects the typical publishers' attitude with the rhetorical question, "What greater gift have we to give to the peoples of the world than the right to read what they please?"—as though the responsibility of a newspaper began and ended with that nebulous conception of it. In a sarcastic little book review of Marshall Field's *Freedom Is More Than a Word*, in the columns of the *Times* Sunday book section, one also finds such a gem as, "The most soundly established newspapers exhibit the greatest independence of any group interest and offer the best news report of minorities' views." The *Daily News* is certainly the most soundly established newspaper in New York, yet its news report of minorities' views is far from being the best, and barely qualifies as a news report at all.

The illustrations are endless, but perhaps they can best be summarized in essence by the Pulitzer prize editorial of 1944, or, more properly, the editorial cited by the Pulitzer prize jury in giving its award for distinguished editorial writing to George W. Potter, chief editorial writer of the Providence (Rhode Island) *Journal-Bulletin*. The award was given for Mr. Potter's editorials on freedom of the press, and with admirable candor the Advisory Board which recommends the prize winners, a board composed of prominent publishers and editors, cited one editorial particularly "which best expressed the view that the Advisory Board itself holds on the subject. . . ."

This editorial, then, may be said fairly to reflect the opinion of a cross section of newspaper ownership and editorial direction. It is certainly about as clear an expression of such a viewpoint as one could ask. The meat of the editorial is contained in a single paragraph:

"Some people in this country do not understand or deliberately misinterpret what freedom of the press actually is. They father the idea that it is a right belonging to newspapers solely, giving them the privilege of doing as they please. As a matter of fact, freedom of the press is a specific grant of a right by the Constitution not to the newspapers solely but to all the people for their protection. We have the freest press in the whole world, thanks not alone to a jealously guarded popular right but also because the American press is economically independent, stands on its own two feet without subsidy or subvention and can pay its own way, depending upon its own competency for survival. Through our cooperative system of newsgathering, which serves newspapers of all shades of opinion, the American people are assured of objective news."

Here may be discerned the foundation upon which the majority of American publishers rest. It is a foundation compounded of the argument that the guarantee of a free press rests ultimately with the people, which conveniently relieves the newspapers of responsibility; further, that the American press is the freest in the world, which is true but does not make it nearly as free as it should be in a democracy; further, that the threat of government control is paramount in ownership thinking, rather than the idea that newspapers could never be controlled by government if they truly represented the people; finally, that "our cooperative system of newsgathering"—freely translated, this means the Associated Press—is a guarantee of objective news, although it is incontrovertible fact that the AP report is frequently manipulated by member papers to suit their political views, and even oftener is carried under policy-slanted headlines—leaving entirely aside the fact of editorializing in news columns by a newspaper's own writers.

To sum up the argument, it seems plain that there is only one answer, speaking in general terms, to the problem of making the American press really free by ending the abuses of its freedom perpetrated by its own members. The reform cannot and must not come from government; it should ideally, but cannot practically, come from the people; it can and must come from the newspaper business itself.

This is anything but a new idea; apparently, however, it is one that has been lost in the shuffle. The American Society of Newspaper Editors adopted a code called "The Canons of Journalism" at its first annual meeting in 1923. The society is an organization whose membership comprises all the large dailies of any consequence in America, and the code it devised is a good one. It contained such sound standards as these:

"The right of a newspaper to attract and hold readers is restricted by nothing but considerations of public welfare. The use a newspaper makes of the share of public attention it gains serves to determine its sense of responsibility, which it shares with every member of its staff. A journalist who uses his power for any selfish or otherwise unworthy purpose is faithless to a high trust. . . .

"Partisanship in editorial comment which knowingly departs from the truth, does violence to the best spirit of American journalism; in the news columns it is subversive of a fundamental principle of the profession. . . .

"Headlines should be fully warranted by the contents of the articles which they surmount. . . .

"Sound practice makes clear distinction between news reports and expressions of opinion. News reports should be free from opinion or bias of any kind."

These are canons to which virtually all newspaper publishers would subscribe. Adherence to them would curb the kind of personal journalism which the Patterson-McCormick papers practice and would end the abuse of privilege for which the newspaper business is paying an increasingly heavy price.

Frank Luther Mott may argue, as he has in his history of American journalism, that the society was not organized as a court and therefore could not enforce its own canons, but that is not proof that the canons are therefore unenforceable. The primary requisite is for publishers as a whole to recognize their own dilemma and determine collectively to enforce these standards, which are after all fundamental and already generally agreed upon. Once determined, the various publisher organizations—ANPA, ASNE, Inland Press Association and all the others—could unite, police their own ranks and guarantee a truly free press, truly representative of the people they serve—simply by demanding that publishers live up to the fundamental ethics of journalism, the judges to be their fellows.

At present there is little tendency of any consequence in this direction, but those of us who love the newspaper business more for what it could be than for what it is hope that the reform comes before it is too late.

# Chapter 3

# ASSESSMENT

GEORGE WILLIAM CURTIS, a contemporary of Joseph Medill, may have unwittingly written an estimate of the McCormick-Medill-Patterson dynasty when he noted, "It is not observed in history that families improve with time. It is rather discovered that the whole matter is like a comet, of which the brightest part is the head; and the tail, although long and luminous, is gradually shaded into obscurity."

This is certainly true of the McCormick and Medill families. The Colonel, for example, would be an extraordinary branch on any family tree, but he is not the forceful, strong character that Cyrus McCormick was, nor does he exemplify the flowering of the dynasty he represents. Moreover, when he dies, the McCormick family will be "shaded into obscurity" at a rapid rate. Of the numerous descendants, there is not one who promises to be another titan. Medill was the head of a very short-tailed comet. His grandchildren carried on his temperament, but the Medill family itself petered out after his death.

Only the Pattersons have improved with time. Worthy man though he was, Dr. Robert W. Patterson was overshadowed by other figures. Tough-minded, powerful Captain Patterson was by all odds the most striking figure the family ever produced, and Cissy is one of the most colorful, if nothing more. Yet there the Patterson potential virtually ends. Now that the Captain is dead, the last strong man of the family has passed.

Substantial properties like the *Tribune* and the *News* will probably continue to prosper without their owners at the helm, and their editorial policies may even stay the same, but they will inevitably lose their personalities under other direction.

It is possible, therefore, to anticipate the verdict of history to some extent and make a preliminary estimate of the dynasty's impact on American life. Obviously there must be some entries on the credit side of the ledger, the most important of which is Joseph Medill's contribution to American political history. Whatever his real motives may have been, Medill's sponsorship of Lincoln and the *Tribune's* influential backing of the Lincoln Administration were factors in saving the Union. Yet, having helped save it, Medill and his *Tribune* did little to preserve it thereafter. The *Tribune* was seldom on the side of democracy after the Civil War. Medill in those years set the pattern for individual, irresponsible journalism which was not a quarter as dangerous in his time as it became in the twenties and thirties of our own century, when the circulation of the printed word reached hitherto undreamed-of peaks.

Another entry on the credit side of the dynasty is Cyrus McCormick's list of inventions, which gave so much to American agriculture, and the part that he played in the making of Chicago. The McCormicks helped create the business structure of that great city and the fortunes created by family members were sometimes turned to wise and beneficial uses.

When we come down to the present generation, however, there is little that can be said to the family credit, or at least to the credit of its three principal figures. The chief indictment against the family is that its members used their newspapers as political weapons to advance their own prejudices and opinions. Moreover, these newspapers, with their total circulation of nearly five million, were used at a time of national peril to advocate ideas which, it can be argued, were not in the public interest.

It is all very well to argue for freedom of editorial opinion, to say that Colonel McCormick has a right to think that everyone else is out of step, to insist that the McCormick-Patterson papers be free to print whatever their private ownership chooses. These freedoms presuppose that their users will be restrained by a sense of responsibility to the people and an obligation to present the news as accurately as it is humanly possible. Yet the Colonel and his cousins apparently have felt no such restraint. When this country was at war, when all our people and our institutions were imperiled, they insisted arrogantly on the right to do as they pleased, a right which they seemed to think was conferred on them by virtue of wealth and property ownership. This lack of responsibility is not the sole possession of McCormick and the Pattersons. They are the worst offenders; there are other publishers only slightly less guilty.

In terms of practical politics, it appears, the influence of McCormick-Patterson thinking is negligible, but no one can estimate the extent of its influence on American minds, where it may be expressed in more subtle ways than the direct method of the ballot box. For example, that thinking must be to blame at least in part for the continued political existence of such men as Gerald L. K. Smith, Senator Theodore Bilbo, Representatives Clare Hoffman and John Rankin; and such institutions as the Christian Front, publisher Frank Gannett's Committee for Constitutional Government, and all the numerous festering movements whose catchwords "American" and "Christian" attract the forces of bigotry, chauvinism and intolerance.

The voices of anti-democracy find powerful allies in the *Tribune*, the *Daily News* and the *Times-Herald*, and although neither the papers nor their owners admit to any connection with those voices, it is still true that both owners and papers are quoted continually and approvingly by the individuals and publications devoted to the cause of "Christian Americanism" in its several ugly forms.

John Ruskin long ago set forth an ideal, toward whose fulfillment the members of this or any other newspaper dynasty might well set their faltering footsteps. Ruskin wrote:

"The power of the press in the hands of highly educated men, in independent position, and of honest purpose, may indeed become all that it has been hitherto vainly vaunted to be."

# INDEX

# INDEX